I0030965

BUSINESS PROCESS MANAGEMENT CAPABILITIES

Janne Ohtonen

Sarja/Series A-6:2015

Turun kauppakorkeakoulu
Turku School of Economics

Custos: Professor Jukka Heikkilä
                   Turku School of Economics

Supervisor: Professor Jukka Heikkilä
                   Turku School of Economics

Pre-examiners: Professor Samuli Pekkola
                   Tampere University of Technology

                   Professor Peter Trkman
                   University of Ljubljana

Opponent: Professor Peter Trkman
                   University of Ljubljana

Copyright Janne Ohtonen & Turku School of Economics

The originality of this thesis has been checked in accordance with the University of Turku quality assurance system using the Turnitin OriginalityCheck service.

ISBN   978-952-249-437-5 (print) 978-952-249-438-2 (PDF)
ISSN   0357-4652 (print) 1459-4870 (PDF)

Publications of Turku School of Economics, Series A

Suomen yliopistopaino Oy – Juvenes Print, Turku 2015

ABSTRACT

This thesis focuses on analysing Business Process Management (BPM) Capabilities (BPMC) through a practical approach based on design science. The research questions are (i) which capability factors are related to the success and failure of BPM initiatives and (ii) how can organisations take these capability factors into account in their respective environments.

This research started from the personal interest of the researcher on BPM. The researcher has been working between the academic and practical worlds over time and knew that although there is a lot of research on the success and failure factors of BPM, that information has not been put to good use in the practical world. This led to an idea to gather the most important factors and to design a practical BPM capability factors artifact.

This artifact helps organisations to identify and improve their BPMCs. The artifact is built based on an extensive literature review, expert interviews and case studies. The artifact consists of 35 key capability factors that affect the success and failure of BPM initiatives. It also includes a process that organisations can use to take those capability factors into account in their BPM initiatives.

This research contributes by identifying recent important BPM capability factors as well as using design science combined with interviews, surveys and case studies to build the artifact. From a practical perspective, this research was able to produce a process that can be used in organisations first to evaluate their BPMCs and then to improve them. The information produced by using the BPM capability artifact was found to be both useful and interesting by all participating real-life case organisations.

Keywords

Business process management, business process management capabilities, design science, case study, expert interview, building the artifact, evaluating artifact, survey, success and failure

TIIVISTELMÄ

Väitöskirja keskittyy analysoimaan liiketoimintaprosessien hallinnan kyvykkyyksiä (BPM) Design Science menetelmän avulla. Tutkimuskysymykset ovat (i) mitkä kyvykkyydet liittyvät liiketoimintaprosessien kehittämisen onnistumiseen ja epäonnistumiseen sekä (ii) kuinka organisaatiot voivat ottaa nämä kyvykkyydet huomioon omassa toimintaympäristössään.

Tutkimus on saanut alkunsa tutkijan kiinnostuksesta liiketoimintaprosessien kehittämiseen ja hallintaan. Tutkija on työskennellyt molemmissa sekä akateemisissa että käytännönläheisissä ympäristöissä. Sitä kautta hän on havainnut että vaikka liiketoimintaprosessien kyvykkyyksistä sekä kypsyysmalleista on tehty paljon tutkimusta, sitä ei ole sovellettu organisaatioissa laajasti. Tämä johti Design Science menetelmän käyttämiseen käytännönläheisen kyvykkyyksien arvioimisen työkalun kehittämiseen.

Kyseinen työkalu (artefakti) auttaa organisaatioita tunnistamaan heidän liiketoimintaprosessien kehittämisen kyvykkyydet sekä arvioimaan miten parantaa onnistumisen mahdollisuutta kyvykkyyksien kehittämisen kautta. Työkalu on perustuu laajaan kirjallisuuskatsaukseen, asiantuntijahaastatteluihin sekä kolmeen tapaustutkimukseen. Työkalussa on tunnistettu 35 avainkyvykkyyttä, jotka vaikuttavat liiketoimintaprosessien kehittämiseen. Väitöskirjassa esitellään myös tutkimukseen perustuva prosessi, jota organisaatiot voivat käyttää omien kyvykkyyksiensä arvioimiseen.

Väitöskirja myötävaikuttaa tieteellistä tutkimusta tunnistamalla uusimmat liiketoimintaprosessien kehittämiseen vaikuttavat kyvykkyydet. Lisäksi työ yhdistää ainutlaatuisella tavalla Design Science menetelmän asiantuntijahaastatteluihin sekä tapaustutkimuksiin. Käytännönläheisestä näkökulmasta työ myötävaikuttaa organisaatioiden toimintaa esittelemällä menetelmän kyvykkyyksien arvioimiseen. Tutkimukseen osallistuneet tapausorganisaatiot pitivät työkalun avulla saatua tietoa liiketoimintaprosessien kehittämisen kannalta hyödyllisenä.

Avainsanat

Liiketoimintaprosessi, kyvykkyys, tapaustutkimus, design science, haastattelututkimus, prosessi

ACKNOWLEDGEMENTS

"Made it all possible."
Jesus – Our Saviour and Lord.

"Made it academically possible."
Professor Jukka Heikkilä, Professor Hannu Salmela, Professor Peter Trkman,
Professor Samuli Pekkola, Dr. Timo Lainema, Dr. Klara Palmberg-Broryd,
Dr. Kai K. Kimppa, Hongxiu Li, Timo Leino, and Jonna Järveläinen

"Made it mentally possible."
Hanna Norvanto-Ohtonen, Daniel Ohtonen, Arja Ohtonen, Jarmo Ohtonen,
Miika J. Norvanto, Jukka Norvanto, Liisa Norvanto, Elisa Norvanto, Pirita
Norvanto, Mira Ohtonen, Mikael Jaakkola, Minna Karjalainen, Mikko
Karjalainen, Toni Karjalainen, Nea Karjalainen, Miral Ismail,
Tommi Hännikkälä, Tomi BGT Suovuo,
and all other family and friends.

"Made it financially possible."
Suomen Koulutusrahasto, Liikesivistysrahasto, Suomen Kulttuurirahasto –
Kainuun jaosto, Turku School of Economics Association, Affecto Finland Ltd,
BizLog Services Ltd, Turku School of Economics, Kela, Arja Ohtonen,
University of Turku, Tracker Connect Pty, Appelsiini Oy
and my personal wallet.

"Supported me on the way."
Harri Kulmala, Davor Markota, Markku Tuomola, Petri Reiman, Prof. Jan
vom Brocke, Dr. John C. Maxwell, Martina Beck-Friis, Satu-Päivi Kantola,
Shahid Ahmed Osmani, Dr Feras Abou Moghdeb, Malou Järgården, Jose Juan
Hernandez, John Macdonald, Jason Edlin, Karl Walter Keirstead, Stephen
Nicholson, Minna Hellgren, Liisa Venho, Mark Smith, Shaida Aboo, Timo
Mäkelä, Tommi Eklund, Tuukka Heinonen, Päivi Kanerva,
Aino Halinen-Kaila, Kirsi Tammi,
and all the other people that helped me on the way.

TABLE OF CONTENTS

LIST OF TABLES

LIST OF FIGURES

1 INTRODUCTION

1.1 Background

Recent studies (e.g. Gartner 2009; Gartner 2010; Hill and McCoy 2011; Lopez 2011; Pöppelbuß and Röglinger 2011) identify business process improvement as the number one business and technology priority of CIO's. Škrinjar et al. (2010) have claimed that more process-oriented companies perform better than less process-oriented companies. Business Process Management (BPM) is seen as one way of managing improving processes (Mathiesen et al. 2011). The main goal of BPM initiatives is to enhance an organisation's performance by adopting a process view of the organization (Škrinjar et al. 2010). According to Bandara et al. (2009), BPM has become a powerful competitive tool for organizations. However, the implementation of a BPM concept can be a complex and time-consuming effort (Škrinjar et al. 2010; Bowers, Button and Sharrock, 1995). Business Process Management as a domain contains a wide variety of activities leading to an increasing need for multi-disciplinary practitioners trained in a variety of process techniques (Mathiesen et al. 2011; Harmon & Wolf 2010).

This research started from the personal interest of the researcher in this topic as he saw this advantage in his professional work. The researcher has been working between the academic and practical worlds his entire career and has found a lot of research on the success and failure capability factors of BPM (presented in more details in literature review chapter of this thesis). For researcher, many times it seemed like, this information has not been put to use in the practical world through easy-to-use tools that practitioners could apply themselves, creating a research gap and need for this study. Researcher agrees to Mathiesen et al.'s (2011) view, "*as organizations become more process oriented and BPM tools and techniques continue to evolve, the need for BPM expertise increases*". Also Spanyi (2003) has stated that only a handful of organizations can coordinate beyond functional departments to form end-to-end process and improve process-based activities efficiently. Nowadays organizations do not coordinate only internally, but many times in network of stakeholders. This led to an idea to gather the most important capability factors together and to create a BPM Capability (BPMC) artifact, which will enable of practitioners to evaluate capabilities in a practical way. This thesis

14

will be different from various maturity models (such as Rosemann and de Bruin 2005; Hammer 2007; Lee et al. 2007; Weber et al. 2008; Rohloff 2009) in that it does not present a staged maturity model to follow to highest maturity level but rather a tool for measuring and understanding the state of BPM capabilities in the organisation currently based on their operating environment. Nor the focus of this work is to focus on finding new BPM capabilities and to work on those, but to use existing scientific knowledge on BPM capabilities to build a novel artifact that is practical.

According to Niehaves et al. (2014), *"contemporary BPM research is no longer only about methods, procedures, or tools for managing or modeling processes but about assessing and developing BPM capability in organizations"*. Researcher9 follows that idea in this thesis that focuses on, *which capability factors are related to the success and failure of BPM and how can organisations take these capability factors into account in their BPM initiatives*. In this thesis, capability factors are divided into two subcategories, i.e. success and failure, according to their effect on BPM initiatives. The first part of this research question is answered in chapter 0 and the latter part of the question in chapter 0. There has been a lot of research done on BPM capabilities, as this work will show. Recent literature (e.g. Becker et al. 2010) also reports an increasing academic interest in maturity models. However, most of that research has had the purpose of presenting a maturity model, which implies that there is some predetermined path for organisation to follow (Benbasat et al. 1984; King and Kraemer 1984; Prananto et al. 2003; de Bruin et al. 2005; McCormack et al. 2009). As discussed later in this thesis, this work takes a different approach basing the capability development on the environmental fit and market situation rather than on a levelled maturity path. Such maturity models have been claimed to neglect the potential existence of multiple equally advantageous paths (Teo and King 1997; Pöppelbuß and Röglinger 2011). Based on the literature presented in this thesis, previous maturity or capability models have been theoretical exercises where this thesis has its roots on design science in order to design an artifact that will benefit process practitioners and consultants around the world. The main focus of this work is not the originality of the found capability factors (which makes sense since they are mainly based on the existing literature), but in using design science to create a useful and meaningful artifact, which will have value not only to practitioners, but also to academics. This work is to present the relevant processes for utilising the artifact in various organisational environments, which has not been done in previous studies.

This research combines a literature review with the use of the design science method and case studies. Design science is especially of importance in a research oriented to the creation of successful artifacts (Peffers et al. 2008).

The goal of the research was to create an artifact that enables organisations to evaluate their BPMCs. For empirical data collection, researcher used interviews and surveys. Researcher developed the artifact developed based on the literature review combined with expert interviews and one case study. Then, it was evaluated in its natural use environment through three case studies. The advantage of using design science as a research method was to produce an artifact that can be practically used in organisations. For example, two international consulting companies have been using a version of this research's results for consulting purposes, which is explained in more details in chapter 7.3. Design science enables us to use the scientific information accumulated through the literature review and expert interviews in a practical way. In this research, the artifact was both built and evaluated using the design science method. The case study method was used to evaluate the artifact further in the case organisations.

This thesis is organised into seven main chapters. The first chapter introduces this study and the background to it. The second chapter focuses on the theoretical background of this study. The third chapter contains the literature review and proposal for the first version of the BPMC artifact. The fourth chapter explains the methodological choices of this study regarding design science. The fifth chapter focuses on building the BPMC artifact further through expert interviews. The sixth chapter finalises the building of the artifact and evaluates it in practical use through case studies. The seventh chapter contains conclusions and a summary of this study.

1.2   Motivation for the research

The researcher of this study has been working full-time and studying information technology systems since early 2000. Järvinen (1999) states *"every researcher has his/her own personal motivation to perform a scientific study"*. Improving an organisation's efficiency and profitability through information technology systems was fascinating and seemed to bring tangible results for customers. However, there was constant pain between the implemented IT systems, processes and people. This caused the researcher to wonder why so many organisations either were not having purposeful BPM at all or were failing at doing it. In 2009, the researcher participated in a process certification training, which demonstrated some elements of BPM that may cause those initiatives to succeed or fail in organisations. As Song and Zhu (2011) and Spanyi (2003) have discussed, only some of the organizations are able to integrate and coordinate beyond functional departments to form end-to-end process, which is from the customers to final results, and improve process-based activities efficiently. This has motivated the researcher also to conduct this research.

After training, the researcher started to implement customer-centric thinking into information technology system projects. The results of that thinking were easy to see, since the gap between the business and IT systems people was getting smaller through successful BPM. In 2010, the researcher started as a PhD student in the Turku School of Economics information systems science department and it seemed natural to conduct scientific research on the success and failure capability factors that the researcher had seen in practical work while consulting organisations on BPM.

The motivation for this research is different from traditional BPM maturity models (e.g. Fisher 2004; Rosemann and de Bruinn 2005; Rosemann et al. 2006; Hammer 2007; Lee et al. 2007; Rohloff 2009; Weber et al. 2008). The idea was not to build yet another maturity model to tell the organisation at what level they are (following BPM maturity critique presented in Niehaves et al. (2014) as well as Pöppelbuß and Röglinger (2011), but rather to have a tool for easily and clearly understanding what capability factors should be in place to promote BPM success in companies. The BPM field has not been very organised in giving practical guidance on capabilities and the researcher found this gap through his practical consulting work. The main motivation to carry out this research was to find out which capability factors are related to the success and failure of BPM and how organisations can take them practically into account in their BPM initiatives. The basis of the research comes from theory, and that knowledge is then practically used by building an artifact, which is also evaluated. The researcher found maturity models to be impractical in his consulting work and this has been expressed also by Niehaves et al. (2014) in their research as the following quote expresses (p. 91):

> ...we challenge this maturity model perspective on BPM capability development which generally implies that BPM routines corresponding to the highest maturity levels are the most desirable ones. Based on existing literature on dynamic capability evolution and a real-life case study, we argue that organizations neither develop necessarily on the paths described by existing maturity models nor should they be recommended unconditionally to do so. Instead, a constant alignment with their respective environment seems needed.

This has inspired the researcher to design a practical artifact, which can be used to understand current level of BPM capabilities in organizations in their respective environment. Figure 1 shows the motivation for this research in brief. The column on the left side contains matters against the research and the column on the right side contains matters for the research. These are discussed in more detail below the figure.

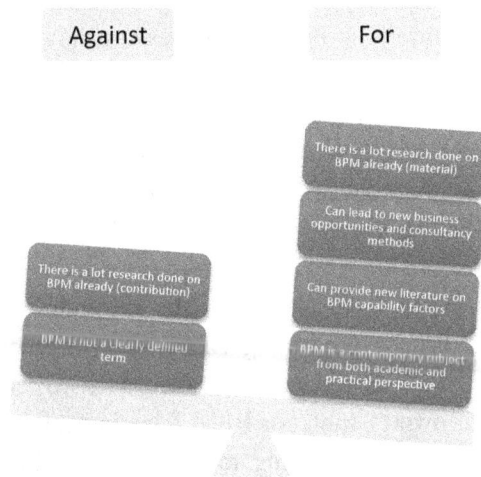

Figure 1.   Pros and cons for this research

BPM is not a clearly defined term (Palmberg 2009). Therefore, it is important first to define the term BPM in the context of this research. This research focuses on BPM capability factors. The researcher's view of BPM is explained in chapter 1.4.

A lot of research has already been carried out on BPM (Bandara et al. 2009). Generally speaking, there is a lot of material on BPM, as the literature review of this research shows. This matter can be used as an advantage in this research when searching for the success and failure capability factors that other researchers have found in their studies (which contributes to the 'for' side), but it is difficult to find new contributions on BPM (which contributes to the 'against' side). However, this research aims to contribute by formulating existing and new information on BPMC factors into a unique artifact that will enable organisations to evaluate their capabilities for succeeding at BPM.

BPM is a contemporary subject from a practical perspective and it can lead to new business opportunities and consultancy methods (vom Brocke and Rosemann 2010). Oracle (2008) published a whitepaper stating that the estimated size of the BPM market was around 5.5B$ in 2011. Also Gartner Group (2009) has indicated that business process management continues to stay as an important business priority. BPTrends (2010) made a survey where they asked respondents to describe organization's current interest in business process initiatives. 52% said their organizations had either a strategic commitment to becoming process-centric, or were engaged in one or more major business process change projects. An additional 45% said they were exploring opportunities or had made an initial commitment. This implies that the markets are growing and demand for BPM services is increasing. Thus, it is important for organisations be able to measure how capable they are at BPM. According to Oracle's (2008) whitepaper, organisations are likely to pursue the following corporate initiatives within the next two years: business process improvement, technology upgrades and new products or services expansion. BPM may be able to help organisations succeed in each of these initiatives by making business processes visible (see the Oracle's 2008 whitepaper for more details).

Even though Oracle (2008) has paid for the research mentioned above and it has its own agendas for promoting BPM, several other enterprises have awoken to BPM as well. Big companies such as IBM, SAP and Lombardi have developed their own IT tools for BPM. This indicates an interest in BPM in the business field. Also according to Houy et al. (2011), BPM is not a temporary fashion but an evolving trend.

BPM is a contemporary subject from an academic perspective and research on it can provide new literature on BPM factors. This research provides new information on the success and failure capability factors of BPM. The literature review collects the most important success and failure factors found for BPM. This information is then used to design a unique artifact for evaluating BPM success and failure capability factors. According to Niehaves et al. (2013), *"developing BPM capabilities constitutes a key challenge for organizations"*.

The results of this research may be used as a basis for providing new consulting services and improving contemporary ones. Several studies state that managers do not necessarily know how to use research outcomes and therefore do not know how to utilise them (Whitley 1984; Gill and Johnson 1991). That is why it is important to have a practical approach to utilising scientific research results that explain phenomena and provide managers with the possibilities to understand the theory behind the action. To achieve that goal, this research is based on design science, which is used to create a useful artifact for practical use based on theory. Chapter 6.5.3 explains in more detail, how to use the artifact in practical environment.

Most of the benefits of this research's outcomes come as knowledge and a deeper understanding of the capability factors required in organisations to carry out BPM. This enables us to design consultancy and measuring systems for finding out how ready organisations are for BPM and for which areas it should focus on more to be successful at BPM.

1.3   Research problem

This research focuses on *which capability factors are related to the success and failure of BPM and how can organisations take these capability factors into account in their BPM initiatives.* The purpose of this work is to design a tool, which can be used to systematically assess and improve capabilities (i.e. skills or competences) in order to reach business process excellence. Related to the research question presented in this thesis, Niehaves et al. (2013) have written, *"divergence theory appears to be better able to inform decision makers for building dynamic capabilities than maturity models"*. BPMC artifact does not present a maturity model with desirable predetermined stages, but rather functions as a practical tool for understanding the level of current capabilities, which then enables organisation to define their desired stage based on their environment and other variables (requiring help from BPM professional). According to Curtis and Alden (2007), most maturity models contain only a set of capability areas and descriptions of capability and maturity levels, and leave the actual identification of improvement measures to the model user. BPMC artifact has been designed to help with that challenge by giving instructions on how to do the improvement measurement using the artifact and then using the skills of a BPM professional to design appropriate improvement actions to be taken by the organisation.

Based on design science (March and Smith, 1995), the research is carried out in two phases: building the artifact and evaluating it. Most of the building is carried out in the literature review part of this research, which aims to answer the first part of research question: *"Which capability factors are related to the success and failure of BPM?"*. That knowledge is complemented with a quantitative analysis of the capability factors found in the literature review and expert interviews with BPM professionals all over the world.

The artifact is evaluated with case organisations and focuses on the second part of the research question: *"How can organisations take these capability factors into account in their BPM initiatives?"*. The purpose of the cases is to use the artifact in a practical environment to see how well it performs. The case studies showed that the BPMC artifact performs well in use and is able to produce useful and important information for organisations. As part of using the artifact, one difference to existing maturity models is to enable the artifact to be more flexible and therefore address the issue related to rigidity of such models (Mettler and Rohner 2009). This research question also addresses the desire of King and Kraemer (1984) who have written that maturity models should not focus just on a sequence of levels toward a predefined desirable end-state, but on factors driving evolution and change in an organisation.

In design science, building the artifact is the first part of the research (March and Smith, 1995). Peffers et al. (2008) could be seen having in this first phase the following steps: problem identification and motivation, definition of the objectives for a solution, design and development. Then second phase may consists of demonstration, evaluation, and communication according to Peffers et al. (2008). In this research, the artifact is a list of capability factors in BPM, which is build based on the principles described by March and Smith (1995) and Peffers et al. (2008). That artifact is then evaluated with case examples. According to the Collins Cobuild English language dictionary (1987), an artifact is *"an object that is made by a person, for example, a tool or an ornament"*. Building the list of capability factors is based on a wide range of BPM articles presented in this research, looking for the factors that have contributed to the success or failure of BPM initiatives.

According to Quinton and Smallbone (2006), *"critical management research requires an open attitude and an expectation that we do not see the results before they appear. The role of a modern critical researcher is to open the way for discourse rather than to find the one true way"*. This research can open up discussion on which capability factors may affect success in BPM. As the literature review of this research shows, there have been a lot of studies of these factors, but no one has made one collective and practical tool using design science for evaluating whether an organisation has the needed capabilities to succeed at BPM. Based on Quinton and Smallbone (2006), this research does not claim to show all the capability factors in one holistic tool, but rather opens up the discussion and provides organisations with something to start improving their own capabilities towards successful BPM. Future studies should be performed to refine the results and to show why these certain capability factors affect BPM success.

Based on Järvinen (1999, 59), constructive research aims to search for answers to questions such as *"can we build a certain artifact and how useful is a particular artifact?"*. The contribution of this research is building the BPMC artifact and evaluating its usefulness. This research also provides a base for the knowledge on what kinds of capability factors are related to BPM. As an answer to the first part of the research problem, the researcher was able to find 35 BPMC factors, which are presented in chapter 7.1. For the latter part, the researcher developed a process based on case studies to use the BPMC artifact, which is presented in chapter 6.5.3.

1.4   Key concepts, terms and glossary

The researcher sees BPM as a management approach that may promote business effectiveness and efficiency while striving for innovation, flexibility and integration with a process–oriented perspective on organising the company and its resources (loosely based on Ongaro 2004). BPM can be seen as attempting to continuously improve processes. It could therefore be described as a *'process optimisation process'*. BPM also focuses on business process automation and modelling. Since BPM is quite vague as a term (e.g. Lee L. L. 2005; Palmberg 2009), it is described more accurately through the literature analysis in this study.

A business process is defined as a collection of related, structured activities that produce a service or product that meet the needs of the organisation's clients (Bund 2005). These processes are critical to any organisation as they generate revenue and often represent a significant proportion of costs. The business is driven by business events and for each business event there is an associated business process to be executed. A business process coordinates the execution of business activities and the execution is carried out in accordance with business rules.

According to Song and Zhu (2011), business process management (BPM) will become one of the most popular business and technology management methods in the recent years. BPM is an approach to integrate a *'change capability'* to an organisation - both human and technological. It seems that there is no one single definition for the term BPM (Palmberg 2009; Lee L. L. 2005). Therefore, it is important to define what this research means by BPM. This is done in chapter 2.1 in this study.

BPMC is an abbreviation of Business Process Management Capabilities, which refers to the artifact that is built and evaluated in this study. BPMC factors refer to those factors that are important from BPM capability perspective. Those factors are thought to affect the success or failure of BPM initiatives. The artifact aims to make the evaluation of these capabilities practical.

'Success' is a complex phenomenon according to Seddon et al. (1999). Success in this study is defined to be any BPM initiative that is able to bring the organisation positive results when intended goals of the BPM initiative are met to a satisfactory level (adapted from Bandara et al. 2009). This means that the BPM initiative is able to add value to organisation in some way. When using the literature in this study, success is seen as the original authors describe it in their articles. Failure is seen as the opposite of previous, taking value from organisation more than giving it. Strict definition of terms success and failure are not that important in this study, because the artifact focuses on more holistic perspective in building useful capabilities in organisations.

When this work is referring to 'positive' or 'positive results' or similar, it means that the organisation will receive outcomes that are beneficial for it. This could mean better adoption of process methods, favourable reception by employees, increased revenue or other business related positive outcomes. 'Negative' or 'failure' or seen as opposite to previously described.

The factors by themselves cannot produce value without resources. They may include such matters as management, organisation, processes and knowledge (ITIL 2007). This study will focus on the leadership, change and IT factors in BPM context. Capability factor is determined to be a factor, which aids successful outcome of a BPM initiative. Failure factor is just the opposite of previous, aiding BPM initiative to fail.

The definition of capability factors follows Laamanen and Tinnilä (2009), who state "*capability is the ability, in practice, to act in a purposeful way*". Helfat and Peteraf (2003) claim that for something to qualify as a capability, it must at least work in a reliable matter. This thesis is also following Rockart's (1979); Magal et al.'s (1988) and Bandara et al.'s (2009) define capability factors as key areas where 'things must go right' in order for the BPM initiative to proceed efficiently and be completed successfully. In this dissertation, we are looking into abilities to evaluate how capable an organisation is at this moment of conducting a BPM initiative. Capability factors are explained in more detail in chapter 2.3.

1.5   Introducing the literature part of the study

There is a lot of previous research in the field of BPM, as the literature review of this research shows. BPM seems to be a vast field of study with several focuses on different matters. As Bandara et al. (2009) quotes several sources, a well structured literature review can provide a foundation for further research in new or very narrow topics such as BPM (Seuring and Muller 2008) and can help to identify conceptual content and develop theories (Meredith 1993; Seuring and Muller 2008). Also Jurisch et al. (2014) write that the BPM research field "*builds on a wealth of knowledge derived from a large number of case studies. All of these case studies provide comprehensive reviews of past failures and successes. This rich pool of knowledge has remained largely unexploited.*" Ray et al. (2005) have said that capabilities can only be of value if they are exploited in the organisation's processes. And this is one of the underlying reasons for this thesis also (to build a practical artifact from years of scientific research).

The search results with keywords *business process management* from databases[1] produced about 140,000 results in October 2014. For the keywords *"business process management"*, the databases presented earlier provided about 70,000 results and for *"capability management"* about 40,000 results around the same time. The search word *BPM* resulted in about 3,700 articles. For *"business process management factors"*, we got about 70,000 results. This study uses over 200 relevant sources as the basis for the literature review.

The literature review is divided into two parts: prior to 1999 and after that. This is following the division presented in Harmon's book (2007, chapter 1) where Internet changed also how BPM is perceived in 1990s and 2000s in a different way. Dividing the sources into these two categories enabled the researcher to see how the BPM domain has developed during different time periods (although that was not the main goal). The researcher found that the factors contributing to success differed little in these time periods and the final BPMC artifact joined those factors together. This helped the researcher evaluate whether some factors have become outdated in recent years.

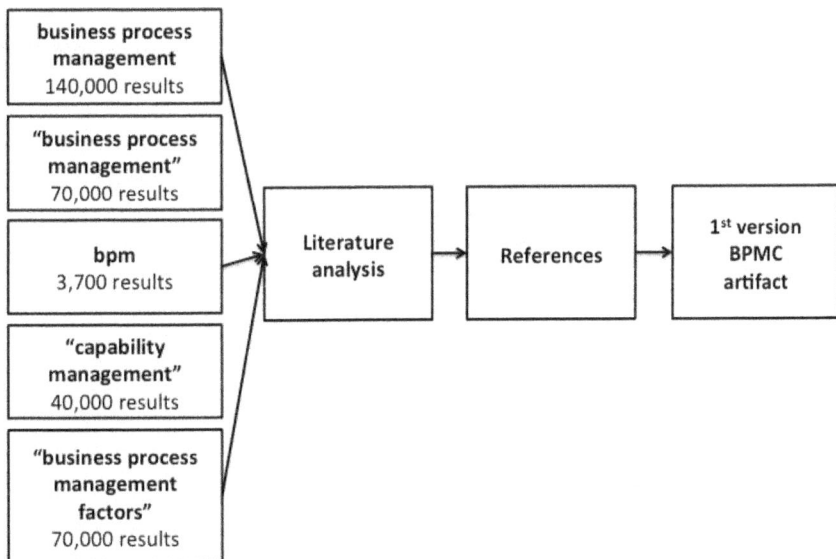

Figure 20.   Literature Search Keywords

The most referenced sources for this research were articles by Al-Mashari and Zairi (1999); Hammer and Stanton (1999), McAdam and Donaghy (1999); Paper, Rodger and Pendharkar (2001); Abdolvand, Albadvi and Ferdowsi

---

[1] Computer + Info Systems (CSA), Science Citation Index (ISI), Web of Science (ISI), Web of Knowledge (ISI), SCIRUS (Elsevier), ACM Computing Classification System, ACM (Association for Computing Machinery), Volter - Turun yliopisto and Ebrary.

(2008); Palmberg (2009) and Trkman (2010). These articles contained most interesting research regarding the topic of this study. Through the literature review, it was possible to find over 50 positive capability factors and 30 failure capability factors. The first proposition for the BPMC artifact is based on those success and failure factors and it contains 26 positive capability factors and 27 failure factors.

1.6   Introducing the empirical part of the study

In the design science, empirical methods are important for the investigation of the actual effects, the efficiency and other characteristics concerning the practical usage of innovative design artifact (Fettke 2010). The researcher is following the ideas presented by Niehaves et al. (2014) in the following quote: *"Qualitative research has a long tradition in the field of IS (Kern and Willcocks 2002; Mingers 2003; Remenyi and Williams, 1996) and is especially suitable when the research area is still emerging (Bandara et al. 2005; Yin 2003) and not controllable by the investigators (Yin 2003). Our field of BPM capability development is such an area (Rosemann 2010)."* The empirical data collection of this study is two-fold: 1) interviewing BPM professionals to build BPMCs and 2) case studies in organisations to design and evaluate the BPMC artifact further. The picture below shows the two approaches used to design and evaluate the artifact and their empirical data collection methods. These are explained in more details in chapters 0 and 6.

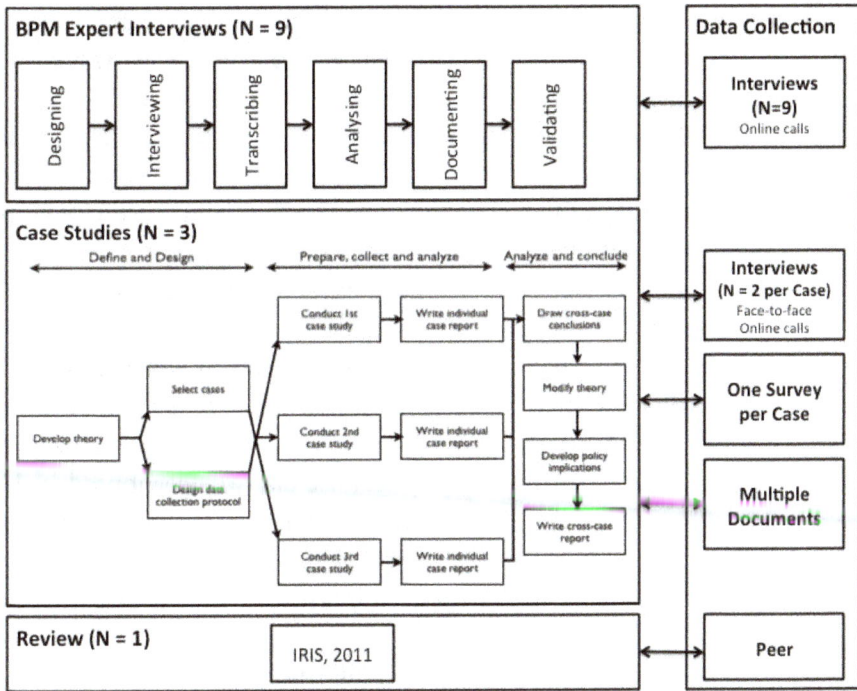

Figure 21.   Introducing the empirical part of the study

Expert interviews. As Eriksson and Kovalainen (2008, 78) present in their book, "*interviews consist of talk organized into a series of questions and answers*". In this research, nine expert interviews are used to ask BPM professionals about their views on the BPMC artifact. These results are analysed and used to refine the artifact, which in the first phase is based on the findings from the literature review. BPM professionals are chosen to be the target group for interviews, because they have practical experience of success and failure in BPM initiatives. Interviews were held face-to-face whenever possible, but otherwise they were conducted through recorded online calls. The purpose of these interviews was to produce empirical material for building the artifact. As a result of the nine expert interviews, the success and failure factors were put together, because many failure capability factors were reversed versions of other success capability factors as described in chapter 5.3.1. Further, the categorisation of BPMC factors changed from the first proposed version to a simpler format.

Case studies. In this research, the case is seen as one organisation, which is the target of BPM initiatives. The study is not labelled case research, because in this study the cases are used more as a data collection method than as a research approach. The role of case studies in this thesis is two-fold: to do an iterative round of designing the artifact further and to evaluate the artifact in real-world use. Even though March and Smith (1995) claim that evaluation is not needed, because this research is producing new research outcomes, Järvinen (1999, 68) states *"although the outcome itself is the merit, the potential importance of the new construct, model, method and instantiation can be evaluated"*. The researcher complies with Järvinen's view that in this study the built artifact should be evaluated in actual use to see its potential importance. Also Peffers et al. (2008) mention the importance of evaluation of the artifact in design science. The purpose of using cases in this study is to the evaluate ease of use, practical usefulness, completeness, simplicity, elegance and understandability of the built artifact (March and Smith 1995). As this thesis will show later, the first case study resulted in small design changes to the wording of a few BPMC factors. Two other case studies were used to verify the BPMC artifact in practical use and whether it produced useful and interesting information for the participating case organisation. Each case study is described in more details in chapter 6. Especially chapters 6.2.1, 6.3.1and 6.4.1 contain more information on who were interviewed in each case and when.

Review. The findings from literature were peer reviewed in IRIS (2011) conference. The article written based on this thesis was discussed amongst the academic practitioners in the conference. The feedback received from this event was used to improve the way the artifact is presented in this thesis. The article can be found using the reference Ohtonen and Lainema (2011) from the end of this thesis.

1.7   The organisation of this study

This research follows the design science principles set by March and Smith (1995), Hevner et al. (2004) and Peffers et al. (2008). Design science is concerned with *"devising artefacts to attain goals"* (Simon 1981, p.133). According to Peffers et al. (2008), design science is of importance in a discipline oriented to creation of successful artifacts. Purpose of using design science in this research is to create *"a thing"* that serves human purposes. Rather than producing general theoretical knowledge, design scientists produce and apply knowledge of tasks or situations in order to create effective artefacts (March and Smith 1995, p.253). Design science consists of two basic activities, build and evaluate. Building is the process of constructing an artifact for a specific purpose; evaluation is the process of determining how well the artifact performs (March and Smith 1995, 254).

Building is the process of constructing the BPMC artifact for a specific purpose; evaluation is the process of determining how well the BPMC artifact performs (March and Smith 1995, 254). Design is both a process (set of activities) and a product (artifact). It describes the world as acted upon (processes) and the world as sensed (artifacts) (Hevner et al. 2004, 78). The design process is a sequence of expert activities that produces an innovative product (i.e., the design artifact). The evaluation of the artifact then provides feedback information and a better understanding of the problem in order to improve both the quality of the product and the design process. In this research, expert interviews are used as the main tool for acquiring information for building phase. Then case studies including surveys and interviews are used to evaluate the artefact as well as to iterate the build-and-evaluate loop, which is typically iterated a number of times before the final design artifact is generated (Hevner et al. 2004, p.78).

The focus of this study is not to create software, but to device an artifact, which can be used for giving useful knowledge about current state of an organisation regarding BPM capabilities in current environment. It is left for future research to create software, which will use BPMC artifact as a basis. This study does not use action design science (Sein et al. 2011), because researcher wanted to build and evaluate the BPMC artifact first, before taking it into organisations to change them. That is left for future research.

This thesis is outlined into seven main chapters, which are shown in a picture below. The first chapter introduces this study and the background to it. The second chapter focuses on the theoretical background of this study. The third chapter contains the literature review and proposal for the first version of the BPMC artifact. The fourth chapter explains the methodological choices of this study regarding design science. The fifth chapter focuses on building the BPMC artifact further through expert interviews. The sixth chapter finalises the building of the artifact and evaluates it in practical use through case studies. The seventh chapter contains conclusions and a summary of this study.

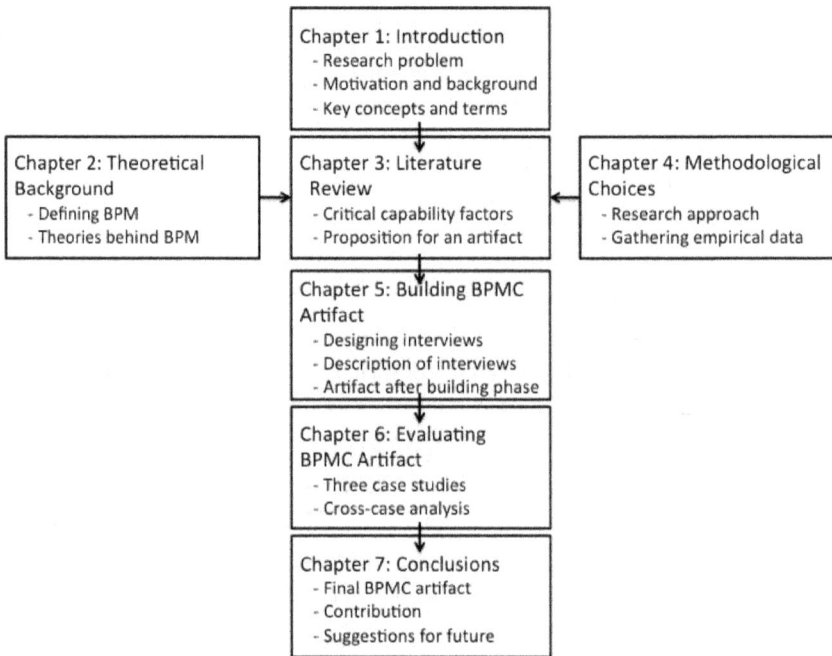

Figure 23. Chapters in this study

The table below shows how this research is organised in relation to structures presented by March and Smith (1995), Hevner et al. (2004) and Peffers et al. (2008).

Table 9.   Research chapters in relation to design science approaches

Thesis Chapter	March and Smith (1995)	Hevner et al. (2004)	Peffers et al. (2008)
Chapter 1.	Justify	Guideline 2. Problem relevance Guideline 7. Communication of Research	Activity 1. Problem identification and motivation. Activity 2. Define the objectives for a solution. Activity 6. Communication.
Chapter 2.	Theorize	Guideline 7. Communication of Research	Activity 6. Communication.
Chapter 3.	Build	Guideline 1. Design as an artifact	Activity 2. Define the objectives for a solution.
Chapter 4.	Theorize	Guideline 5.	Activity 3. Design

		Research rigor Guideline 6. Design as a Search process	and development.
Chapter 5.	Build	Guideline 1. Design as an artifact Guideline 5. Research rigor	Activity 3. Design and development.
Chapter 6.	Evaluate	Guideline 3. Design Evaluation	Activity 4. Demonstration. Activity 5. Evaluation.
Chapter 7.	Justify	Guideline 4. Research contribution Guideline 7. Communication of Research	Activity 6. Communication.

1.8   Limitations

This study has some limitations. One is that this research is not able to show why the BPMC factors discovered herein are important. The research is not able to compare different industries or cultures either. Since the focus of this research is a practical approach to developing the BPMC artifact, some parts of the theory could be researched deeper, especially in the area of originality of the identified capability factors. Also, it remains important to discover how the chosen capability factors are related to each other.

Another limitation concerns the use of the BPMC artifact. Only process professionals who have enough knowledge to adjust to the use of a tool to suit the target organisation and environment can use it. The BPMC artifact also requires enough knowledge to analyse and interpret the results. However, it is very important to let organizations know where they are today (Song and Zhu 2011). By following this thesis, organizations may be able to do the evaluation themselves using the information presented in this thesis.

It is not within the scope of this thesis to start evaluating possible new capability factors related to BPM that have not emerged from the literature or through the case studies of this thesis. The researcher suggests conducting another study of the new capability factors presented in this research to see how relevant they are. This thesis follows the previous research results identified in the literature review section of the study to create first iteration version of the artifact. This causes some limitations to the originality of the factors in this work. However, as the results chapter at the end of this thesis will show, this work is clearly a unique and original work, which has succeeded to add to the domain of business process management capabilities.

This research is able to identify that certain capabilities are important for organisations and based on the literature these are related to the success or failure of BPM initiatives. Like Larsen and Myers (1997) have said, *"it is difficult in practice to identify those factors, which led to success or failure."* What this research did not focus on was to what extent each of these capabilities actually affects success and how that success can be quantified and measured. The definition of 'success' in this context can be put under debate also. Larsen and Myers (1997) described this dilemma in following way *"the extent to which a project is successful or not is not easy to determine, particularly if the viewpoints of various stakeholders are taken into account."*

This research is a snapshot from the case organisations. It might be beneficial to revisit these organisations after a suitable period of time to reevaluate how their BPMCs have developed. Naturally, this is more useful with those case organisations that are aiming to purposefully improve their BPMCs in the future. The limitation of this research is showing how organisations can and will develop those capabilities over time (longitudinal research).

This research is mainly based on design science method, though it has abductive elements in it also (as discussed in chapter 2). For this reason generalizability of the results of this research may be limited to those case organisations presented in this study. The goal of this work has not been to find a definitive list of new capability factors, but to find the ones that are in BPM capability literature already and then design an artifact based on them through iterative design rounds. Another potential research method could have been action research, but the researcher analysed this phase to be early for action research, since BPM capabilities are not clearly articulated so far in this form. Another potential research method could have been Action Design Science, where the artifact is built and used to change an organisation, but researcher didn't choose this research method, because he concluded that it would be more suitable for future research once this first version of the artifact is built. In future research this artifact could be refined through Action Design Science where the artifact is developed further and used to change some case organisation.

The proposition is that in BPM, certain capability factors contribute to the success or failure of that initiative. These capability factors may not necessarily be only BPM-specific; they may also be generic skills that are useful in other organisational improvement initiatives (this is left for future studies to find out). Such skills may be for example:

- Mindset of the people
- Attitude towards change
- Ability to '*think outside the box*'
- Ability to question the '*status quo*'
- Focus towards customers' needs

This work is not able to show any concrete improvements resulting from business process management (Anyanwu 2003). BPMC artifact is designed for measuring current level of business process management capabilities and therefore does not directly aid in improving such capabilities.

Regarding expert interviews and case studies conducted in this thesis, some results are a matter of interpretation and reading of case narratives written by other researchers. Here, other researchers will probably derive slightly different findings. Although some aspects may be a matter of discussion, this research has gone through several stages of review (e.g. thesis review and interview review by the participants) and therefore several academics (e.g. thesis supervisor, thesis reviewers, expert interview participants) have agreed on the presented interpretation. Hence, the researcher argues that case reading presented in this thesis is empirically sound and valid. Second, the generalizability of this study is limited as the researcher only studied three case organisations.

2 THEORETICAL BACKGROUND

2.1 Defining BPM

Process management is almost 100 years old concept (Shewhart 1931; Davenport and Stoddard 1994). It has been seen as a challenger to product control concepts. The basic idea of business processes and their management has been to create value for the customer through activities in an organisation (Laamanen and Tinnilä 2009; Hammer and Stanton 1999; Bund 2005) and to fulfil other strategies such as providing returns to stakeholders (Guha and Kettinger 1993; Strnadl 2006). The development of process methodologies started in the 1970s, while Business Process Reengineering (BPR) and other methods were introduced from the 1990s onwards. Palmberg (2009) has researched the history and development of BPM. Palmberg concludes, based on a wide literature review, that there is no clear definition of BPM (also Møller 2008; Ko 2009; Bandara et al. 2010). She states that it is to be seen more as a collection of certain matters rather than as one clear term. Also Lindsay (2003), writes *"definitions of business process given in much of the literature on Business Process Management are limited in depth and their related models of business processes are correspondingly constrained"*. Still, process management has stayed on the surface of business management concepts throughout the years. Contemporary organisations need to reengineer and organise themselves to be more efficient in such a challenging competitive environment (Aler et al. 2002). According to research reports (e.g. de Bruin and Rosemann 2007; Oracle 2008; Gartner 2009; Song and Zhu 2011; Houy et al. 2011), BPM is found to be one of the top development priorities in organisations. You may note that change management and BPM can easily be seen to be interrelated since BPM is designed to change the functionalities of the organisation with the support of appropriate change management.

BPM summary by Palmberg (2009) finds that even practitioners have different perspectives on what BPM really is. Even though it is possible to analyse the term, there is no easy way out from the fact that there is no one truth in that. Business aims to accumulate wealth through one's work. Process as a term is described according to Palmberg (2009) differently depending on the author. 'Process' is a word, which is appears in many different disciplines, and for different people, it has different meanings (Gulledge and Sommer

2002) She identifies six components from these definitions: input and output, interrelated activities, horizontal: intra-functional or cross-functional, purpose or value for customer, the use of resources, and repeatability. A basic process definition is described in Figure 3.

A horizontal sequence of activities...

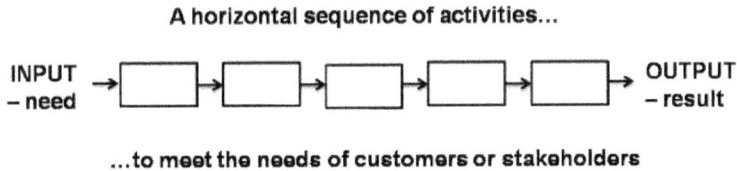

...to meet the needs of customers or stakeholders

Figure 3.   A horizontal sequence of activities (Palmberg 2009)

Processes may be related to the different functional areas in an organisation (Laamanen and Tinnilä 2009). Organizations may have processes such as marketing or manufacturing (Zairi 1997). Moreover, the complexity of the processes may vary greatly and flow of processes between functional areas has been found challenging (Davenport 1993; Earl 1994; Rummler and Brache 2012; Davenport 2013). Researcher suggests reading a book by Rummler and Brache (2012) for a method that can be used to improve organisational performance across functional departments and processes. People participate in processes as part of their work through activities. Palmberg (2009) identifies two important roles related to processes: process owner and member. The first is responsible for the process and the second for participating in it (Laamanen and Tinnilä 2009, 24).

Palmberg (2009) summarises the results and analysis of her literature review. The model is described in Figure 4 and it shows well what people perceive BPM to be generally.

Process definition	A horizontal sequence of activities that transforms an input (need) to an output (result) to meet the needs of customers or stakeholders
Process categorizations	Strategic, Operational, Supportive Process → Sub-process → Activity → Task
Process roles	• Process owner • Process team members
Purpose of process management	• Remove barriers • Control and improve the processes • Improve quality of products & services • Identify opp. for use of technology • Improve collective learning • Align with strategic objectives • Improve organizational effectiveness • Improve business performance

Definition of process management	(A) A structured systematic approach to analyze and continually improve the process	(B) A holistic manner to manage all aspects of the business and a valuable perspective in determining organizational effectiveness
Approaches for process management	1. Process selection 2. Process description and mapping 3. Organizing for quality 4. Process measurements 5. Process improvements	• Process architecture • Process visibility • Monitoring mechanisms • Improvement mechanisms
Tools for process management	• Process mapping • Process measurement • Process re-engineering or re-design • Models for continuous improvement • Instrument for benchmarking	

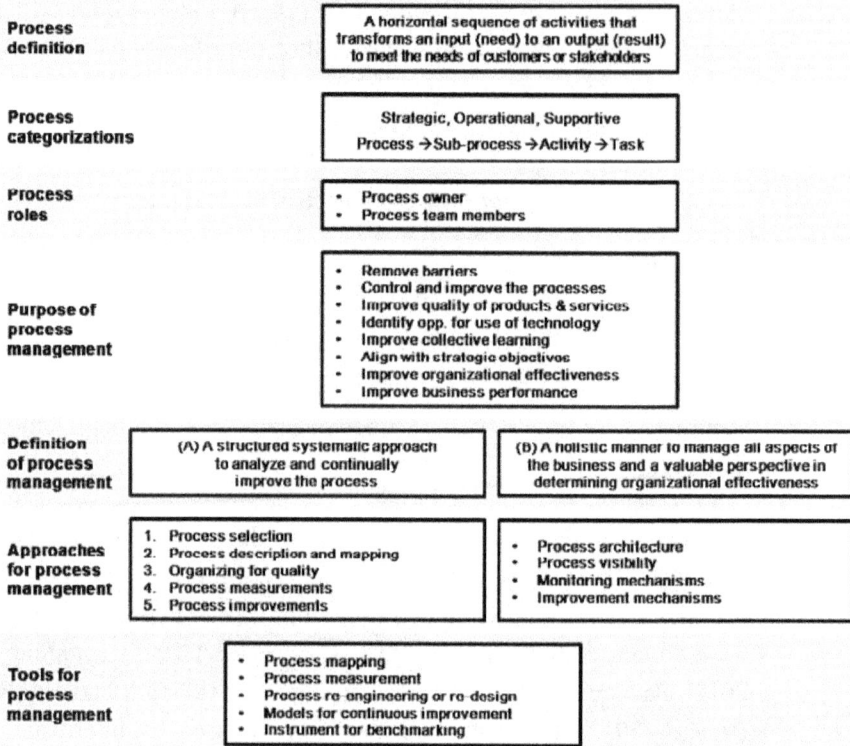

Figure 4.   Process definition

We can briefly examine this model from a BPM factors perspective. The process definition was described in more detail earlier. The idea of a process as a sequence of tasks, from inputs to outputs, is that it aims to produce more value to customers and stakeholders (Laamanen and Tinnilä 2009; Egnell and Klefsjö 1995). There is not really any business unless customer organisations see the services of the provider organisation to be so valuable that they are willing to pay for them. Thus, there is no business without customers (Drucker 1954), and without the customer, the process becomes obsolete. Another point in process thinking is not to make people do more, but to do things differently, so that the value comes through the process (Laamanen and Tinnilä 2009). That may be one reason for the words 'radical change' being mentioned so often when talking about BPM, though Manfreda et al. (2014) have claimed that the radicalness of change depends a lot on the absorptive capacity of the organisation (in other words, that radicalness depends a lot on how radical employees of an organisation perceive that change to be).

Process categorisation is an interesting subject, since people seem to have a natural tendency to categorise things. From a BPM factors perspective, the categorisation of success and failure factors is more important than the actual categorisation of processes. However, the categorisation of processes is also important in organisations that have several core or strategic processes.

The roles of people in processes are a key issue in BPM. Organisations are usually based on some kind of hierarchy. Several researchers (e.g. Zairi and Sinclair 1995; Woolfe, 1993; Hammer and Stanton 1999) have shown that support from top and middle management is crucial for process improvement efforts to succeed, as this thesis will show. It is important to have responsible people for processes and they are key factors in successful BPM (Møller 2008). Even though process improvement may cause revolutionary changes in an organisation, at least from employee perspective, it should never be uncontrolled. As Manfreda et al. (2014) express in their research, *"the radicalness of changes depends on the difference between the individual or organizational perception and the scope and extent of proposed changes"*, which is an interesting perspective on people side of BPM. Niehaves et al. (2013) have regarded BPM as a management approach for achieving both evolutionary and revolutionary improvements in business processes.

The purpose of process management is to describe the very nature and reason for why BPM exists. The purposes described by Palmberg (2009) are easily seen through this research as well. Since we described the nature of the process itself earlier, it is logical for BPM to be aligned with it. The focus of BPM is more the management of the processes and ensuring that they are able to provide the benefits and outcomes that are important for customers. Organisations recognise the value of BPM as a way of attaining strategic alignments and effectively creating and implementing business strategy (Ariyachandra and Frolick 2008). Thus, the definition of the purpose of process management leads to some requirements for BPM factors.

Palmberg (2009) defines process management from two perspectives: a structured systematic approach and a holistic manner to manage all aspects of the business. Palmberg (2009) quotes Lee and Dale (1998, 213) to summarise the two perspectives as follows:

> *Business Process Management is both a set of tools and techniques for improving processes and a method for integrating the whole organization and it needs to be understood by all employees. (c.f. Palmberg 2009)*

This also conforms to the other findings in this research concerning the importance of employees understanding what kind of work system in the organization they are part of. Personally, I would also add the purpose for the organisational system to exist is to serve customers following Drucker (1954).

There are several approaches to BPM. This research does not look into the differences between them, but aims to extract the common factors. The tools for process management also vary and there are several methods for the actual implementation of BPM. This requires the process owner and team to understand and know several BPM approaches and tools to pick the one that is right for their organisations and purposes. Nowadays, many businesses are either directly or indirectly related to IT. Therefore, strategic alignment with BPM and IT means that the goals and activities of the business are in harmony with the information technology systems that support them (Woolfe 1993). As Woolfe (1993) states, IT's impact on business performance depends on the extent to which it enables business processes to be changed. Woolfe (1993) particularly recommends using IT to model and improve processes. However, IT is not the only and not even always the best way of improving processes. It is more important to do the right things, rather than only do things right.

BPR is one of the closest terms to BPM. It has attracted much interest in the academic and practitioner literature (Larsen and Myers 1997). BPR has existed as a term since the 1990s (Hammer M. 1990; Davenport and Short 1990), but there have been several definitions for it over time; therefore, it is not clear to everyone what it means (Zairi and Sinclair 1995; Palmberg 2009). The term has been used for different meanings in different situations, and managers have abused the term for downsizing efforts (Ligeti 1994; Hammer and Stanton 1999). Choi and Chan (1997) review the definitions of BPR and they find various different versions of it. The literature review presents the findings from three perspectives: what BPR concerns, how to deal with it and expectations towards BPR. Based on their analysis, they conclude:

> *There is consensus that, in performing reengineering work, it should aim to achieve a dramatic improvement.*

This same matter is also stated by Zairi and Sinclair (1995), namely that the goal of BPR is radical improvements in business processes. BPR is interested in business processes from both internal and external perspectives (Maull, Tranfield and Maull 2003). Another finding is that BPR is based on the proactive and radical redesigning of business actions (Choi and Chan 1997).

BPR is seen more as a rapid and dramatic performance improvement effort than as an incremental improvement (Ardhaldjian and Fahner 1994). It is intended for improving product and service quality, cost and speed. Maull, Tranfield and Maull (2003) state that BPR efforts can be divided into three characteristic approaches: strategic BPR, process-focused BPR and cost-focused BPR. It is important to see processes rather than functionalities to improve the whole chain of actions in an organisation. Davenport and

Stoddard (1994) conclude that successful BPR is not an IT initiative, but a business initiative with the purpose of improving business practices to satisfy the needs of customers.

Eardley et al. (2008) stated that the original definition of BPR given by Hammer and Champy (1993) was too narrow and so they rewrote it as follows:

> BPR is the fundamental rethinking and radical redesign of appropriate business processes to achieve dramatic improvements in critical, contemporary measures of performance, such as cost, quality, service and speed. Such redesign and pace of implementation to be suited to the individual organization, contingent upon the "gap" between the present state of the organization's structure, culture and IT infrastructure, and the state required to implement the new business processes successfully. An ideal state would be one in which BPR was an ongoing, proactive process.

Therefore, what are some of the differences between BPR and BPM? BPM may be seen more as a holistic approach to processes, including everything around the processes. BPR is more focused on processes and optimising them, while BPM looks into the processes, resources, roles, people, infrastructure and other aspects of the overall process management of an organisation. In BPM, it is no longer only about redesigning the processes, but also actually naming the process owners and giving them the authority to act as needed. The focus has shifted from unit goals to process goals (Hammer and Stanton 1999). As Ko et al. (2009) explain, BPM and BPR are not necessarily the same thing:

> Whereas BPR calls for a radical obliteration of existing business processes, its descendant BPM is more practical, iterative and incremental in fine-tuning business processes.

Workflow management is also often discussed in the BPM literature. There are a few different perspectives on the relationship between BPM and workflow management. Hill et al. (2008) describe this difference as follows:

> Business process management (BPM) is a process-oriented management discipline. It is not a technology. Workflow is a flow management technology found in business process management suites (BPMSs) and other product categories.

Service-oriented architecture is also mentioned in the BPM literature. BPM is a process-oriented management discipline aided by IT, while service-oriented architecture is an IT architectural paradigm (Ko, Lee and Lee 2009).

2.2 Theories behind BPM

BPM is a young field in the academic world and it has been considered to be quite non-theoretical so far (Karimi, Somers and Bhattacherjee 2007; Melão and Pidd 2000). Also Houy et al. (2011) have come to a conclusion that the development of original BPM theories is still in its early stages. According to them design-oriented research and the development of artefacts which are useful for practical application are more in focus than building theory in the classical sense. That conclusion may also be drawn from most of the capability factor articles handled in this research, which seem to be case studies or otherwise lacking a theoretical framework for BPM. In this study the author attempts to describe in detail how the study was conducted and which issues influenced the research process. But before we get to that, let's look at some of the theories behind BPM, which are relevant for this work. Trkman (2010) suggests that BPM is based on contingency theory (CT), dynamic factors theory and task–technology fit theory (TTF), which may be used as a basis for the evaluation of success capability factors in BPM. This follows the ideas presented by Houy, Fettke, and Loos (2011) where they listed 11 important theories used in empirical BPM research. Trkman (2010) sees that these three base theories can be used to categorise the success (and failure) capability factors for further discussion and more general use. Trkman (2010) explains how these three theory frameworks are related to BPM in the following quotation:

> *Firstly the fit between the business environment and business processes is needed (as claimed by the contingency theory). Then proper organization and continuous improvement efforts are needed to assure sustained benefits from BPM (as stipulated by [dynamic factors] theory). Also, the proper fit between the tasks in the business processes and information technology/systems must exist (as found by task–technology fit theory).*

Every organisation has some purpose for existing, its so-called mission, and that mission is carried out by the strategy. BPM efforts need to be firmly linked into an organisation's purpose and strategy so that it will support them. If BPM is not responding to those needs, it is either slowing the organisation down or even keeping it back. It is not effective to focus only on processes or technology; all this must be connected and intertwined for a greater purpose. That is why Trkman (2010) suggests looking into capability factors of BPM from more interconnected perspective, than just taking separate variables and thinking that they have no effect on one another. All this provides the basis for the research presented in this thesis, since there is no point trying to formulate a universal recipe for successful BPM that fits all situations and organisations (that being unrealistic to researcher's opinion). We can anyway try to identify the most common success and failure factors and offer suggestions based on them. If the base is not solid in an organisation, there may not be opportunities for greater success either.

Additional to Trkman's (2010) three background theories, this thesis suggests extending the technology acceptance model (TAM) theory with TTF and we also present a fourth background theory for BPM: Outside-In, which can be also called being customer-oriented. This is dealt with in more detail in the following chapters. There is no reason for business processes to exist at all without the customer, which provides the greater purpose for BPM generally. This thesis presents the following four background theories for BPM (Figure 5).

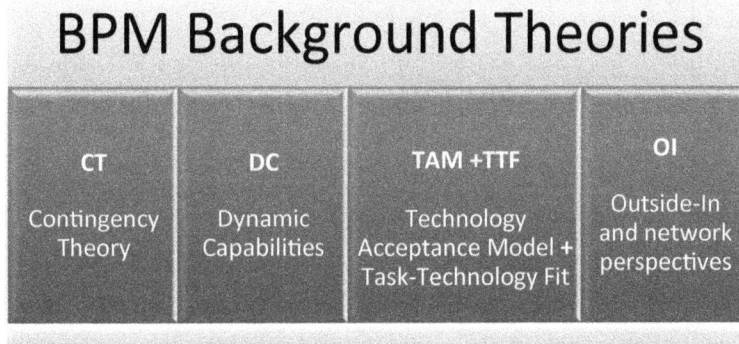

BPM Background Theories

CT	DC	TAM +TTF	OI
Contingency Theory	Dynamic Capabilities	Technology Acceptance Model + Task-Technology Fit	Outside-In and network perspectives

Figure 5.   BPM background theories (based on Trkman 2010)

In common language, we could say that based on CT, business processes are not something that organisations can just copy from each other and successfully implement if the environment or other dependents vary. Based on dynamic factors, BPM is not a single project; it needs to continue all the time. TAM and TTF state that infrastructure and technology must support the tasks people need to do in an organisation. TTF may be sufficient for BPM purposes, but TAM gives a wider perspective on technology adoption in an organisation. An outside-in philosophy gives a purpose for business processes to exist, and thus a reason to manage them. These are discussed in more detail in the following subchapters.

2.2.1   CT – Contingency Theory

Fiedler (1964) more than 40 years ago found that there is no best way of organising. One organisational style may be successful in one situation, but not in another. The best way of doing things is dependent on the internal and external environment (Trkman 2010). CT is a theoretical lens that is used to view organisations (Sousa and Voss 2008). The fit between the business environment and business processes is needed (Trkman 2010; Niehaves et al. 2014) and therefore it is important to understand the contextual conditions in which BPM is effective (Sousa and Voss 2008). No any one process model fits all organisations, but organisations need to fit their actions based on the environment. This might have some indications on the factors behind the success or failure of BPM initiatives. Figure 6 shows a proposed environment of the BPM fit that may contribute to BPM success.

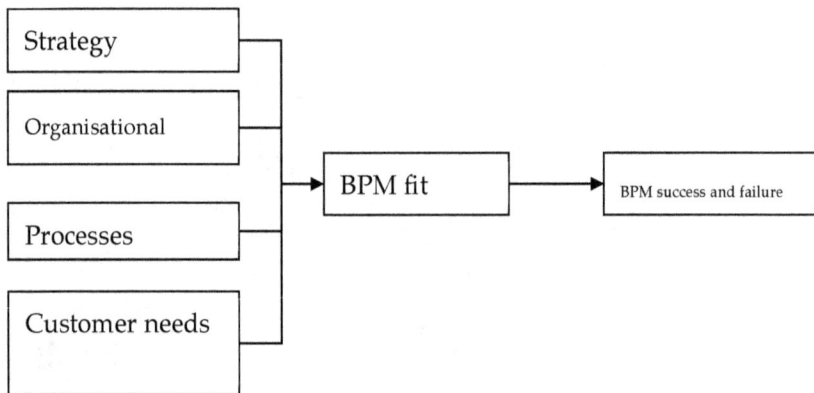

Figure 6.   Proposed BPM fit

Rogers, Miller and Judge (1999) state that strategy is an important component in organisations when examining processes. They also emphasise the alignment of strategy and structure on the competitive environment.

Organisational structure affects everything that the organisation does: from an internal perspective, the organisation is the providing party for customers, and from an external perspective, organisational structure and especially its efficiency is perceived by customers as needs fulfilling or not.

The fit between the characteristics of the adopting organisation and process designs embedded into an adopted system affects the likelihood of BPM success (Morton and Qing 2008).

Organisations operate in an environment, which contains a lot of contingencies. One of those is the customer, who is unpredictable. Organisations may be able to fulfil some of the customer's needs and those needs have to be managed in the business environment (Customer Experience Management). Some organisations may also choose to fulfil different needs of the same customer than others (note also the relation between the strategy of an organisation and customer needs).

It is not simply possible to copy successful business processes to another organisation and get the same results (Trkman 2010), as can be seen from the components of CT in BPM. Too many contingencies affect the whole picture, meaning that BPM fit varies from organisation to organisation, thus leading to different BPM success in different organisations. For this reason it is not possible to find "perfect" case organisations either, since there are too many potential combinations of BPM fit. The artifact will be designed to be suitable for use in various BPM fit and organisational contexts and also to be flexible, so that it can be changed to fit the environment where the organisation operates in. However, this will cause some challenges to generalizability of the results of this thesis. This is not a problem since purpose of design science is to design artifacts that can be used in real-world cases and therefore what this research may miss in theoretical generalizability, it may make up in practicability.

Trkman (2010) finds in his research BPM capability factors from the following areas: strategic alignment, level of IT investment, performance measurement and level of employee specialisation. Those success capability factors related to CT contribute to the BPM fit of an organisation.

2.2.2 DC – Dynamic Capabilities

Plattfaut (2011), have mentioned in their research that developing BPM capabilities in a real-life organization has become one of the key topics in BPM practice and it is becoming a central element in BPM research as well. Let's start by taking a look at the definitions of dynamic capabilities in the context of this research. Niehaves et al. (2013) claims, *"from a theoretical perspective BPM can be understood as a collection of dynamic capabilities to adapt existing business processes and create new ones to achieve a fit with the organizational environment"*. Teece, Pisano and Shuen (1997) define dynamic capabilities as exploiting existing internal and external firm-specific resources to address changing environments. Eisenhardt and Martin (2000) define dynamic capabilities, following the ideas of Teece, Pisano and Shuen (1997), as:

> *The firm's processes that use resources—specifically the processes to integrate, reconfigure, gain and release resources—to match and even create market change. Dynamic capabilities thus are the organizational and strategic routines by which firms achieve new resource configurations as markets emerge, collide, split, evolve, and die.*

The competitive advantage of dynamic capabilities does not lie in themselves, but rather in the combinations of resources that dynamic capabilities change (Eisenhardt and Martin 2000). What dynamic capabilities theory basically says is that organisations need to evolve and change based on the market situation. How and into what organisations change their resources are the dynamic capabilities that enable them to adapt to their current situations (Plattfaut et al. 2011). Researcher agrees with Plattfaut et al's (2011) view that the traditional interpretation often brought forward by maturity models that only highly mature BPM is ineffective and inefficient. They argue that organizations do not develop on a prescribed path but through constant realignment with their respective environment like previously mentioned. Researcher also agrees with Bandara et al. (2010) who state, "*adopting the dynamic capability view, BPM may be defined as a set of techniques to integrate, build and reconfigure an organisation's business processes for the purpose of achieving a fit with the market environment*".

For BPM, this means that BPM projects should not be one-time projects, but rather they need to be continuous improvement projects on business processes (Trkman 2010). What makes one organisation more successful than another is using its dynamic capabilities to arrange its resources in the best possible way for the current situation? Like Platfautt et al. (2011) quote several sources, one major question today is how organizations can and should advance their BPM capabilities. Even though competitors might imitate your organisation's dynamic capabilities, they cannot imitate easily the resources that you have to manage with dynamic capabilities nor the combination of the two. However, Plattfaut (2011) mentions that BPM capabilities are developed if needed for competitive survival and that they are acquired through learning and imitation. Basically this means that companies need to imitate some of the capabilities from each other. To gain that competitive advantage, dynamic capabilities are needed, but they are not sufficient alone (Eisenhardt and Martin 2000).

Through carrying out BPM continuously, an organisation can achieve and maintain its competitive advantage by using the resources it has in the best possible way. This also means that organisational structure and culture has to support BPM (Cooper 1994; Trkman 2010). Schmiedel et al. (2012) have done a research on the connection of BPM and culture and they came to conclusion that culture, which supports BPM objectives, is important for success. They have presented an instrument to measure BPM culture in organisations in their work.

Trkman (2010) finds BPM capability factors from the following dynamic capability areas: organisational change, appointment of process owners, implementation of proposed changes (quick-win strategy) and use of a continuous improvement system. Jurisch et al. (2014) have stated that the reason why some process change initiatives fail while others succeed may be attributed to differences in resources and capabilities. They write that important for the success of a BPM project and the performance of the improved business process is that the organization possesses the necessary capabilities to select, deploy, and organize these resources properly.

While using dynamic capabilities to adjust the resources of an organisation, one has to bear in mind the purpose for the changes. The Outside-In perspective provides the purpose for the changes based on successful customer outcomes and customer needs, which are the underlying reason for changes in markets (from some perspective markets can be perceived as collective customer needs). Niehaves et al. (2014) have argued that in moderately dynamic markets, the evolution of dynamic capabilities is argued to be rather slow. On the other hand they also argue that in highly dynamic markets, effective dynamic capabilities are expected to be adaptive to constantly changing circumstances.

2.2.3   TAM + TTF – TAM extended with TTF

It is hard to avoid using IT in contemporary business. Most businesses are either directly or indirectly linked into IT, and this has brought many good and bad things into play. TTF theory states that IT has a positive impact on work and individual performance if the factors of IT match the activities that workers must perform (Goodhue and Thompson 1995). This has clear indications for BPM, where the automation of routine tasks and easing human-related tasks with IT is the current trend.

As Dishaw and Strong (1999) explain, *"task-technology fit focuses on the match between user task needs and the available functionality of the IT"*. They combine the TTF model with TAM and find that this is able to better explain the variance in IT utilisation that either model alone. Figure 7 shows the integrated TAM/TTF model described by Dishaw and Strong (1999).

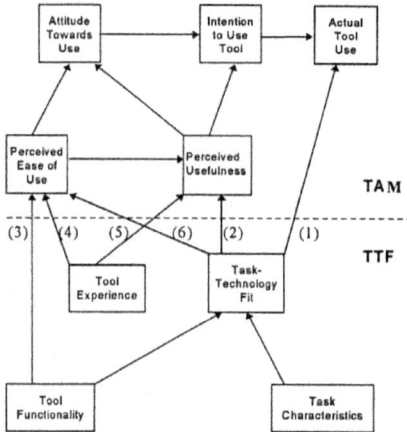

Figure 7.   Integrated TAM/TTF model

From a BPM perspective, we are interested in the TTF side of the model, since business processes are directly related to tasks and IT is seen as supporting processes (and through them tasks). For this reason TAM is not considered in this thesis. As Smith and Fingar (2003) provocatively state: "*IT does not matter, business processes do*". If IT users do not see the perceived usefulness from the technology, they will not use it. Bleistein, Cox, Verner and Phalp (2006) state that the alignment of IT with an organisation's strategy is crucial for business success. That alignment exists when processes are in line with the information technology that supports them (McKeen and Smith 2003). TAM becomes important when new tools are presented to organisations as part of BPM initiatives. Those systems will shape how people do work and how they perceive and actually use such systems like BPMS. TAM can be used to analyse the factors that potentially influence the level of technology acceptance and use of BPM systems.

In BPM, tasks and processes should be kept as simple as possible. There is no reason to overcomplicate work, as it is complicated enough already. If technology is used to help working, it should make the lives of users easier not more complicated. Dishaw and Strong (1999) put it this way: "*IT will be used if, and only if, the functions available to the user support (fit) the activities of the user. Rational, experienced users will choose those tools and methods that enable them to complete the task with the greatest net benefit*". IT has a positive impact on organisational performance only if it matches business processes; therefore, it is important to consider IT as part of the organisation's business strategy (Karimi, Somers and Bhattacherjee 2007). The IT value should be evaluated through the business value that it generates.

2.2.4 Customer and network perspective

In today's business, it is not always enough just to improve internal processes, even though this is also very important. Continuous improving must consider the Outside-In perspective of customer needs and market requirements as a crucial part of improving business processes (Zinser, Baumgartner and Walliser 1998; Laamanen and Tinnilä 2009). An organisation's business processes should be able to respond to these changes accordingly (Siha and Saad 2008). In this thesis, the term 'Outside-In' (also sometimes spelled as 'Outside In') refers to being a *customer-oriented*. Outside-In has been referred in consulting and practical literature (e.g. Manning and Bodine 2012; Day and Moorman 2010), but it may not have solid enough academic base yet. However, principle of having customers as integral part of companies has been discussed for some time already (e.g. Drucker 1954). A term 'Inside-Out' has been used as the opposite of Outside-In, focusing on the internal workings of an organisation.

The basic idea of business processes and their management is to create value for the customer through activities in an organisation (Laamanen and Tinnilä 2009; Hammer and Stanton 1999) and to fulfil other strategies such as producing returns for stakeholders (Guha and Kettinger 1993; Strnadl 2006). Business value is no longer created in traditional, hierarchical organisations with the separation of organisations and their clients and potential supplier network. Networking has become an increasing trend and since it sometimes is not possible to get benefits only from optimising internally, both external and internal resources are compulsory assets for today's organisations (Zinser, Baumgartner and Walliser 1998; Palmberg 2009). Organisations need their customers to participate in their actions and to help them improve their businesses, so that they grow to be strategic partners to customers (Laamanen and Tinnilä 2009). Competition has not been local for some time now, but it has become international, which puts more effort on cross-organisational cooperation and customer centricity (Zinser, Baumgartner and Walliser 1998). As Zinser, Baumgartner and Walliser (1998) state, *"there is a need for organizational structures that bring together market and technology with the aim to assure a long-range survival and competitiveness of the company"*.

As you may note from the literature review in this dissertation, the customer is not included in most of the matters dealt with in the existing BPM literature. There has been an evolution from process-centric business process improvement methods through Six Sigma, TQM and others to BPM, which has a more holistic perspective than previous ones, but still lacks a customer-centric and cross-organisational networking focus on the process development of the organisation. However, that is very much needed as stated earlier, as the customer is becoming the king of all organisations though globalisation and freedom of choice as well as many companies produce value for their customers in value networks. We as customers want the organisations that we do business with to show that they understand what we need and are able to deliver it (Bund 2005).

This could potentially lead to a next generation of BPM, which is based on the Outside-In and value network perspectives. Outside-In has been used as a synonym for customer-centric. Bund (2005) is thought to be one of the original thinkers of this philosophy. She refers to Drucker (1954) as one of the first authors saying that that the customer is the reason for a business to exist. The researcher sees customers as the main reason for processes to exist (otherwise they would not be needed) and therefore Customer Experience Management (external perspective) could potentially be seen as a first stage of Business Process Management (internal perspective). Also those processes may be divided into internal to the organisation (i.e. that is how the products or services are produced) or external (i.e. how the customer will use and benefit from those products).

The problem with traditional BPM perspectives is their focus on internal actions that seemingly contribute to delivering outcomes to customers. We spend our time focusing on those actions without realising that they do not necessarily contribute to successful customer outcomes. That will lead to doing the wrong activities very efficiently; emphasis is on fixing the causes of work rather than their effects. There should be more emphasis on customer-focused results that go beyond basic customer satisfaction measurements, because customer relationships and engagement are better indicators and measures of the future success of the organisation (Malcolm Baldrige National Quality Program 2009, 53).

The Outside-In perspective's central thesis is that all organisations ought to be built and designed with a keen focus on achieving successful customer outcomes (Bund 2005). It is not a new idea to focus on customers, but the BPM literature is missing mentions of them quite widely; why is that? Does it really help organisations to do the things more efficiently through task optimisation such as Six Sigma when there is no clear picture on what the organisation should even be doing? Successful customer outcomes help organisations align their initiatives to the real needs of their customers. Willaert et al. (2007) discuss in their work on the importance of the link between customers and processes. According to them, *"customers are valuable information sources for process improvement*". They also say that becoming a process-oriented organisation requires the organisation to adapt its internal processes to the different customers and their wishes.

This may be seen as the next generation of BPM, taking a holistic perspective on all the tasks that we carry out in an organisation. This also leads to some success and failure capability factors considering the customer centricity of an organisation. Therefore, the Outside-In philosophy may be one of the dominant theories behind contemporary BPM, taking it to the next level from a mere task optimisation perspective. CT, dynamic factors and TTF are all important theories behind the execution of BPM, but Outside-In is the overall reason for BPM to exist, namely satisfying the needs of the customers that pay for our business processes to exist. That is why this thesis suggests adding Outside-In as a fifth theory behind BPM and leaves more detailed exploration of this idea for future research.

In this study, Outside-In perspective is used not only to include the customers as part of the capability artifact, but also in a way that the artifact can be used. Relevant capabilities can be measured from customer perspective also, targeting the survey in the artifact to organisation's customers instead of just employees. This could potentially also reveal gaps between perception of capabilities between these different stakeholders. The artifact could be also utilised to understand the business process management capabilities in the value network the organisation has.

2.3 Capability factors

Many methods are available for enhancing the organisation's capabilities to run processes. However, in this dissertation, we are not looking into the capabilities of organisations to run processes, but into the factors of an organisation to conduct BPM. One thing that is similar to both perspectives is the importance of learning and quality. Anything a person does leads to some kind of learning (at least if that learning is extracted from the experience). Also we may assume that organisations thrive because of the good quality of their products and services (we may be able to assume that otherwise customers would not buy them voluntarily, unless they were forced for some reason). These two perspectives set some expectations for both running processes and conducting BPM. Laamanen and Tinnilä (2009) state *"capability is the ability, in practice, to act in a purposeful way"*. Helfat and Peteraf (2003) claim that for something to qualify as a capability, it must at least work in a reliable matter. In this dissertation, we are looking into abilities to evaluate whether an organisation is capable, in practice, of conducting BPM or not. The artifact designed helps the organisation to do a gap analysis of their existing and desired capabilities. Laamanen and Tinnilä (2009) write about knowledge, competences, skills and qualifications as part of the organisation's process factors. Different kinds of capability models are useful to depict a roadmap to a certain level of capability. Laamanen and Tinnilä (2009) describe the process maturity model, which values process maturity using five levels. This dissertation aims to develop a simple capability model for BPM, so that organisations can evaluate how ready they are for process improvements, which can then be evaluated against their desired state, if they so will. However, one must bear in mind the limitations of the situation explained by CT. This endeavour is an important one for organisations as described in the following quote from Forstner et al. (2013):

> *Capability development is an essential task of organizational design and corporate decision-making, particularly in a world where numerous organizations face strong competition and a progressively dynamic environment (Pavlou and El Sawy 2011; Wernerfelt 1984). Despite elaborate theoretical underpinnings such as the resource-based view of the firm and dynamic capability theory, scholars and practitioners still struggle when deciding which capabilities they should develop to which extent in order to sustain competitive advantage. In fact, capability development is closely related to business process management (BPM) because capabilities and processes refer to the same phenomenon (Ortbach, Plattfaut, Pöppelbuß, and Niehaves 2012; van Looy, de Backer, and Poels 2011)*

This thesis wants to do its part to help practitioners to understand their current level of capabilities and to use that information as a basis for choosing which capabilities need to be developed into what extend based on the market environment potentially leading to a gap analysis. Since the case organisations in this thesis were not able define their desired states due to time restrictions, such gap analysis is not evaluated as part of the artifact (this is left for future research to do).

3   REVIEW ON BPM CAPABILITY LITERATURE AND PROPOSITION OF ARTIFACT

Capability factors can be seen as enablers for an organisation to do something. In this research, we discuss the factors related to BPM. The focus of this research is finding out the success and failure capability factors for BPM to process them into a simple checklist. Before we can discuss in more detail these success and failure capability factors, we need to define what does success or failure in BPM mean. Trkman (2010) claims that most of the research carried out so far has been missing this definition. Thus, he gave this definition for the success of BPM:

> *Since BPM can be initiated for a variety of different reasons and the definition of success may differ by unit of analysis (e.g. project, organization) a very general definition of success is proposed: BPM is successful if it continuously meets pre- determined goals, both within a single project scope and over a longer period of time.*

This general definition of the success of BPM is suitable for our purposes since, as stated by Trkman (2010), the unit of analysis may affect the degree of success. As such, there is no need for us to make a more specific claim about successful BPM efforts. It is important to note, however, that the goals must be met both from a short- and from a long-term perspective and they need to be predetermined. This has a strong correlation to BPM's relation to an organisation's strategy and mission. Jurisch et al. (2014) write in their work:

> *Performance differences between BPC projects – why some fail while others succeed – can be attributed to differences in resources and capabilities. Research shows that the resources, which are needed for a successful BPC project, do not present a source of competitive advantage by themselves but are rather mere input factors (Melville et al. 2004). Important for the success of a BPC project and the performance of the improved business process is that the organization possesses the necessary capabilities to select, deploy, and organize these resources.*

There has been a lot of research on the capability factors of BPM, as can easily be seen from this research. Daniel (1961) was one of the early researchers to mention capability factors related to an organisation's information technology. Further, Anthony, Dearden and Vancil (1972) also talk about an organisation's capability factors. Rockart (1979) defines capability factors to be areas where successful results will assure good performance. Unlike Rockart (1979), this research does not focus on the capability factors of an organisation, but on the capability factors of BPM efforts (including readiness for process-oriented management, implementation of process improvement initiatives, etc.) in an organisation. Thinking about capability factors helps an organisation understand the reasons why a particular BPM effort may fail. By observing these capability factors, organisations can effectively manage the key contextual variables that influence the success or failure of a BPM effort (Ariyachandra and Frolick 2008). Failure factors can be seen as opposite capability factors. They are areas where failure will result in unsuccessful BPM performance. BPM has several challenges in many categories such as organisational, managerial, information technology and even social problems (Trkman 2010). This has led to difficulties in clearly categorising and making BPM factors general; there will always be case-specific matters to deal with.

This thesis divides the literature two prior and after year 2000 to make it easier to compare those two in future studies and to structure this thesis to be easier to read on the literature review part. Song and Zhu (2011) wrote, *"the concept of BPM is mainly evolved from Business Process Reengineering (BPR), which once attracted many researchers' attention during 1990s (Davenport and Short 1990; Davenport 1993; Hammer 1990; Hammer and Champy 1993)"*. This kind of division was done also to follow the structure presented in Harmon's book (2007, chapter 1) where Internet changed how BPM is perceived in 1990s and 2000s in a different way. The combination of Internet becoming more popular and BPR turning into BPM may have caused changes in the success and failure factors also (this remains for future research to evaluate). However, it is not included in the scope of this thesis to do any deep analysis of development of the BPM concept between different decades.

The researcher has chosen the literature included in thesis using the following process:
1. Search of relevant articles in business process management capabilities as described in chapter 1.5 Introduction
2. Reading the abstracts of the articles searching for mentions about matters relevant for success or failure of BPM initiatives or references to capability factors or maturity models.

3. Speed reading over 500 articles to find the ones that give some relevant information and capability factors from the perspective of this thesis.

4. Reading carefully the chosen of the articles, that is about 300.

5. Referencing the articles presented in this thesis (over 200).

The researcher read the articles having the research questions in mind and thinking how the information given in any particular article potentially could contribute into understanding what capabilities are important in successful (or failure) BPM initiatives and how that information could be used to build the artifact presented in this thesis. Also articles recommended by BPM practitioners and experts during the interviews and reviews of this work have been included where relevant. The researcher received suggestions from esteemed professors and PhD's in BPM field. Some of the articles were also discussed in blogs written by the researcher to get feedback from a wider audience (especially from process specific, independent website called BPMLeader).

The capability factors were identified in those articles through the following mechanisms:

- The author clearly articulated the BPM capability factors as such.
- The author reported the capabilities as contributing either to success or failure of BPM initiatives.
- The researcher interpreted the author to discuss about BPM capability factors for example through their case studies, conclusions, literature review, etc. based on the definitions of BPM capability factors described earlier in this thesis.

The following subchapters contain tables of capability factors identified from literature divided into two tables based on their time of publication (prior and after 2000). These two tables could be combined, but have been left separately for future research use (such as comparing development of BPR/BPM over time). Capabilities are also divided into success and failure capabilities (either positively or negatively contributing to BPM initiatives). On top of the tables listing the factors, some of the articles that were perceived more valuable for this thesis than the others are handled in more detail. Those articles have been referenced by several other articles and may be perceived as some kind of milestones in the scientific history of researching BPM capability factors. Another reason for those articles being discussed in more details than others is that the researcher analysed those articles to be important from the overall perspective of the purpose of this thesis, contributing to developing the final artifact presented at the end of this thesis. Categorisation of capability factors is also subject that the researcher will work on in this chapter. Some articles presented in more details did similar kind of work, forming their view of different ways to categorise the factors. This has helped to make the research trail and design of categorisation of capability factors for this thesis more visible.

3.1 Success and failure capability factors before 2000

Table 1.   Capability factors before 2000

Capability Factors	Research contributors
Top and middle management commitment and support	Hall, Rosenthal and Wade 1993; Feltes and Karuppan 1995; Maul, Weaver, Childe, Smart and Bennett 1995; Holland and Kumar 1995; Kotter 1995; Grover, Jeong, Kettinger and Teng 1995; Alavi and Yoo 1995; Zinser, Baumgartner and Walliser 1998; Zairi and Sinclair 1995; Woolfe 1993; Hammer and Stanton 1999; Ives and Olson 1984; Savolainen 1999; Kiely 1995; Attaran and Wood 1999; Hammer and Champy 1993; Robb 1995; Bartlett and Ghoshal 1995.
An effective, trained reengineering team	Leith 1994; Feltes and Karuppan 1995; Alavi and Yoo 1995; Grover, Jeong, Kettinger and Teng 1995; Zinser, Baumgartner and Walliser 1998; Zairi and Sinclair 1995; Hammer and Champy 1993; Caron, Jarvenpaa and Stoddard 1994
Targeting of correct processes to be reengineered, strategically significant processes	Leith 1994; Holland and Kumar 1995; Hyde 1995; Zairi and Sinclair 1995; Keen 1997; Kiely 1995; Attaran and Wood 1999
Set specific outcomes and measurements in relation to performance, benchmarking, customer needs etc.	Johnson S. 1993; Hall, Rosenthal and Wade 1993; Leith 1994; Feltes and Karuppan 1995; Grover, Jeong, Kettinger and Teng 1995; Holland and Kumar 1995; Guimaraes and Bond 1996; Zairi and Sinclair 1995; Forsberg, Nilsson and Antoni 1999; Pritchard and Armistead 1999
Synergistic use of IT and process redesign methods	Johnson S. 1993; Leith 1994; Smith B. 1994; Alavi and Yoo 1995; Maul, Weaver, Childe, Smart and Bennett 1995; Guimaraes and Bond 1996; Zinser, Baumgartner and Walliser 1998; Woolfe 1993
Ensure project breadth and depth, goal for big enough improvements	Hall, Rosenthal and Wade 1993; Maul, Weaver, Childe, Smart and Bennett 1995; Holland and Kumar 1995; Zinser, Baumgartner and Walliser 1998; Robb 1995
Empowerment of 'process owners'	Goll and Cordovano 1993; Hall, Rosenthal and Wade 1993; Smith B. 1994; Willmott 1994; Maul, Weaver, Childe, Smart and Bennett 1995; Wellins and Murphy 1995; Kotter 1995; Rothwell 1995; Guimaraes and

	Bond 1996; Lee and Dale 1998; Hammer and Stanton 1999; Pritchard and Armistead 1999
The reengineering effort must be straightforward and practical	Johnson S. 1993; Leith 1994; McAdam 1996
Organisations must possess the capacity and willingness to change	Johnson S. 1993; Grover, Jeong, Kettinger and Teng 1995; Halachmi 1996; Zairi and Sinclair 1995; Willmott 1994
Existing organisational culture must be adaptable to change	Davidson W. 1993; Morris and Brandon 1993; Grover, Jeong, Kettinger and Teng 1995
Plan and implement the reengineering project concurrently	Woolfe 1993; Feltes and Karuppan 1995; Grover, Jeong, Kettinger and Teng 1995
Use enablers	Johnson S. 1993; Feltes and Karuppan 1995; Grover, Jeong, Kettinger and Teng 1995; Caron, Jarvenpaa and Stoddard 1994; Sarker and Lee 1998
Pilot new process designs	Hall, Rosenthal and Wade 1993; Caron, Jarvenpaa and Stoddard 1994
Assign an implementation team	Hall, Rosenthal and Wade 1993
Ensure implementation competency, in particular information technology and IT proficiency	Grover, Jeong, Kettinger and Teng 1995; Zinser, Baumgartner and Walliser 1998; Zairi and Sinclair 1995; Woolfe 1993
Enlist customers	McAdam and Donaghy 1999; Zairi and Sinclair 1995
Knowledge of process tools and methods	Elzinga, Horak, Lee and Bruner 1995; Forsberg, Nilsson and Antoni 1999; Attaran and Wood 1999; Hammer and Champy 1993; Robb 1995
Continuous improvement	Forsberg, Nilsson and Antoni 1999
Sufficient resources, time and energy to the effort	Forsberg, Nilsson and Antoni 1999; Kiely 1995
Reward the team	Goll and Cordovano 1993; Feltes and Karuppan 1995; Pritchard and Armistead 1999
Modelling as-is and future states of processes	Hunt 1996; Carr and Johannson 1995

The table presented above is based on researcher's previously described method. The table above would probably contain different kind of categorisation of capability factors if done by someone else. This could explain also why different studies on BPM capabilities have different results, though along the same lines (as discussed in chapter 0). For example,

McAdam and Donaghy (1999) categorise capability factors into the following categories:

- Management support
- Communication/empowerment
- Change management
- Others/miscellaneous grouping

Their categorisation is close to that presented by Abdolvand, Albadvi and Ferdowsi (2008) done 10 years later. McAdam and Donaghy (1999) survey several kinds of departments in the public sector and find that certain things are important overall, while some factors are more questionable than others. The most important factors are:

- Top management understanding, support and commitment for BPR
- Communications of reasons to all staff
- Regular communication of progress
- Realistic expectations
- Readiness and receptiveness for change
- Maintenance of job security
- Willingness to dismantle existing structures
- Empowering employees

Many of these factors conform to the literature review for earlier years and also for recent findings. Many of the mentioned matters have changed little compared with recent research. However, if we look at the number of mentions of some capability factors (between this and the next subchapter), it makes the researcher to wonder whether some factors have potentially been a bit less important 10 years earlier than now. This is left for future research to evaluate in more detail. For example, following two factors seem to be less popular in pre-2000s literature than in 2000s:

The use of IT, even though Woolfe (1993) says maybe even over eagerly that IT is very important in BPR.

The involvement of customers and stakeholders, even though Zairi and Sinclair (1995) saw customer involvement as important for BPR.

Research has found that customers are involved in business processes Al-Mashari and Zairi (1999), since they are the primary reason for business to even exist Drucker (1954). In addition, IT has advanced rapidly in the past 10 years, enabling more complex tasks to be automated. These capability factors may be used to reason the factors that are needed in BPM efforts. Al-Mashari and Zairi (1999) focus on a literature review and do not test the factors found in the case organisations in that research. Figure 8 summarises the success and failure factors found by Al-Mashari and Zairi (1999).

Factors by Al-Mashari and Zairi (1999) contain multiple elements that are noted to exist in later research as well. Several points are related to the research by Abdolvand, Albadvi and Ferdowsi (2008). The empowerment of people is seen as important in both research efforts. The culture for change and building a vision for new process improvement efforts are also both critical. Both studies also state that knowledge and understanding of BPM efforts, goals and objectives are important; thus, people need to be trained properly. As Zinser, Baumgartner and Walliser (1998) describe in their research, in many BPR efforts, teams focus too much on removing the symptoms rather than fixing the causes. That may be one of the issues related to BPM generally, since there is little point in fixing the wrong things.

3.2   Success and failure capability factors in the 21st century

Table 2.   Capability factors in the 21st century

Capability Factors	Research contributors
Top, senior and middle management commitment and support	Siha and Saad 2008; Paper, Rodger and Pendharkar 2001; Ahmad, Francis and Zairi 2007; Laamanen and Tinnilä 2009; Trkman 2010; Ranganathan and Dhaliwal 2001; Grant 2002; Ariyachandra and Frolick 2008; Hartlen 2004; Griffin 2004; Biehl 2007; Eckerson 2006; Fui-Hoon, Nah and Zuckweiler 2002; Havenstein 2006; Korogodsky 2004; Politano 2007; Nah, Lau and Kuang 2001; Ongaro 2004; Gunasekaran, Chung and Kan 2000; Bandara, Gable and Rosemann 2005; Davidson and Holt 2008; Kovacic 2001; Hammer M. 2007; Ahadi 2004
An effective, trained reengineering team	Paper, Rodger and Pendharkar 2001; Lu, Huang and Heng 2006; Ariyachandra and Frolick 2008; Wixom and Watson 2001; Fui-Hoon, Nah and Zuckweiler 2002; Kovacic 2001; Willaert et al. 2007
Targeting of correct processes to be reengineered, strategic alignment to the organisation's strategy	Siha and Saad 2008; Paper, Rodger and Pendharkar 2001; Palmberg 2009; Trkman 2010; Ariyachandra and Frolick 2008; Biehl 2007; Frolick and Ariyachandra 2006; Fui-Hoon, Nah and Zuckweiler 2002; Poon and Wagner 2001; Stiffler 2006; Watson 2006; Zeid 2006; Maull, Tranfield and Maull 2003; Gunasekaran, Chung and Kan 2000; Davidson and Holt 2008; Kumar, Antony and Cho 2009
Set specific outcomes in relation to process performance measurement, benchmarking and customer needs	Siha and Saad 2008; Palmberg 2009; Trkman 2010; Terziovski, Fitzpatrick and O'Neill 2003; Maull, Tranfield and Maull 2003; Schiff 2008; Škrinjar, Bosilj-Vuksic and Indihar-Štemberger 2008; Hammer M. 2007; Tucker and Dimon 2009
Synergistic use of IT and process redesign methods. IT to support BPM efforts.	Paper, Rodger and Pendharkar 2001; Ahmad, Francis and Zairi 2007; Trkman 2010; Grant 2002; Ariyachandra and Frolick 2008; Ongaro 2004; Kovacic 2001; Sandhu and Gunasekaran 2004; Eardley, Shah and Radman 2008; Subramoniam, Tounsi and Krishnankutty 2009; Kirschmer 2009
All the needed resources (money, time,	Paper, Rodger and Pendharkar 2001;

tools, etc.) and training of people are available	Mabin, Forgeson and Green 2001; Ahmad, Francis and Zairi 2007; Lu, Huang and Heng 2006; Ariyachandra and Frolick 2008; Biehl 2007; Eckerson 2006; Wixom and Watson 2001; Davidson and Holt 2008
Do not ignore the human factor and empowerment of 'process owners' and teams	Siha and Saad 2008; Paper, Rodger and Pendharkar 2001; Ahmad, Francis and Zairi 2007; Mabin, Forgeson and Green 2001; Laamanen and Tinnilä 2009; Tonnessen 2000; Trkman 2010; Grant 2002; Maull, Tranfield and Maull 2003; Irani, Hlupic, Baldwin and Love 2000; Kuwaiti 2004; Ongaro 2004; Hammer M. 2007; Attaran 2004; Willaert et al. 2007
Organisations must possess the capacity and willingness to change, while the existing organisational culture must be adaptable to change	Siha and Saad 2008; Paper, Rodger and Pendharkar 2001; Ahmad, Francis and Zairi 2007; DeToro and McCabe 1997; Rentzhog 1996; Laamanen and Tinnilä 2009; Ongaro 2004; Hammer M. 2007; Bandara et al. 2009
Change is carefully planned, change management, managing uncertainty of people, management of resistance	Paper, Rodger and Pendharkar 2001; Ahmad, Francis and Zairi 2007; Laamanen and Tinnilä 2009; Herzig and Jimmieson 2006; Ariyachandra and Frolick 2008; Frolick and Ariyachandra 2006; Gruman 2004; Hartlen 2004; Poon and Wagner 2001; Gunasekaran, Chung and Kan 2000; Davidson and Holt 2008
Quality management system	Ahmad, Francis and Zairi 2007; Palmberg 2009
Continuous and iterative improvement	Siha and Saad 2008; Paper, Rodger and Pendharkar 2001; Trkman 2010; Ariyachandra and Frolick 2008; Poon and Wagner 2001; Vessel 2005; Al-Mashari, Irani and Zairi 2001; Attaran 2004
Effective communication at all levels	Smith M. 2003; Laamanen and Tinnilä 2009; Trkman 2010; Grant 2002; Lee and Pai 2003; Biehl 2007; Chan, Sabherwal and Thatcher 2006; Eckerson 2006; Fui-Hoon, Nah and Zuckweiler 2002; Hirschheim and Sabherwal 2001; Jensen and Sage 2000; Nah, Lau and Kuang 2001; Politano 2007; Gunasekaran, Chung and Kan 2000
Teamwork/working in teams, team	Ahmad, Francis and Zairi 2007; Ongaro

ownership	2004; Paper, Rodger and Pendharkar 2001; Al-hudhaif 2009; Willaert, van den Bergh, Willems and Deschoolmeester 2007
BPM project management	Ahmad, Francis and Zairi 2007; Burlton 2001; Laamanen and Tinnilä 2009; Trkman 2010; Grant 2002; Ongaro 2004; Bandara, Gable and Rosemann 2005; Davidson and Holt 2008; Al-Mashari, Irani and Zairi 2001
Knowledge and use of BPM technologies, tools and approaches, BPM-specific expertise	Palmberg 2009; Laamanen and Tinnilä 2009; Grant 2002; Schiff 2005; Al-Mashari, Irani and Zairi 2001; Hammer M. 2007; Alibabaei, Bandara and Aghdasi 2009; Antonucci and Goeke 2010; Mathiesen et al. 2011; Niehaves and Henser 2011
Both initial quick wins and long-term solutions should be sought	Trkman 2010
Reward the team, use of appropriate incentive systems and training	Siha and Saad 2008; Ahmad, Francis and Zairi 2007; Mabin, Forgeson and Green 2001; Trkman 2010; Gunasekaran, Chung and Kan 2000; Willaert et al. 2007
Customer-centric focus on BPM and customer-orientation	Reijers 2006; Willaert et al. 2007; Schmiedel et al. 2012
BPM champion who promotes it in an organisation	Ariyachandra and Frolick 2008; Eckerson 2006; Fui-Hoon, Nah and Zuckweiler 2002; Jensen and Sage 2000; Nah, Lau and Kuang 2001; Reich and Benbasat 2000; Wixom and Watson 2001
Users are involved in the development of a BPM solution and engage in specific responsibilities and tasks related to the BPM effort	Ariyachandra and Frolick 2008; Biehl 2007; Eckerson 2006; Shin B. 2003; Wixom and Watson 2001; Davidson and Holt 2008
Support for data management	Ariyachandra and Frolick 2008; Biehl 2007; Eckerson 2006; Politano 2007; Poon and Wagner 2001; Reich and Benbasat 2000; Wixom and Watson 2001; Gunasekaran, Chung and Kan 2000; Davidson and Holt 2008
Prepare for potential emergencies and ensure continuity of operations	Malcolm Baldrige National Quality Program 2009
Involve all personnel	Sandhu and Gunasekaran 2004; Sentanin, Santos and Jabbour 2008
Understanding existing and future processes	Danesh and Kock 2005; Kohlbacher 2010

As Table 2 shows, many capability factors have been found to be related to success in BPM. Table 3 shows the failure capability factors that the literature has mentioned to contribute to BPM failure.

Table 3.　　　Failure factors in the 21st century

Failure Factors	Research contributors
Lack of indirect impact on customers, customer needs are not considered	Siha and Saad 2008; Laamanen and Tinnilä 2009
Failure to have stakeholder participation (involve both suppliers and customers etc.)	Siha and Saad 2008; Laamanen and Tinnilä 2009; Bandara, Gable and Rosemann 2005; Davidson and Holt 2008
No linkage to the overall business goals and objectives or the organisation's strategy	Siha and Saad 2008; Paper, Rodger and Pendharkar 2001; Trkman 2010; Bandara, Indulska, Chong and Sadiq 2007; Ariyachandra and Frolick 2008; Davidson and Holt 2008
Missing understanding of BPM terms, concepts and tools	Laamanen and Tinnilä 2009; Attaran 2004; Grant 2002; Kemsley 2006; Kovacic 2001; Al-Mashari, Irani and Zairi 2001
Targeting wrong processes (won't lead to profit, better customer service, etc.)	Siha and Saad 2008; Laamanen and Tinnilä 2009
Lack of top or middle management support	Siha and Saad 2008; Ahmad, Francis and Zairi 2007; Laamanen and Tinnilä 2009; Garvare 2001; Trkman 2010; Terziovski, Fitzpatrick and O'Neill 2003; Grant 2002; Ariyachandra and Frolick 2008; Schiff 2006; Davidson and Holt 2008; Kovacic 2001
Negligence of work environment aspects	Siha and Saad 2008; Paper, Rodger and Pendharkar 2001; Ranganathan and Dhaliwal 2001
Issues with infrastructure and IT	Ariyachandra and Frolick 2008; Attaran 2004
Internal politics and resistance	Ariyachandra and Frolick 2008; Schiff 2006; Attaran 2004
Process improvement efforts are not seen as important	Siha and Saad 2008; Davidson and Holt 2008
People who are involved in process do not understand the whole system that they are part of	Paper, Rodger and Pendharkar 2001; Laamanen and Tinnilä 2009
Managerial attitude remains as "command and conquer" and behaviour doesn't change	Paper, Rodger and Pendharkar 2001; Laamanen and Tinnilä 2009; Trkman 2010; Irani, Hlupic, Baldwin and Love 2000
Organisation is unwilling to dedicate resources, time and energy to the effort	Paper, Rodger and Pendharkar 2001; Ahmad, Francis and Zairi 2007; Garvare 2001; Grant 2002; Ariyachandra and Frolick 2008
Bureaucratic documentation procedures	Garvare 2001
Problems in communication	Smith M. 2003; Laamanen and Tinnilä 2009; Trkman 2010; Lu, Huang and Heng 2006; Grant 2002; Ariyachandra and Frolick 2008

Lack of customer involvement, old mindsets are keeping the organisation back	Bund 2005
Lack of integrated and coordinated interorganisational business processes	Chabrow and Sullivan 2004; Bala and Venkatesh 2007; Ongaro 2004
Organisation does not use consultants/external experts even if it would be useful	Schiff 2006
Over-customisation of the BPM system, too much custom code	Kemsley 2006
Too much of a technical approach to BPM initiatives	Al-Mashari, Irani and Zairi 2001

Thinking of failure factors that may contribute to BPM initiatives, the researcher agrees, based on his experience, with Palmberg (2009), who explains how the mental model of traditional, hierarchical organisations may restrict the organisation in improving its business processes. Sometimes practitioners call such organisations as 'silo organisations'. This is becoming a more important factor in organisations, since new generations of employees grow up in the Internet era with ever-growing possibilities. This may cause new failure factors to emerge (which is left for future research to explore). BPM requires organisations to be able to reorganise according to current business needs and environment. For this reason these failure factors presented above might change even more in next ten years than what they have changed in the past.

Abdolvand, Albadvi and Ferdowsi (2008) researched BPR based on a literature review and a survey in two companies. They find factors that affect success in BPR efforts. They categorise these factors into six categories, of which five are capability factors and one is for failure factors. Their findings are based solely on the literature review and they test the factors in two case companies. The testing is not focused on the actual factors themselves, but on using them in a real context and analysing the readiness status of the companies.

Based on reading various articles for this study, the researcher analysed that the article presented by Abdolvand, Albadvi and Ferdowsi (2008) was most suitable to be used in the context of this work. They presented profound results for listing and categorizing capability factors in their study, which can be used as a basis for designing the artifact in this work. The list presented below also makes it easier to see how the list of capability factors identified by the researcher differs from previous studies. The categorised factors stated by Abdolvand, Albadvi and Ferdowsi (2008) are as follows:

A) Egalitarian leadership
    1. Shared vision/information

2. Open communication

3. Confidence and trust in subordinates

4. Constructive use of subordinates' ideas

B) Collaborative working environment

5. Friendly interactions

6. Confidence and trust

7. Teamwork performance

8. Cooperative environment

9. Recognition among employees

C) Top management commitment

10. Sufficient knowledge about the BPR projects

11. Realistic expectations of BPR results

12. Frequent communication with BPR team and users

D) Change in management systems

13. New reward system

14. Performance measurement

15. Employee empowerment

16. Timely training and education

E) Use of IT

17. The role of IT

18. Use of up-to-date communication technology

19. Adoption of IT

F) Resistance to change

20. Middle management fear of losing authority

21. Employees fear of losing job

22. Scepticism about project result

23. Feeling uncomfortable with new working environment

Factors are also based on the research by: Crowne, Fong and Zayas-Castro 2002; Dennis, Carte and Kelly 2003; Grant 2002; Guimaraes 1999; Maull, Tranfield and Maull 2003; Motwani, Subramanian and Gopalakrishna 2005; Ranganathan and Dhaliwal 2001; Reijers and Mansal 2005; Terziovski, Fitzpatrick and O'Neill 2003. Factors and their presence in previous research can be seen more accurately in the research by Abdolvand, Albadvi and Ferdowsi (2008, 500). Factors with numbers 3, 5, 6, 9 and 13 are most questionable based on the literature review. They appear only in a few sources, but that does not necessarily mean that they are not important for BPR readiness. Naturally, a sole literature review is not strong enough to cause these 5 factors listed above to be discarded; they need to be researched in more detail, preferably empirically.

3.3   Summary of factors in the literature

The researcher has chosen some most significant articles for this work from the list of capability factors to be discussed in more detail in this work. Before moving into listing the summary of factors identified from the literature, let's discuss the differences a bit further. Choi and Chan (1997) review the reasons for success and failure, since not all BPR projects seem to be failing. They create a three-level categorisation for the factors and review the reasons for both success and failure. The categories used by Choi and Chan (1997) are definition, human and skill. The first category is related to the concepts and utilisation of BPR. Since actions are based on humans, the second category involves management and personnel issues. The third category is related to the skills of the people carrying out BPR. This category also contains issues related to IT and project management.

There are some differences in the results of Abdolvand, Albadvi and Ferdowsi (2008) and Choi and Chan (1997) when it comes to the details of failure reasons. The research by Abdolvand, Albadvi and Ferdowsi (2008) concerns more positive factors, while Choi and Chan (1997) look into negative capability factors. These two studies strengthened each other's expectations of BPR, change resistance, top management commitment and worker involvement. However, Choi and Chan (1997) point out a few important points on failure factors that add value: the concepts and methodology of BPR, project management of BPR efforts and scope and objective of BPR in an organisation. It is important for an organisation to understand the definition of BPR and the concepts around it. Otherwise, BPR efforts may fail, since they are not BPR efforts at all (Ligeti 1994). Even though BPR has been stated to be a difficult concept to understand (Bartram 1994), it holds a specific meaning (Choi and Chan 1997). Another important aspect raised by Choi and Chan (1997) is BPR-related project management. According to their findings, there should not be too long a time between starting a BPR project and delivering results (Zairi and Sinclair 1995). If a project takes too long a time to produce results, people will start to depart from the project and forget about it. An even more important subject is the scope and objectives of the reengineering project (Matthews 1995). Processes need to be prioritised and reengineering should focus on the most important matters. Benefits recognition is also important for the project to succeed, so that people can be encouraged (Choi and Chan 1997).

What is interesting between the mentioned studies is the timeframe. These studies were carried out 10 years apart and still the results seem to be quite likeminded. One reason could be that both were based on literature reviews and therefore contribute to each other through references. However, the researchers tested these results empirically and seemed to find most of the found factors relevant.

Figure 9 summarises the capability factors for BPM found in the literature.

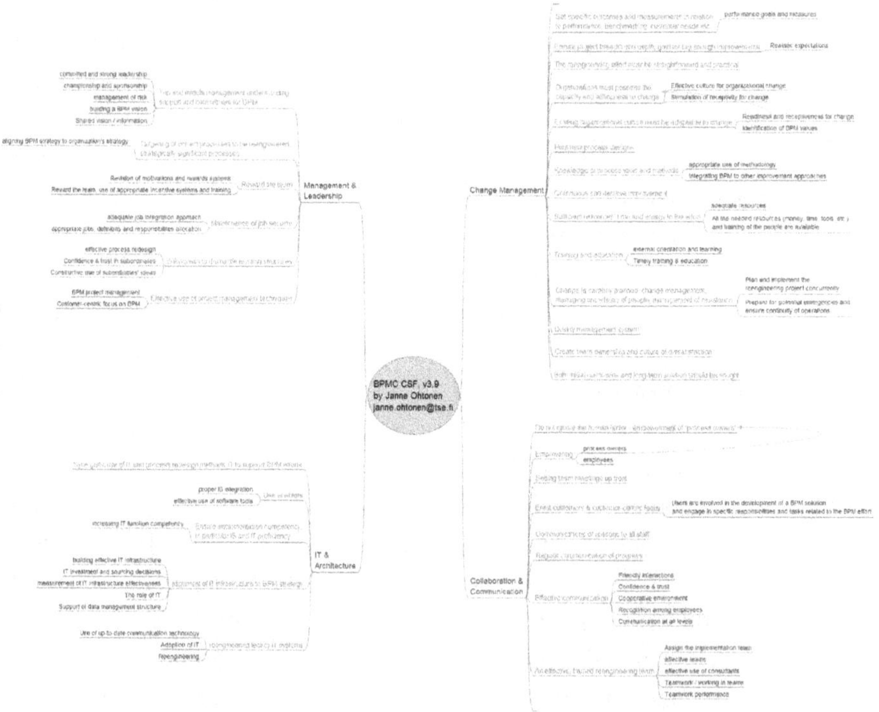

Figure 9.   Mind map of the success capability factors

In this phase, all the found success and failure capability factors are divided into four groups to make it easier to handle them. The empirical part of this study focuses more on these categorisations and their validity through interviews with BPM professionals. The blue text on the mind map shows the categorisation, while green levels are capability factors. The red level is a factor under another higher-level category.

Figure 10 shows a summary of the failure capability factors.

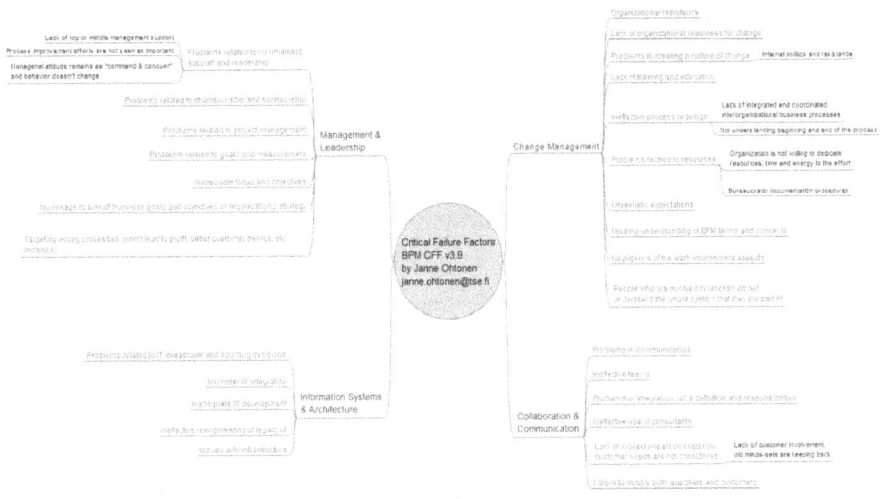

Figure 10.   Mind map of the failure capability factors

These failure capability factors follow the same logic. The blue (1st) level is the categorisation, the green (2nd level) is the higher-level capability factors, and the red (3rd) levels are below them.

3.4   Proposition for the BPMC artifact based on literature

This proposition for the BPMC artifact is based on the literature review presented earlier (based on BPR and BPM readiness and implementation success and failure factors) and the researcher's ideas accumulated from the literature. It seems that improving business processes takes more than just adding more resources into action, even though resources are also important (Feltes and Karuppan 1995). BPM is a complex field, since it involves challenges from several aspects such as organisational, managerial, information technology and even social problems (Trkman 2010). This proposition contains aspects related to current resources as well as changes that radical BPM efforts entail. Understanding this whole picture is the key factor to success in all BPM efforts. The picture below shows how this proposed BPMC artifact was accumulated through literature review.

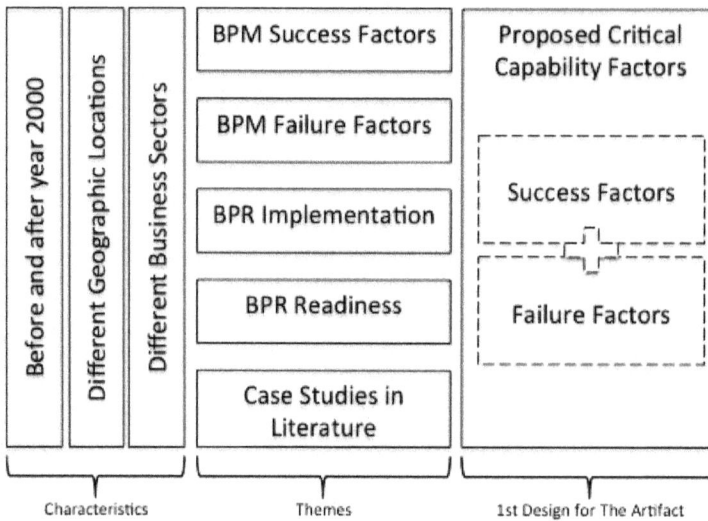

Figure 24. Proposed Capability Factors Based on Literature

The picture above shows the thinking process the researcher had while conducting the literature review to find the capability factors used in designing the first version of the artifact (which is presented later in this chapter). Characteristics used in the picture above have emerged from the literature while the researcher was reading the case studies. In similar way themes and finally the 1st design for the artifact emerged from the hundreds of articles read by the research to create the artifact.

As it shows on the left-hand side (first three vertical columns), these are the characteristics that govern the used literature. These characteristics govern through all the literature used in this thesis. The researcher divided the literature review into two sections based on the years for the reasons discussed earlier in this thesis (before and after year 2000). Different geographic locations of studies and cases used from the literature have been listed also in chapter 3.4.4 though they haven't been seen as important for the results of this thesis, but they have been briefly discussed for the sake of the international nature of this research (i.e. case studies from different countries). Culture has significant impact on BPM initiatives as discussed earlier and therefore it is left for future research to identify differences caused to capability factors by cultures and geographical locations. In the context of this research, the artifact has been designed to be used in global scale and not to be tied down to any specific region or culture. Neither the artifact presented in this doctorate thesis is targeted to any specific business sector, but to be used across various sectors, both private and public. Business sectors that rose from the literature used in this thesis have been described in chapter 3.4.4.

The second block of columns (5 horizontal ones) describes the main themes that were identified in the literature review while searching for capability factors. A lot of literature reviewed in this thesis contains discussion and case studies on BPM success and failure factors. And as mentioned earlier, since the literature refers more to BPR prior to year 2000, BPR implementation and readiness are seen as themes in the literature reviewed. This thesis does not discuss BPM/BPR implementation or readiness in detail, but uses the findings from those themes to jointly list important capability factors in this work.

The last column in the above picture shows how the identified capability factors were listed in two categories: success and failure. Later researcher's thinking evolved from having separate lists of success and failure capability factors combined in to one list of capability factors that combine both success and failure perspectives. That was done mainly based on the suggestions received through expert interview presented later in this thesis. But since the nature of designing this artifact has been iterative, the success and failure capabilities were kept as separate in the 1st version of the design of the artifact.

In summary, the researcher has followed the guidelines given for design science to bring the process for creating the artifact clear also in the literature review part. The thinking has evolved from the 1st draft of the artifact (designed based on the literature review) into final version designed based on the empirical findings. Capability factors identified from the literature were looked in the light of time, geographical location and business area. Then researcher used BPM and BPR studies having different themes to find relevant capability factors. Last phase in the thinking process was to design the first draft of the artifact, having success and failure capability factors.

The following lists for 'categories of capability factor' as well as lists of 'success capability factors' and 'failure capability factors' are built through the thinking process described earlier in this chapter. The researcher used the lists presented in chapters 3.1, 3.2 and 3.3 to design the content presented in this chapter 3.4. The main method of deriving the lists in this chapter is based on reduction (removing duplicates and similar things) and combining them into a sensible list that could be used as an artifact. This was then taken further with empirical research as this thesis later shows.

3.4.1   *Categories of capability factors*

The following categorisation of capability factors is based on the categories found in the literature review, modified by the researcher to be suitable for the BPMC factors matrix presented in the next chapter:

Management and leadership (ML)

IT and architecture (ITA)

Change management (CM)

Collaboration and communication (CC)

3.4.2 *Success capability factors*

Management and leadership (ML)

S1   Managers share vision and information with their subordinates

S2   Managers place confidence in supervisors and their subordinates

S3   Managers constructively use their subordinates' ideas

S4   Top management generally has realistic expectations of projects

S5   Top management usually has sufficient knowledge about projects

S6   Top management frequently communicates with the project team and users

S7   Top management generally supports changes in processes

S8   The organisation has empowered process owners who are responsible

S9   Performance measurements adequately correspond to the processes and changes in them

S10 Employees are empowered to make decisions

IT and architecture (ITA)

S11 IT is integrated into the business plan of the organisation

S12 The organisation extensively uses information technology

S13 There are efficient communication channels in transferring information

S14 Legacy information technology are reengineered if necessary

S15 IT is aligned with BPM strategy

S16 Does everyone know the cost of customer acquisition, the annual value of a customer and the cost of a customer complaint?

Change management (CM)

S17 The reward system adjusts to serve employees after changes

S18 Training and/or educational programs update employees' skills

S19 BPM concepts and methodologies are known and understood

S20 The project plan for reengineering processes is adequate

S21 People are eager to improve the existing state of processes

Collaboration and communication (CC)

S22 There is open communication between supervisors and their subordinates

S23 Co-workers have confidence and trust in each other

S24 Teamwork between co-workers is the typical way to solve problems

S25 There is performance recognition among co-workers

S26 Customer expectations are considered in discussions about the organisation's business

3.4.3 Failure capability factors

Management and leadership (ML)

F1 Top management is not committed to process improvement

F2 Top management expects to get benefits of < 30%, 30–50%, >50% from BPM

F3 Top management feels uncomfortable with delegating power to lower - level management

F4 Business process improvement efforts are not seen as important

F5 Process improvement projects do not have clear goals and measures

F6 It is hard to change the organisational structure

IT and architecture (ITA)

F7 The organisation does not have a clear understanding of information technology investments, structures and infrastructure

F8 Information technology systems are not integrated

F9 Legacy information technology systems are not renewed

Change management (CM)

F10 Employees are concerned about losing their jobs after the changes

F11 Managers are anxious about losing their authority after the changes

F12 There is scepticism among employees about BPM projects

F13 Employees feel uncomfortable with the new environment

F14 The organisation knows and understands BPM concepts and methodologies

F15 The organisation has a standard methodology for improving processes

F16 The organisation has a well-defined scope and objectives for process improvement efforts

F17 People are punished for complaining about ineffective work processes

F18 Processes are improved only when necessary

F19 The organisation does not have a culture, methodologies or tools for renewing itself

F20 The organisation is not able to respond to changes in markets quickly

F21 People are generally happy with the current situation and no process improvement is needed

F22 There are several corporate initiatives going on

F23 The organisation does not know how to manage change

Collaboration and communication (CC)

F24 The organisation has problems in communications generally

F25 People do not know the whole system they are part of

F26 Customer expectations are not considered in business process management efforts

F27 The organisation does not use external consultants even if they could help

3.4.4 Business sectors and geographical locations in the literature

This research intends to uphold the international perspective on BPM factors. Therefore, the literature review and empirical part contain participants and research from different countries. Also, a wide range of business sectors is evaluated based on the general appliance of BPM efforts. This chapter gives the reader more background information on what kind of literature was used as part of the literature review, which functioned as a basis for the 1st design version of the artifact. This thesis does not compare any differences between specific business sectors or geographical areas, but follows the ideas of Al-Mashari et al. (2001) on general nature of BPM. Also Nieheves et al. (2013) have stated that BPM is an established approach both in private and public sectors. The artifact presented in this thesis has not been deigned to address any one specific business sector or geographic location, but to be agile in various uses. In the literature review of this thesis, the studies that clearly indicated connection to some specific business sector are listed here:

Public sector: McAdam and Donaghy 1999; Hutton 1996; Ahmad, Francis and Zairi 2007; Ongaro 2004; Bouckaert and Halachmi 1995; Linden 1993; Packwood, Pollitt and Roberts 1998; Willcocks, Currie and Jackson 1997; Niehaves et al. 2013

Financial services: Francis and MacIntosh 1997; Trkman 2010

Manufacturing: Francis and MacIntosh 1997; Guimaraes and Bond 1996; Guimaraes 1999; Hall, Rosenthal and Wade 1993; Tonnessen 2000; Zinser, Baumgartner and Walliser 1998; Paper, Rodger and Pendharkar 2001

General services: Francis and MacIntosh 1997; Hall, Rosenthal and
    Wade 1993; Attaran and Wood, How to succeed at reengineering
    1999; Shin and Jemella 2002

Education: Ahmad, Francis and Zairi 2007

And geographical locations mentioned in the studies are as follows:

Iran: Abdolvand, Albadvi and Ferdowsi 2008

US: Choi and Chan 1997; Shin and Jemella 2002; Hall, Rosenthal and
    Wade 1993; Attaran and Wood 1999; Paper, Rodger and Pendharkar
    2001

UK: Choi and Chan 1997; McAdam and Donaghy 1999; Francis and
    MacIntosh 1997; Zairi and Sinclair 1995

Europe: Zinser, Baumgartner and Walliser 1998; Ahmad, Francis and Zairi
    2007; Laamanen and Tinnilä 2009; Tonnessen 2000; Ongaro 2004;
    Gunasekaran;Chung and Kan 2000

Hutton (1996) states that the public sector has many aspects that are unique
to it (at least compared with private organisations; it could be interesting to
compare the public sector with private and NGOs). According to Hutton
(1996), the public sector has inflexible hierarchies and policies. His solution to
this is to focus on human issues, but this is also important in the private sector,
as the literature review has shown. However, more detailed comparison of
differences between public and private sectors is left for future studies.

Al-Mashari, Irani and Zairi (2001) research BPR efforts in Europe and the
US and find few differences between European and US efforts. United States
is a little bit more advanced in their BPR efforts because they have done it
longer, but basically these continents are pretty much on the same level.
Another interesting research result in their paper was that the BPR success rate
is higher (around 55%) compared with the original Hammer and Champy
(1993) who stated it to be only 30%. This may be because organisations are
doing more and more process-oriented business development and when
experience grows, the success rate also rises. However, more detailed
comparison of differences between geographic locations and cultures is left
for future studies.

3.5   Summary of proposed capability factors

As this chapter 3 has shown, design science by nature is iterative and requires
the researcher to think about the research questions and how to best reach it.
Since writing this BPM capability review it was not yet fully understood, how
the artifact will shape out to be, the literature was categorized by timeline and

nature (success or failure) of those capabilities. Possibly thinking about the final version of the artifact this may not have been necessary, but to show the research trail on how the 1st iteration of the artifact was formed based on the literature, it is necessary. Figure 11 shows the summary of the 1st iteration version of the capability factors proposed based on the findings in the BPM capability literature review.

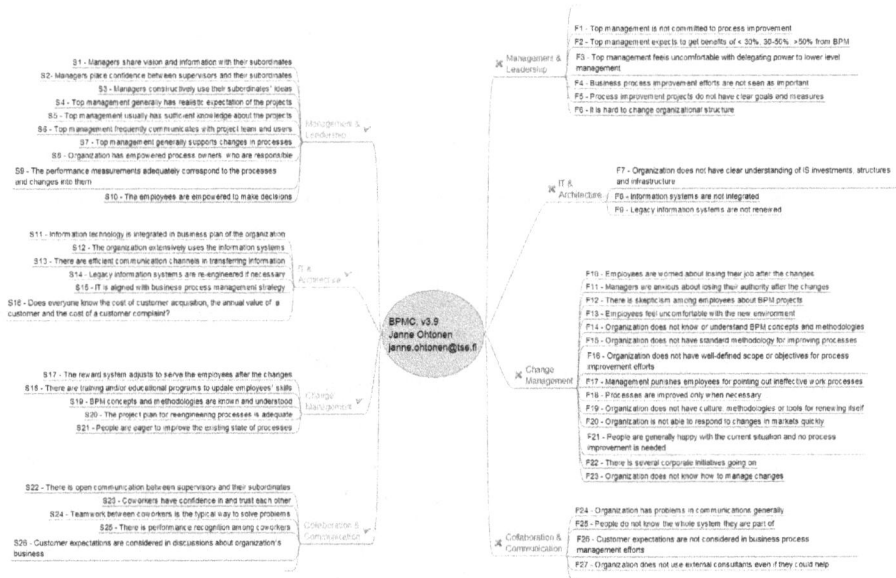

Figure 11.   Mind map of the proposed capability factors

4   METHODOLOGICAL CHOICES

This research is based on design science, which is a constructive research approach (Järvinen 1999). Based on Järvinen (1999, 59), constructive research may search for answers to questions such as *"can we build a certain artifact and how useful is a particular artifact?"*. Kasanen, Lukka and Siitonen (1993) define constructions as entities that provide solutions to specific problem areas. This research focuses on building an artifact that describes the capability factors to the success and failure of BPM initiatives. The choice of this research approach is justified by the research question *"which capability factors are related to the success and failure of BPM and how can organisations take these capability factors into account in their BPM initiatives?"*. The aim of the research question is to find the capability factors and then come up with a way to use them in organisations to evaluate their capability to successfully perform BPM initiatives. This points towards constructing an artifact based on the theoretical findings from the existing BPM literature. The picture below shows the overall organisation of this study with different design science phases and empirical information collection.

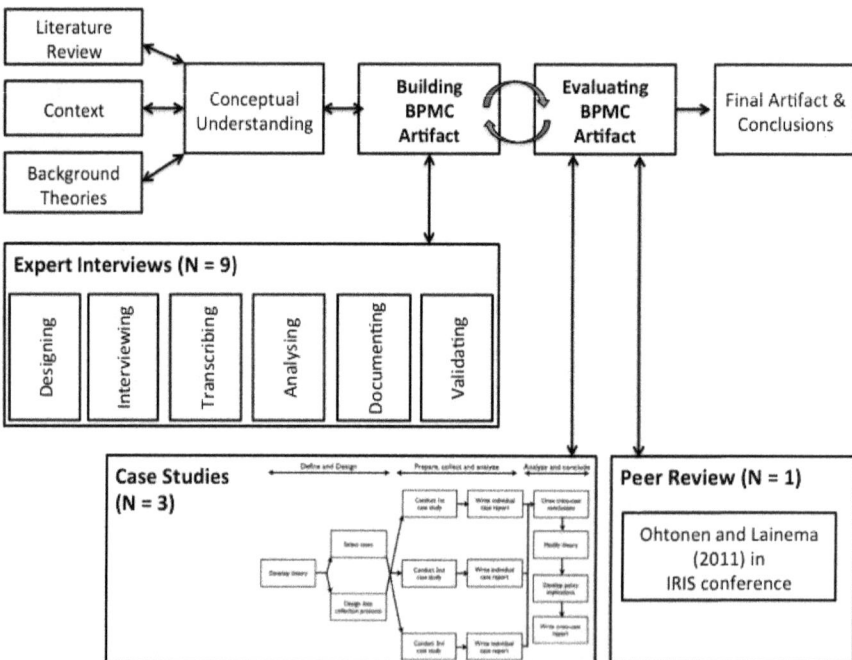

Figure 22.   Overall organisation of this study

Building the artifact started with a literature analysis, which enlightened the research field related to business process and capability management. After that, we conducted empirical research on the most important aspects of the research problem and made conclusions based on the empirical findings. These conclusions were used to build and evaluate the artifact. The main sources for the literature were databases such as: Computer + Info Systems (CSA), Science Citation Index (ISI), Web of Science (ISI), Web of Knowledge (ISI), SCIRUS (Elsevier), ACM Computing Classification System, ACM - Association for Computing Machinery, Volter - Turun Yliopisto and Ebrary. Databases were accessed through Nelliportaali, which is a joint library portal for Finnish universities.

The strategy of this study was to have a proposition for the artifact first before the empirical research, which will evaluate it. Important tasks were to identify relevant concepts, frameworks and other research-related matters that help understand the research problem better (Ghauri and Grønhaug 2002). BPM is a vague term and it was defined first from the researcher's perspective, based on the literature. After that, the research focused on a more specific topic that is the BPMC factors.

This dissertation is published as one single work (monograph), so it does not consists of a series of publications. However, there are publications in conferences derived from this single work (for example Ohtonen and Lainema 2011). Figure 12 shows the main research process followed in this study.

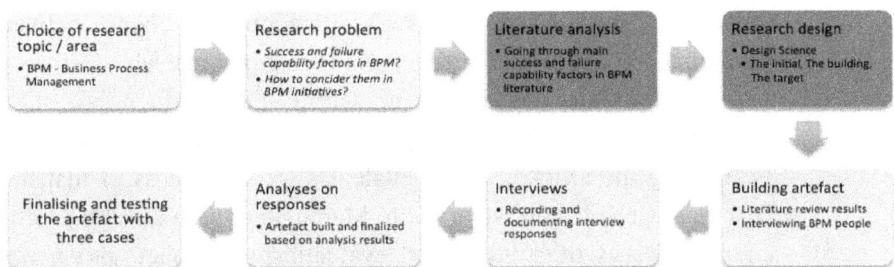

Figure 12.   Research process

The first part of the research process was to form a research plan that can be used to start the research. That plan consisted of choosing the research topic and refining the research problem. The original plan of this research was to define the capabilities of BPM success, but as the study went on, it seemed to be a more useful idea to create an artifact that could be used to evaluate an organisation's capability factors for success in BPM initiatives.

The second phase concentrated on previous research and a literature review. Knowledge acquired from the literature was used to create a proposition about the capability factors that contribute to the success and failure of BPM. There has been a lot of research on these factors, as this study shows, and that information can be used to accumulate the capability factors that others have found in their research. This knowledge led to a research design phase where design science was selected as the tool to build an artifact, thereby benefitting from the scientific knowledge gathered in previous studies in a practical way.

The third stage consisted of the empirical part, where the data were collected and analysed. Building the artifact was based on the empirical research carried out by interviewing BPM professionals. Interviews were used to ask BPM professionals about their views on the BPMC artifact being built. After the artifact had been built, it was evaluated using case organisations.

4.1 Research approach

Choosing a research approach for this research was based on the classification of research methods of (Järvinen 1999, 8). The first step according to Järvinen (1999) is to choose between approaches studying reality and mathematical approaches; this study focuses on studying reality in the context of BPM. The next step in Järvinen's (1999) classification is to choose stressing between what is reality and utility of artifacts. The researcher chooses to stress utility of artifacts, because he sees that as more useful from both theoretical and practical perspectives. The goal of this study is to produce useful outcomes for both sides. The last step in this classification is to choose between artifact-building approaches and artifact-evaluating approaches. Before this study, there did not exist any artifact on BPMC factors; therefore, the researcher chooses the artifact-building approach. Even though this study focuses more on building the artifact, it also evaluates the usefulness of that built artifact. This approach is consistent with March and Smith (1995), where design science consists of building and evaluating an artifact. Järvinen (1999, 10) states: "*in building a new artifact we are designing and constructing a new reality, but by using research approaches of natural and social sciences the object under study is a part of past and present reality*". In this study, past reality is reflected from the literature review and a proposition and present reality are dealt with in the evaluation of the artifact.

Design science is one form of constructive research (Järvinen 1999). It is applied research that may produce a plan, prototype or final product. This study produces an artifact, which can be seen as the first version of the product. Since it is clear already that such an artifact may never be final, but will continue to develop as we get more information on BPM, the results of this study may be seen as the beginning of the BPMC artifact. Järvinen (1999, 59) explains that *"it is typical for constructive research to build a new artifact and this process is based on existing (research) knowledge and/or new technical, organizational, etc. advancements"*. That is also the case in this research, where the base knowledge for BPMC factors is accumulated from the existing research knowledge and refined with empirical study. He also writes that *"the utility of the new artifact is sooner or later evaluated"*. In this study, the utility of the new artifact is evaluated with three case organisations (Järvinen 1999).

Alternative approach to design science could have been the action design research (ADR) introduced by Sein et al. (2011). Their method reflects the premise that *"artifacts are ensembles shaped by the organizational context during development and use"*. To Sein et al. (2011) opinion traditional design science does not fully recognize the role of organizational context in shaping the design as well as shaping the deployed artifact. In this study the researcher deliberately chose to leave the action part for the future study. In next phases it might be sensible idea to use ADR method to develop the artifact further, but for this version of the BPMC artifact the researcher saw the traditional design science method as a more appropriate choice.

March and Smith (1995) divide design science products into four types: constructs, models, methods and instantiations. Comparing to Mettler and Rohner (2009, p.2) who suggest that maturity models are some-how in-between models and methods as they combine state descriptions (i.e., models of distinct maturity levels) with activities (i.e., methods for conducting assessments, recognizing need for action, and selecting improvement measures), this work is closest to constructs, which form a vocabulary of a domain (Järvinen 1999). As part of evaluating the BPMC artifact, there has been done instantiations of the artifact in three case companies. The artifact for BPMC factors can be seen to contain vocabulary for success and failure factors. From an academic perspective, this study contributes to the knowledge of BPMC factors, while from a practical perspective, it offers one kind of construct for evaluating the organisation.

The study is based on a pragmatic perspective, arguing that the research question is the most important determinant of the research methodology adopted (Saunders, Thornhill and Lewis 2007). This research focuses on success and failure capability factors in the BPM context. The research produces a new practical artifact for organisations to use. The use of design science for building the artifact and using several different data gathering methods for building and evaluating it has been found useful in this study.

The researcher has chosen abduction as a logical reasoning method. The logical reasoning method has been called by Perry (1998) as a theories developing approach. There are three generally distinguished logical reasoning methods named deduction, induction and abduction (Hanson 1958; Peirce 1958; Chalmers 1999, 54; Alvesson and Sköldberg 2000, 15-17) and these are illustrated in table below.

Table 10.   Logical reasoning

	Deductive	Inductive	Abductive
Theory		↑	↑
Empirical testing	↓	↑	↕
Empiric			

The table above shows the relationships between logical reasoning methods, employed theory and the context of reasoning. The arrows in table represent the reasoning paths between the theory and the empirical material. Deductive reasoning tries to find generalizations or laws (Möller 1994). To criticize laws and law-like generalizations, Chalmers (1999 215) has written that "*most if not all of the generalities taken to be laws within science fail to qualify*". Yet in deductive reasoning researcher has a prior proven theory that is verified in another form. For example repeated studies in another geographical area involve deductive reasoning. This is why the researcher will have to choose between inductive and abductive reasoning methods in this study. The inductive reasoning method is not used, because it involves the discovery of something empirically, which should be then followed by an attempt to synthesize a theory. Thus, in this study, the researcher moves back and forth between empirical discovery and theory in order to build up a theory that matches already interpreted reality (Gummesson 2003). The abductive reasoning method receives stimulus from literature and existing theories to magnify the guiding principles. In this study the guiding principle has been the idea of creating a BPMC artifact, which is a novel and important topic to be studied. Abductive reasoning begins in the empirical world (as in inductive reasoning), but the view of the empirical world is different due to our chosen frames of references and therefore there exist alternate possibilities and explanations. Abductive reasoning uses existing theories together with empirical material to come up with new concepts (Peirce 1958, 96-97; Grönfors 1982; Gummesson 2000). The arguments presented above favour using the abductive reasoning logic, and therefore this study utilizes abductive reasoning as the chosen logical reasoning method.

This research uses mixed methods as a data collection technique. These methods are used one after the other (e.g. case studies after interviews). Qualitative research data are in the form of words and observations rather than in numerical format (Johnson and Harris 2002). Data collection is described more accurately in chapter 4.4 Gathering empirical data for building and evaluating the artifact.

As a time horizon, this research uses a cross-sectional timeframe. This means that this particular research question is research within the timeframe of this research. The time horizon will not span a long time. The factors needed in organisations doing BPM will develop over time along with the development of BPM itself. Therefore, it is possible to conduct the forthcoming research to update the latest knowledge after this research

4.2   Advantages of this approach

The advantage of using design science in this study is that it provides useful results for both the academic and the practical worlds. The artifact is the beginning of new tools to use in evaluating an organisation's capability factors on BPM.

Producing knowledge depends both on the techniques for collecting, analysing and interpreting data and on the way they are applied (Simon 1980). This study uses different ways of collecting and analysing data to provide different perspectives on the same matter. The advantage of this approach is finding both qualitative and quantitative data, which provide more information than only using one approach.

4.3   Assessing the research

The quality of management research should be assessed in relation to the way the research results are perceived to facilitate finding solutions to actual problems and as the management action science paradigm requires its own quality criteria (Gummesson 2000). The researcher has used various ways to assess this research as explained in this chapter.

Gummeson (2000, 186-187), suggests the following eight points of assessment:

1.   Readers should be able to follow the research process and draw their own conclusions.
2.   As far as realistically feasible, researchers should present their paradigm and pre-understanding.

3. The research should be credible.
4. The researcher should have had adequate access to data.
5. There should be an assessment of the generality and validity of the research.
6. The research should make a contribution.
7. The research process should be dynamic.
8. The researcher should possess certain personal qualities.

The researcher has fostered all the points above while preparing this study. The first point is left for the reader to decide. The second point is described in first chapter of this study. The third point has been ensured through bringing the research process visible. The fourth point was ensured through research agreement and the researcher did not lack any information. The fifth point is commented later in this chapter. The sixth point regarding the contribution of this study is discussed in the last chapter. The seventh point regarding dynamic research process has realised through iteration between the building and evaluating the artifact through three cases. The eight point researcher feels confident with.

Järvinen (1999) recommends a comparison of the building process and its results to the main idea. In this study, the main idea was to produce an artifact that adds value to both academic and practical lives. One criterion for assessing design science research by Järvinen (1999) is assessing not only the artifact itself, but also the building process. This also brings us back to the point presented earlier by Järvinen (1999) about combining natural and social sciences perspectives. With natural science in mind, we can ask, "*what is the artifact?*" and with social science in mind we may ask "*can we build such an artifact that can be utilised?*" One goal for this study is to bring the process of building the artifact evident.

In this case, we do not have an old artifact to evaluate. Therefore, Järvinen (1999) states that we have to at least solve the problem under consideration. In this study, this means that the BPMC artifact has to give an organisation more information about, how it can perform BPM initiatives better, than without using the artifact. Järvinen (1999) also states that to get scientific merit from building a new artifact, the researcher has to describe the building process in detail, argue his selections and explain his decisions.

March and Smith (1995) describe assessing constructs in the following way: "*evaluation of constructs tends to involve completeness, simplicity, elegance, understandability and ease of use*". The article itself does not provide any specific rationale for this list. One proof of previous list realised in this research could be that an international consulting company is using the BPMC artifact as a capability evaluation tool for their customers. One assessing criteria for this work has been also to use Design Science research method successfully in BPM context. Since there are different views on the structure and arrangement of Design Science researches, the researcher has used own structure for this thesis. However that structure can be aligned to important Design Science literature as the table in chapter 1.7 shows.

The researcher has assessed this study against terms validity and reliability (Kirk and Miller 1986). The term validity is discussed in the literature widely (Carmines and Zeller 1979; Cook and Campbell 1979; Kirk and Miller 1986; Peshkin 1993; Creswell 1998; Yin 2009). Validity means the correctness of the methods that are employed to study what the researcher intended to study (Peter 1981; Gummesson 2000; Yin 2009). The quality of this study may depend on internal or external validity and reliability according to Yin (2009). Internal validity is not seen as a crucial aspect for this study since it does not look for causal relationships using a single case study to test hypotheses. But, external validity is important for this study because it shows the domain and making of generalizations from a study (Yin 2009). Yin (2009) has also mentioned that *"case studies, like experiments, are generalized to theoretical propositions and not to populations or universes"*. Both interview and case study protocols are carefully described earlier chapters to ensure validity.

Reliability is another way to assess this study (Lincoln and Guba 1985, 316; Sobo and de Munck 1998; Gummesson 2000, 91; Yin 2009). Reliability often may refer to research techniques. The stability, accuracy and repeatability of research procedures are an essential part of reliability. Babbie (1998) has said that the study is reliable if the research technique produces the same results when applied repeatedly to the same object. Yin (2009) on the other hand states that when processes such as data collection can be repeated with the same results, the study is reliable. This means that the researcher should establish a clear chain of evidence, research report, case study protocols and a case database (Yin 2009). For example, if two or more studies are undertaken on the same phenomenon, for similar purposes, the results should be similar; that is when a study is considered to be reliable. The use of systematic methods increases the probability that the study is valid (Sobo and de Munck 1998). This research has focused on using the Design Science research method in a reliable way, so that it is evident for the reader what the researcher has done to bring the opportunity for the repeatability visible. However, this research contains several qualitative data collection methods, which will cause the results to vary since respondents and case organisations will be different or at least in different situation and time, if research was to be repeated. But the research procedures are described in this thesis accurately to make it possible to follow and repeat, thus increasing reliability. The researcher has established a clear chain of evidence, research report, case study protocols and a case database to show the reliability of this study.

In this study, the validity of BPMC artifact has been optimised by planning and consistently presenting the research design, case and respondent selection and case study and interview strategies. Both interview and case study protocols are carefully described in this thesis. The validity of case study is the fit between theory and reality (Gummesson 2000), which is assured by going back and forth from building the BPMC artifact to evaluating it. The domain of study has been business process management capabilities and different data collection methods have been used to understand the phenomenon.

Interviews were evaluated using the detailed interview checklists provided by Kvale (1983) and Bell (1993). Kvale (1983) has 12 points in his list of important aspects for understanding the qualitative research interview. The research sees the most important characteristics for this study to be qualitative, descriptive, specific and focused on certain themes with openness to change. This is backed up by semi-structured interviews. A checklist provided by Bell (1993) was used to design the interviews. Software tools, which aid in the analysis of case material or interview material, were not employed in this study as they might harm the study's validity (Seidel 1991; Coffey et al. 1996). Use of one researcher in all the interviews and putting clear, understandable questions to people who can answer them reduced the inherent biases of interviewing and increases the reliability of the study. The locations of all interviews were online calls or quiet offices, which were familiar to the respondents. After each interview the researcher checked the notes, ensuring that they were complete, and understandable. Any handwritten notes were typed onto computer files immediately after each interview session. The interviewing situation was recorded, with the permission of the respondent. Professional English transcriptions produced by an external company from U.K. took place immediately after the interview session in order to keep the information fresh.

The data collection and analysis methods in general were documented in much detail. The transcriptions and case narratives were sent back to the respondents who were asked to propose any changes in case the interviewer had misinterpreted or misunderstood something. Due to high quality of notes, the respondents did not have anything to correct in the notes. All interviews were done in English. It is acknowledged here that non-English-native respondents could to some degree hinder the validity of the interviews. However, interviewer made sure the answers were correctly understood during the interviews to minimize this risk.

According to Peffers et al. (2008), design science process includes six steps: (1) problem identification and motivation, (2) definition of the objectives for a solution, (3) design and development, (4) demonstration, (5) evaluation and (6) communication. These six steps were followed as described here:

1. This research has a specific research problem which is formulated in the following research question: *"Which capability factors are related to the success and failure of BPM and how can organisations take these capability factors into account in their BPM initiatives?"*. This question is important to answer to have a practical capability evaluation tool, which does not have the same problems as traditional BPM maturity models. More details are available in chapter 1 of this thesis.

2. The objective of this research is first to identify relevant capability factors from the literature and then formulate those into a usable artifact. The second objective is then to iterate and evaluate that artifact with case studies. The third objective was to define the artifact accurately enough so that other academics and BPM practitioners are able to utilize the artifact. This thesis has been able to meet both objectives. More details are available in chapters 1 and 3.

3. The designed artifact consists of two things: list of BPM capability factors and description of how they can be used to evaluate any organisation's current level of business process management capabilities. More details are available in chapters 4 and 5.

4. This thesis shows 3 instances of solving the stated problem for case organisations. In those instances, the current level of BPM capabilities are measured and reported back to the organisation. More details are available in chapter 6.

5. The designed artifact is evaluated in this thesis. The evaluation consists of internal evaluations of validity of the work as well as external validation through interviewing representatives of the case organisations. More details are available in chapter 6.

6. This whole has been designed to communicate the design process itself as well as results of it. This thesis shows that the identified BPM capability factors are unique compared to other capability and maturity models. More details are available in chapters 1, 6 and 7.

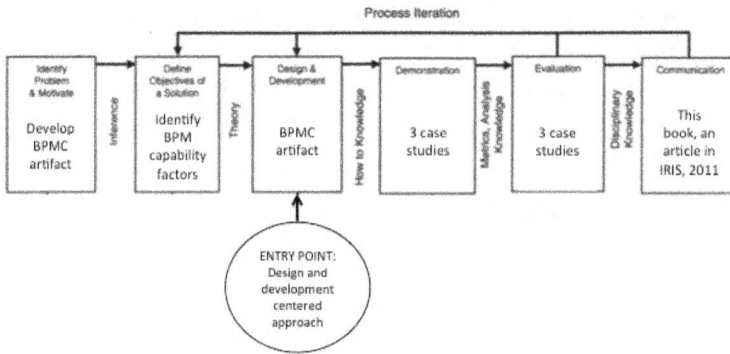

Figure 25.   Peffers et al. (2008) model in this thesis

According to Simonsson et al. (2007), a good capability assessment model has to be valid, reliable, and cost efficient. Validity and reliability have been discussed earlier in this chapter. Cost efficiency of this work comes through instructions on how to use the artifact in any organisation by themselves, saving them time and money. Organisations will benefit from this through saved expenses e.g. in consultation.

As this chapter has pointed out, the assessment of the quality of this study is quite complex. It presented validity and reliability as important topics to evaluate the quality of a study. Various elements were identified that increased reliability and validity and those elements were incorporated into the research design and strategy to further emphasize the quality of the study.

To summarize, multiple cases and interviews were used in order to build and evaluate the BPMC artifact in its real-life context. Literature review, 9 expert interviews and three cases were selected to build and evaluate the BPMC artifact. After three cases enough information about the artifact was received and thereby a fourth case was not necessary for this study. It is left for future study to make more instantiations of BPMC artifact in organisations.

4.4   Gathering empirical data for building and evaluating the artifact

4.4.1   Interviews for building the artifact

Interviews are discussions between the respondent and interviewer with the purpose of receiving certain information from the former (Järvinen 1999). There are different types of interviews, and the selection of type depends on the chosen research approach (Järvinen 1999). In this research, we use a constructive approach with the intention of using interviews to build the artifact. The interviews can be used to ask BPM professionals about the possibilities and restrictions of the artifact in hand. The interviews are used in the same spirit as mentioned in Järvinen (1999): "*Both must cross-educate one another to understand possibilities and restrictions in building and future of the new artifact*". That is why the interview is semi-structured, meaning that the researcher has a list of themes to discuss with the respondent. Discussions however are not limited to any strict questions, and the researcher may ask the respondent unplanned open questions if he sees that as being beneficial for the study. However, the researcher needs to stay as neutral as possible during the interviews to not affect the opinions of the respondent (Ruusuvuori and Tiittula 2005).

These interviews are semi-structured and informal, and the goal of the researcher is to gather descriptions of the life-world of the respondent with respect to the meaning of the described phenomena (Kvale 1983). Semi-structured means that the discussion is not completely free nor it has any strictly structured questions. The questions are used as a guide for advancing through the interviews to get the most valuable information from the respondent regarding this study. If the researcher was to use a strict questionnaire for the interviews, then there would be a possibility to miss information that is important for building the artifact.

According to Myers and Newman (2007) there are seven guidelines to follow in qualitative interviewing:

- Situating the researcher as an actor
- Minimising social dissonance
- Representing various "voices"
- Everyone is an interpreter
- Use mirroring in questions and answers
- Flexibility
- Confidentiality of disclosure
- Ethics of interviewing

Interviews should be recorded whenever possible to be able to return to the interview situation. The interviewer has an effect on respondents and recording interviews helps the researcher identify and react to those situations. Recording also helps the researcher make more accurate notes from interviews, because interviews can be transcribed from the audio format into a textual format. This also helps readers of this researcher see the process of analysing the results (Ruusuvuori and Tiittula 2005).

The interview should be started and ended with a specific style. At the beginning of the interview, the researcher should build rapport with the respondent and then move onto the actual interview part. Agreeing together to start the interview does that. The researcher should ask permission for recording and after the interview has ended, he or she should offer the respondent an interview transcription for inspection. Having trust between respondent and interviewer helps the interviewer get more information from the respondent (Ruusuvuori and Tiittula 2005).

4.4.2 Case organisations for evaluating the artifact

Case study is used to evaluate the BPMC artifact in a practical context. The purpose of a case study is to answer the latter part of the research question: *"how can organisations take these capability factors into account in their BPM initiatives?"* The presented case study will also be able to show how this artifact functions in its intended real-life environment. The case study is organised following the principles presented by (Yin 2009).

5 BUILDING THE ARTIFACT WITH EXPERT INTERVIEWS

5.1 Designing the interviews

According to Flick et al. (2007), developing an overview of the study is important before starting to interview. This chapter focuses on designing the interviews, so that they match the overview of this whole study. The design of this interview follows the interview checklist presented by Bell (1993). The researcher started designing the interview with Bell's list and the results are below. Each number in the list represents the checklist item in Bell (1993) and the researcher comments each sub-list item. The list below does not contain all the checklist items from Bell's work, because some are related more to implementing the interview (the researcher took those items into account while proceeding with interviews).

1. *Decide what you need to know. List all items on which information is needed.*
   a. Respondent's perspective on BPM success capability factors.
   b. Respondent's perspective on BPM failure capability factors.
   c. What scale respondents think should be used to measure these capability factors?
   d. How respondents think those results received with the given scale should be analysed?
   e. What is the potential of this artifact in academic and practical fields?
   f. What limitations might this artifact have?
   g. How should this artifact be developed further?
2. *Ask yourself why you need this information.*
   a. To refine the artifact that was initially built based on the literature review. This information will help identify the good and bad features of this artifact and to refine it.
3. *Is an interview the best way of obtaining information? What alternatives are there?*
   a. An interview is seen as the best way to build this artifact after the literature review, because it gives the researcher the possibility to get qualitative information on the artifact.

b. An alternative for interviews in this research could be a survey. That is not chosen, because it would give only quantitative information and the questions the researcher is looking for answers for are more qualitative in nature.

4. *If interview is the best way to gather this information, begin to devise questions.*

   a. What is your view on the BPM success capability factors presented on this given list?

   b. What is your view on the BPM failure capability factors presented on this given list?

   c. What scale should be used to measure these capability factors?

   d. How should those results be analysed?

   e. What is the potential of this artifact in the academic field?

   f. What is the potential of this artifact in practice?

   g. What limitations might this artifact have?

   h. How should this artifact be developed further?

5. *Decide on the type of interview*

   a. Semi-structured interviews will be used, because this artifact is new and respondents may come up with important information related to it, which might not be received if a strictly structured interview was used. The theme of interviews will be building the BPMC artifact.

6. *Refine the questions.*

   a. The actual interview questions are presented in chapter 5.1.1 Interview format and questions.

The rest of the Bell (1993) checklist items are more related to the actual implementation of the interviews, which the researcher has to take into account while performing the interviews. The list above is shown to bring more visibility to the process of building the artifact with the interviews in this study.

The anonymity of respondents needs to be protected (Ruusuvuori and Tiittula 2005) by renaming all participants with alphabetic letters. The first respondent is called 'Respondent A', the next one 'Respondent B' and so on. If respondents mention names in their interviews, those names are also changed to protect the identities of those people and organisations that are discussed. Respondents will not be asked demographics (age, race, gender, etc.), because their professional qualifications in BPM are perceived to be more important for this study.

The goal is to carry out interviews from as many individuals as needed to get enough information (Flick et al. 2007, 43). However, the resources researcher has limit the amount of respondents: money for transcribing, time for analysing the results and available time to spend on the overall study (Gubrium and Holstein 2002, 86). Owing to a small number of respondents in interviews, the researcher put extra effort into getting good quality people to interview.

The researcher chose participants based on his knowledge of their high BPM skills. After identifying respondents, the researcher had to ask them if they were willing to participate in the interviews (Gubrium and Holstein 2002, 90). The researcher asked 32 people to participate in interviews and 23 of them either promised to participate the research and never replied to any calls or messages ever since or declined because of their busy schedules. Since the researcher was targeting high profile BPM people, that was to be anticipated.

Technically, interviews were recorded with Skype. There is an extension called "Call Recorder for Skype" by Ecamm Network, which is able to record audio in MP3 format. That is suitable for our purposes, since it is possible to easily distribute and edit the recordings for transcription.

5.1.1   Interview format and questions

See the appendix V – Interview format and questions for example of interview questions.

5.1.2   Transcribing interview audio into a textual format

The audio files in this research were transcribed into a textual format as soon as possible. Since the research question of this study focused on building and evaluating the artifact, in this case a convenient level of textual format aimed to have everything said in text with speakers identified. To make sure that respondents agree with what they had said, they were given an opportunity to comment on their own interview text. Before transcribing the audio files, the researcher removed the welcome and thank you speeches to save time in transcription.

An assistant did the transcription from the audio to textual formats in order to save time related to typing and use that time to analyse the results. As a measure of quality assurance, the researcher went through all the audio files and compared them to the text files to make sure that the assistant had made no mistakes in transcription. The researcher made also sure that the text did not contain any names or details to identify respondents.

5.2   Description of interviews

All interviews conducted in this research are analysed in a similar way to make sure the results are comparable. The interviews are analysed based on expert theme interview analysis and joined together with other material and sources of information (Ruusuvuori and Nikander 2010, 373). In this study, one resource is the BPMC artifact given to respondents to evaluate. Another source of information is LinkedIn, which provided a lot of background information about respondents.

These interviews are typical case expert theme interviews, where the interest is not focused mainly on the respondents, but on the subject at hand i.e. BPMC factors (Ruusuvuori and Nikander 2010, 373). The researcher selected a sample of experts to be interviewed because of the assumption that they would able to give good quality comments on the artifact based on their wide experience in BPM. That is why background questions about respondents are mainly about their professional experience in BPM. It is important for these respondents to have practical or academic experience in BPM so that they are able to explain how BPMC factors may affect success or failure in BPM initiatives.

In expert interviews, it is important to know the purpose of how interview material is used and the goal is to find the facts related to that matter (Ruusuvuori and Nikander 2010, 375). In this study, interviews are used to get deeper information about BPMC factors. The goal of the interview analysis is to find out those things as well as how to improve the BPMC artifact.

There are three things to keep in mind while analysing expert interviews: language is just *"noise in the channel through which information flows"*, how honest the respondent is and the researcher is interested in the opinions of the respondent (Alasuutari 1994, 90-92). Because of this expert perspective, transcribing the interviews was also carried out at a less accurate level (not recording every pause etc.), because the researcher is interested in the opinions of respondents, which are conveyed through a medium of spoken or written language. The researcher sees that the information is more in what is said than what is not said verbally. The researcher also had a practical, common sense perspective on reality while he conducted these interviews.

Interaction between researcher and respondent is seen as a way to produce information together (Ruusuvuori and Tiittula 2005). This interaction is not approached as a source of errors in interview data, but it is seen as a useful way to get to the goal (Ruusuvuori and Nikander 2010, 377). While analysing interviews, the researcher has to keep in mind that the information is an interpretation produced from an interaction with the respondent (Ruusuvuori and Nikander 2010, 381). Since English is not the researcher's, and some of

94

the respondents', native language, acquiring that information can be challenging at times. According to Ruusuvuori and Nikander (2010, 412), the researcher has to take this into account while analysing the interviews. The researcher came across this matter while conducting interviews; for example, one of the interview audio recordings was impossible to transcribe because of the unclear pronunciation of English and background noise. The researcher has long experience of using English orally and written, so his language skills to conduct English interviews are adequate. All the material, interviews and analysis are conducted in English, so there is no need for translating anything related to the interviews. The effect of culture is also smaller in these interviews, because the researcher is not focusing on the respondents themselves but rather facts they are giving about the BPMC artifact.

The process for conducting the expert theme interviews is shown in Figure 13 below.

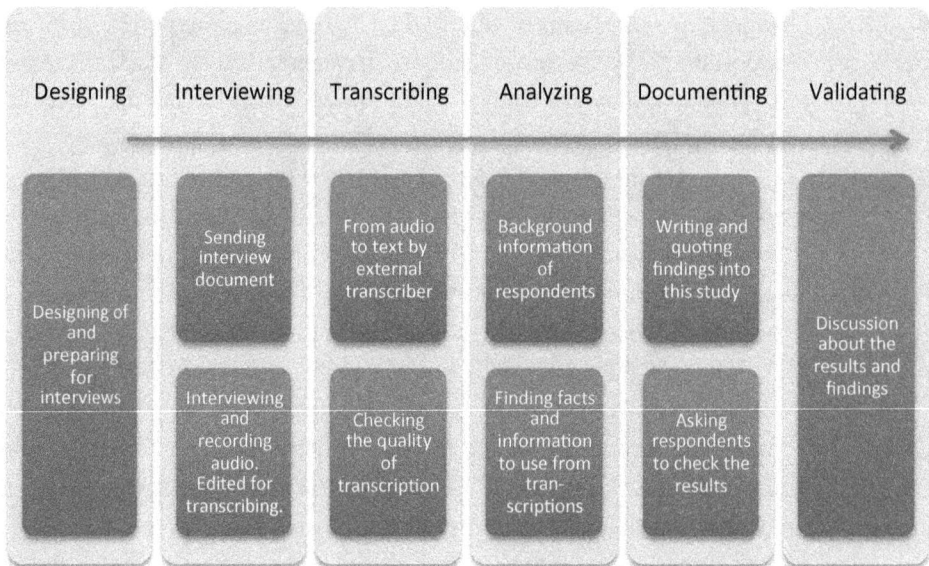

Figure 13.   The process for conducting the expert theme interviews in this thesis

Designing of and preparing for interviews is presented in this chapter. Sending interview document: example can be seen in appendix V. Background information of respondents is presented in the next chapter. Descriptions of interviews are in appendix I. Asking the respondents to check the results were done via email, the appendix I contains the texts that the respondents were asked to check. Discussion about the results and findings can be found later in this chapter.

The goal of these interviews was to get information from BPM professionals about the capability factors that have been identified in the first part of building the artifact through the literature review. To do that, it was important to interview people who are professional and experienced in BPM. To find out how experienced each respondent was, a series of background information questions were asked (Table 4).

Table 4.   Background information on interviewed respondents

Background information questions	Answers		Amount
Where are you from (country)?	•	Australia	2
	•	Canada	2
	•	Netherlands	1
	•	Pakistan	1
	•	Slovenia	1
	•	Sweden	2
How long have you used BPM approaches, tools or methods?	•	10 years or more	3
	•	5–9 years	6
Which BPM conferences or seminars have you attended?	•	BPM conferences	6
	•	Practitioner conferences	3
	•	Academic conferences	2
Have you published articles or books about BPM?	•	Books	1
	•	Articles	2
	•	No/none	6
What kinds of BPM projects have you been involved with?	•	General BPM projects	5
	•	Training	2
	•	Consulting	5
How would you describe your skills and knowledge on BPM?	•	Management perspective	5
	•	IT perspective	4
	•	Customer perspective	4
	•	Practical/professional	6
Are you a member of professional BPM groups or associations?	•	Yes	4
	•	No	5
Is respondent's background in academia, consulting or industry? *	•	Academia	2
	•	Consulting	4
	•	Industry	3
Total number of interviews	9		

* Researcher did not ask this question in the interviews, but he added this information later to the table above based on his knowledge of the respondents as well as how they describe themselves in LinkedIn.

Respondents came from various countries to avoid bias towards any certain working culture. All interviewed persons had work experience on BPM of five years or more. Some of them had also published articles or books about the topic. Most respondents had participated either in BPM-specific or in general conferences on BPM-related topics. Being BPM professionals, many of the respondents work as teachers, professors or professional consultants in the BPM field and many are active members of BPM groups or associations.

Where to end conducting the interviews is guided by saturation, which is a result of the diminishing contribution of each additional interview. When the utility of additional information, according to the researcher's perception, approaches zero, the researcher will not gain more information from continuing interviews. It is important to be aware of the possibility that someone else, with a different pre-understanding, might be able to find further information (Glaser and Strauss 1967). It is also to be noted that the BPMC artifact will be made more accurate during the case studies conducted after these interviews.

In this study, the researcher feels that the information received from interview respondents is sufficient for building the final version of the BPMC artifact in this thesis. Detailed descriptions of the expert interviews can be found in Appendix I - Descriptions of Expert Interviews.

5.3   Changes to the proposed artifact based on interviews

Changes to the proposed artifact were identified through interviews with BPM professionals. They were given the proposed BPMC artifact to evaluate and the researcher interviewed them through Skype Internet calls and email documents. The following chapters contain the most important findings in the following categories: removing and moving capability factors, suggested new capability factors and categorisation of capability factors. This information is used to form the next version of the BPMC artifact after the literature review and expert interviews. Detailed descriptions of the expert interviews can be found in Appendix I - Descriptions of Expert Interviews.

5.3.1   Remove capability factors

As respondent A mentioned, many failure capability factors were reversed versions of the other success capability factors. Respondent C also mentioned that there should not be too many capability factors in the BPMC artifact to make it easier to use. Table 5 shows the failure capability factors that have equivalent success capability factors with the relevant literature references and interview results.

Table 5.   Removed capability factors

Removed Failure Capability Factor	Equivalent Success Capability Factor	References and Interviews (details in appendix I)
F1 Top management is not committed to process improvement	S7 Top management generally supports changes in processes	Refined capability factor: "S7 Top management supports changes and is committed to process improvement." Respondent D said: "*It's the degree of commitment that top management is willing to show for process improvement that affects the level of success in BPM projects.*" Related references in literature: Siha and Saad 2008; Ahmad, Francis and Zairi 2007; Laamanen and Tinnilä 2009; Trkman 2010; Grant 2002; Ariyachandra and Frolick 2008
F2 Top management expects to get benefits of < 30%, 30–50%, >50% from BPM	S4 Top management generally has realistic expectations of projects	Respondent G said: "*The scale for percentages depends on the organisation.*" Respondent I said: "*As such, it is extremely difficult to put a percentage against the benefits as a whole.*" References in literature: McAdam and Donaghy 1999; Abdolvand, Albadvi and Ferdowsi 2008
F3 Top management feels uncomfortable with delegating power to lower-level management	S10 Employees are empowered to make decisions S8 Organisation has empowered process owners, who are responsible	Related references in literature: Paper, Rodger and Pendharkar 2001; Laamanen and Tinnilä 2009; Trkman 2010; Irani, Hlupic, Baldwin and Love 2000
F5 Process improvement projects do not have clear goals and measures	S4 Top management generally has realistic expectations of projects S9 Performance measurements adequately correspond to the processes and changes to them S20 The project plan for reengineering processes is adequate	Related references in literature: Abdolvand, Albadvi and Ferdowsi 2008

F7 The organisation does not have a clear understanding of information technology investments, structures and infrastructure	S11 IT is integrated into the business plan of the organisation S12 The organisation extensively uses information technology S15 IT is aligned with the BPM strategy	Related references in literature: Ariyachandra and Frolick 2008; Al-Mashari and Zairi 1999
F8 Information technology systems are not integrated	S11 IT is integrated into the business plan of the organisation S12 The organisation extensively uses information technology systems S13 There are efficient communication channels in transferring information	Related references in literature: Ariyachandra and Frolick 2008; Attaran 2004; Al-Mashari and Zairi 1999
F9 Legacy information technology is not renewed	S14 Legacy information technology is reengineered if necessary	Related reference in literature: Al-Mashari and Zairi 1999
F11 Managers are anxious about losing their authority after the changes	S2 Managers place confidence in supervisors and their subordinates S10 Employees are empowered to make decisions	Related reference in literature: Al-Mashari and Zairi 1999
F12 There is scepticism among employees about BPM projects	S21 People are eager to improve the existing state of processes	Related references in literature: Al-Mashari and Zairi 1999; Siha and Saad 2008; Paper, Rodger and Pendharkar 2001
F14 The organisation knows and understands BPM concepts and methodologies	S19 BPM concepts and methodologies are known and understood	Respondent I said: "*I found F14, F15 and F16 as contributors to BPM success rather than failures.* Related references in literature: Al-Mashari and Zairi 1999; Laamanen and Tinnilä 2009; Grant 2002; Schiff 2005; Al-Mashari, Irani and Zairi 2001
F16 The organisation has a well-defined scope and objectives for process improvement efforts	S4 Top management generally has realistic expectations of projects S20 The project plan for reengineering	Refined capability factor: "*S20 The project plan for process improvement is adequate.*" Respondent I said: "*I found F14, F15 and F16 as*

	processes is adequate	*contributors to BPM success rather than failures."*
F17 People are punished for complaining about ineffective work processes	S22 There is open communication between supervisors and their subordinates S23 Co-workers have confidence and trust in each other S24 Teamwork between co-workers is the typical way to solve problems	Related references in literature: Smith M. 2003; Laamanen and Tinnilä 2009; Trkman 2010; Lu, Huang and Heng 2006; Grant 2002; Ariyachandra and Frolick 2008
F18 Processes are improved only when necessary	S1 Managers share vision and information with their subordinates S3 Managers constructively use their subordinates' ideas S4 Top management generally has realistic expectations of projects S20 The project plan for reengineering processes is adequate	Related references in literature: Siha and Saad 2008; Paper, Rodger and Pendharkar 2001; Palmberg 2009; Trkman 2010; Ariyachandra and Frolick 2008; Biehl 2007; Frolick and Ariyachandra 2006; Fui-Hoon, Nah and Zuckweiler 2002; Poon and Wagner 2001; Zeid 2006
F19 The organisation does not have the culture, methodologies or tools for renewing itself	S21 People are eager to improve the existing state of processes S19 BPM concepts and methodologies are known and understood S11 IT is integrated into the business plan of the organisation	Related references in literature: Paper, Rodger and Pendharkar 2001; Ahmad, Francis and Zairi 2007; Laamanen and Tinnilä 2009; Herzig and Jimmieson 2006; Ariyachandra and Frolick 2008; Frolick and Ariyachandra 2006
F21 People are generally happy with the current situation and no process improvement is needed	S21 People are eager to improve the existing state of processes	Related references in literature: Paper, Rodger and Pendharkar 2001; Ahmad, Francis and Zairi 2007; Grant 2002
F23 The organisation does not know how to manage changes	S3 Managers constructively use their subordinates' ideas S7 Top management generally supports changes in processes S9 Performance measurements adequately correspond to the processes and changes to them	Related references in literature: Paper, Rodger and Pendharkar 2001; Ahmad, Francis and Zairi 2007; Laamanen and Tinnilä 2009

	S17 The reward system adjusts to serve employees after the changes	
F24 The organisation has problems in communications generally	S1 Managers share vision and information with their subordinates S22 There is open communication between supervisors and their subordinates S23 Co-workers have confidence and trust in each other S24 Teamwork between co-workers is the typical way to solve problems	Related references in literature: Smith M. 2003; Laamanen and Tinnilä 2009; Trkman 2010; Grant 2002
F26 Customer expectations are not considered in BPM efforts	S26 Customer expectations are considered in discussions about the organisation's business	Related references in literature: Reijers (2006)

The researcher used comparison above to link failure capability factors to success ones. Respondents also mentioned a few linked factors. In the interviews, respondent G said: "*We need functional silos. Staff simply have to come out of these silos to do work and then they can return to their silos.*" However, the literature does not seem to support that statement, so factor F6 was not removed.

In the final version of the built artifact, those failure factors are removed that are in the left-hand side of Table 5. The researcher sees that those failure factors are already included in the capability factors that are in the middle column of the table. As mentioned earlier in this thesis, elegancy is one of the evaluation criteria for this artifact. Removing capability factors that are the inverse of others makes the artifact more elegant.

5.3.2 *Move capability factors*

Respondents A, C, D and E suggested combining success and failure capability factors into one list. In this way, users of the BPMC artifact are not put into a positive or negative mindset. As one of the respondents mentioned, it is nicer to think about the positive sides of things. Table 6 contains the proposed failure factors transformed into new success capability factors that are positive inverses of the negative ones.

Table 6.   Transformed capability factors

Proposed Failure Capability Factor	Transformed into a new Success Capability Factor
F4 Business process improvement efforts are not seen as important	Business process improvement efforts are important for the organisation
F6 It is hard to change the organisational structure	The organisational structure can be easily changed when needed
F10 Employees are concerned about losing their jobs after the changes	No one has to be concerned about losing their jobs because of process changes
F13 Employees feel uncomfortable with the new environment	Employees feel comfortable with the new working environment
F15 The organisation does not have a standard methodology for improving processes	The organisation has a standard methodology for improving processes
F20 The organisation is not able to respond to changes in markets quickly	The organisation is able to respond to changes in markets quickly
F22 There are several corporate initiatives going on	Initiatives are heading in the same direction. (Suggested by respondent F.)
F25 People do not know the whole system they are part of	People know the whole system they are part of
F27 The organisation does not use external consultants even if they could help	The organisation uses external consultants when needed

Failure capability factor F15 was already in a positive format, so it does not require transformation. Respondent A suggested moving S16 under the proposed collaboration and communication category. On the other hand, respondent C suggested moving it into the new customer category. Moving these two factors is discussed in more detail in the following chapter about the categorisation of capability factors. Since S16 is the only capability factor in a question format: *"Does everyone know the cost of customer acquisition, the annual value of a customer and the cost of a customer complaint?"*, it is better to change the wording to match the other capability factors: *"Everyone knows the cost of customer acquisition, the annual value of a customer and the cost of a customer complaint"*.

5.3.3 Suggested new capability factors

Most respondents had their own ideas for new capability factors. This shows how difficult it is to come up with solid capability factors that will work in every situation. It also supports reducing the number of capability factors, because most of them are not general enough. Respondents suggested the following new capability factors (Table 7).

Table 7.   New capability factors

Suggested new capability factor	Interviews (details in appendix I)
Internal expertise within the organisation (BPM personnel), people who are experts in process management. "*Add competence and experience of process owners to change management category.*" Leader of BPM initiative should have certain capabilities such as "*be intelligent enough, have excellent personal skills because he/she is just about to change a culture*".	Respondent A. Respondent C. Respondent H.
Capability factor: Have a communication plan for external customers. Failure factor: Organisations can go wrong when they map their processes only from an internal perspective and do not include their customers in it. Capability factor: Who is responsible for customer interactions? Everyone in an organisation should focus more on customer needs. Capability factor: Has management evaluated customer expectations when establishing the organisation's vision.	Respondent B. Respondent C. Respondent D. Respondent E.
Capability factor: Know why you need BPM and process modelling and such.	Respondents B and F.
Failure capability factor: Internal power struggle between the BPM team and IT.	Respondent A.
Capability factor: Have a BPM roadmap for upcoming years.	Respondent B.
How able is your top management to adopt BPM? The degree of commitment that top management is willing to show to process improvement affects the level of success in BPM projects.	Respondent D.
S8 could be extended to include process organisations.	Respondent F.
Do you have the ability to choose the right business process management system (list of vendors, business process management suites, etc.) that best	Respondent G.

suits your meets? And if you don't, do you consider using consultants?	

It is not within the scope of this thesis to start exploring possible missing capability factors related to BPM that have not already risen from the literature review of this thesis or through iterating the design of the artifact through cases. It is left for future research to do a wider exploration of potential new or missing capability factors. The researcher suggests carrying out another study on these new capability factors to see how relevant they are. In the context of this thesis, these suggestions are handled from the perspective of which will affect the proposed capability factors in the BPMC artifact.

The comments by respondents A, C and H about the competence of process owners are reasonable. Knowledge and use of BPM technologies, tools and approaches along with BPM-specific expertise is thought to be important by many researchers: Palmberg 2009; Laamanen and Tinnilä 2009; Grant 2002; Schiff 2005; Al-Mashari, Irani and Zairi 2001; Hammer M. 2007. Proposed capability factor S8, "*The organisation has empowered process owners who are responsible*", does not address the competence of those process owners. However, capability factor S19, "*BPM concepts and methodologies are known and understood*", addresses this issue from a more general perspective. Thus, the combination of capability factors S8 and S19 may be able to measure both the responsibility and competence of process owners at a general level.

Respondents B, C, D and E commented on managing customer expectations from communication, process mapping, customer responsibility and the organisation's vision perspectives. In the proposed BPMC artifact, capability factor S26, "*Customer expectations are considered in discussions about the organisation's business*", is related to this issue. In the literature, stakeholder participation (Siha and Saad 2008; Laamanen and Tinnilä 2009; Bandara, Gable and Rosemann 2005; Davidson and Holt 2008), customer involvement (Bund 2005) and a customer-centric focus on BPM (Reijers 2006) are perceived to be important. Capability factor S26 can be seen to be somewhat similar to respondent E's suggestion: "*Has management evaluated customer expectations when establishing the organisation's vision*", but the difference is that respondent E's suggestion is clearer than S26, which mentions a vague term about the organisation's business. The wording of this respondent's suggestion is in a question format, which is different to the other capability factors. Thus, the researcher proposes replacing S26 with the following enhanced capability factor: "*Management evaluates customer expectations when establishing the organisation's vision*".

Respondent A suggested a new failure capability factor: "*Internal power struggle between the BPM team and IT*". This can be seen to be included in the following proposed capability factors in general: S23, *"Co-workers have confidence and trust in each other"*, and S24, *"Teamwork between co-workers is the typical way to solve problems"*.

Respondent F suggested extending capability factor S8 to contain a process organisation perspective. That would make the question contain two parts, one for process owners and one for the organisation itself. In addition, defining the meaning of process organisation would take more research to clarify; so adding this into S8 at this stage does not seem to be reasonable. Respondent F's suggestion and the rest of the new capability factors require more studies before making any conclusions.

5.3.4   *Categorisation of capability factors*

Respondents provided several suggestions on changing the categorisation of the capability factors in the BPMC artifact. Respondents C and D suggested having a fifth category with a customer heading. Another suggestion by respondents E and F was to shift the IT and architecture capability factors to the bottom of the list.

Respondent F gave clear instructions to change the category 'Change Management' into 'Transformation Management' and 'Collaboration and communication" into 'Culture'.

Respondent H suggested not talking about success or failure factors, but rather facts. This respondent suggested having only three categories called "people skills, technical skills and process skills". This suggestion is reasonable since success and failure are subjective matters that everyone perceives differently. Success in one organisation may be failure in another. Therefore, the researcher agrees with respondent H's suggestion about not talking about success and failure factors. Further, the respondent's suggestion on having only three categories sounds reasonable and has a similar structure to the Business Process Maturity Model categorisation by Fisher (2004). The categories aim to help use the capability factors in the BPMC artifact by making them simpler and easier to understand.

5.4   Final artifact introduced after the building phase

The following final BPMC artifact contains all the changes based on the interview results described earlier.

People BPMC Factors

BPMC1   Managers share vision and information with their subordinates

BPMC2   Managers place confidence in supervisors and their subordinates

BPMC3   Managers constructively use their subordinates' ideas

BPMC4   Top management generally has realistic expectations of process improvement projects

BPMC5   Top management usually has sufficient knowledge about process improvement projects

BPMC6   Top management frequently communicates with the project team
and users

BPMC7   Top management generally supports changes in processes

BPMC8   The organisation has empowered process owners who are responsible

BPMC9   Employees are empowered to make decisions

BPMC10   There is open communication between supervisors and their subordinates

BPMC11   Co-workers have confidence and trust in each other

BPMC12   Teamwork between co-workers is the typical way to solve problems

BPMC13   There is performance recognition among co-workers

BPMC14   Management evaluates customer expectations when establishing the organisation's vision

BPMC15   The organisation uses external consultants when needed

Process BPMC Factors

BPMC16   Performance measurements adequately correspond to the processes and changes to them

BPMC17   Everyone knows the cost of customer acquisition, the annual value of a customer and the cost of a customer complaint

BPMC18   The reward system adjusts to serve employees after changes

BPMC19   There are training programs to update employees' skills

BPMC20   BPM concepts and methodologies are known and understood

BPMC21   The project plan for process improvement is adequate

BPMC22   People are eager to improve the existing state of processes

BPMC23   Business process improvement efforts are important for the organisation

BPMC24   The organisational structure can be easily changed when needed

BPMC25 No one has to be concerned about losing his or her job because of process changes

BPMC26 Employees feel comfortable with the new working environment

BPMC27 The organisation has a standard methodology for improving processes

BPMC28 The organisation is able to respond to changes in markets quickly

BPMC29 Initiatives in the organisation respect each other and are heading in the same direction.

BPMC30 People know the whole system they are part of

Technical BPMC Factors

BPMC31 IT is integrated into the business plan of the organisation

BPMC32 The organisation extensively uses information technology

BPMC33 There are efficient communication channels in transferring information

BPMC34 Legacy information technology is reengineered if necessary

BPMC35 IT is aligned with the BPM strategy

The numbering of the capability factors has been renewed to make it easier to use. The final BPMC artifact now consists of 35 capability factors.

6 EVALUATING THE ARTIFACT WITH CASE STUDIES

Case study is used to evaluate the BPMC artifact in a practical context. The purpose of case study is to answer the latter part of the research question: *"How can organisations take these capability factors into account in their BPM initiatives?"* Case study can also show how this artifact functions in its intended real-life environment. The case studies are organised following the principles presented by Yin (2009). Figure 14 shows the overall process used in this thesis (based on Yin 2009, 1):

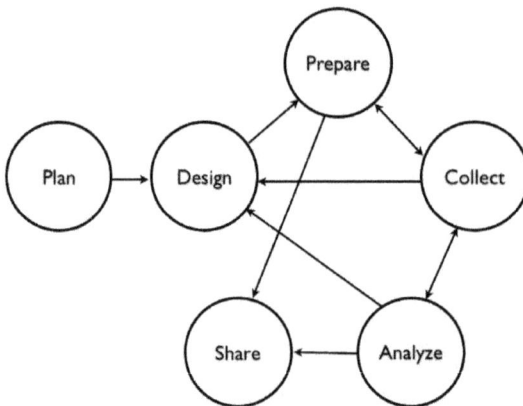

Figure 14.   Case study overall process used in this thesis

The following chapters describe in more detail how this case study was conducted. The first phase was to *plan* the case study. This will help us determine whether building the artifact was successful from a practical perspective and indicate the contribution of this work for practical use in BPM initiatives. The reason for choosing case study as a method is that the research question is looking to answer the question "how". This study is examining contemporary events, but without manipulating relevant behaviours. The researcher will take this artifact into an organisation, but he will not change the organisation to see what happens. Using the BPMC artifact in this stage can be seen more as measuring and analysing the case organisation rather than directly changing it. Naturally, the results of those analyses may lead to changes in the case organisations. However, the researcher did not choose experiments or other research methods, because the goal is not to actively control the behaviour of cases. The downside of using case study in evaluating the artifact is the large amount of work required doing it and scientific generalisation may be difficult. To diminish those downsides, the researcher has done his best to report case evidence reliably.

The *design* phase contains the case study protocol and unit of analysis. The researcher sees that it is better to have a multiple-case study over a single-case study, because in a single case it could be possible that the artifact functioned or did not function by chance. Evaluating the artifact with multiple cases helps make a cross-case analysis for the usefulness of the artifact. The design of this case study is explained in even more detail in the chapter called 'Case study protocol'.

Preparation of this case study consisted of honing the skills of the researcher, training for a specific case study and developing the case study protocol further. The researcher participated in several courses at the Turku School of Economics to learn more skills for data gathering and analysing. As Yin, (2009) suggests, researchers need to have good skills for asking questions and interpreting the answers. The researcher carried out 'Certified Coach Training' at the JTO School of Management to improve skills. The researcher also needs to have a firm grasp of the issues being studied (Yin 2009), which the researcher has acquired over the years as a professional BPM consultant. The important part of preparation was also to gain approval for human subjects protection using Research and Non-Disclosure Agreements.

The *collection* phase of a case study includes collecting evidence from multiple sources in case organisations. The information used during a case study may contain, for example, interviews, notes, documents, tabular materials and narratives (Yin 2009). These data are contained in a case study database, which has all the information acquired during the case study research. The researcher then follows the interaction between the case study report, database, citations to specific evidentiary sources, case study protocol and case study questions (Yin 2009).

Case study data are *analysed* through several methods. Cross-case synthesis is used to analyse the results from each case. This allows the researcher to handle each case as a separate study and synthesise the results. The research question and propositions described in this research about the BPMC artifact are the guidelines for the analysis. Data are also analysed to ascertain rival explanations for the phenomenon. The goal of the data collection phase is to get enough data to show that the researcher has sought out as much evidence as needed to be able to answer the research questions. The researcher has also used his expert knowledge in this case study (Yin 2009).

The *share* phase of the case study process includes documentation in this study. The cases are shared with two audiences in mind: academic colleagues who read this with scientific eyes and BPM practitioners who want to take this knowledge and use it in practice. As the documentation method, we use multiple case versions of single case studies, which means that there are narratives of each case separately as well as cross-case analysis and results. The compositional structure of this case analysis is linear-analytic, that is cases are presented in a linear order. The goal of documenting these cases is to provide enough information for readers to make their own conclusions.

6.1   Case study protocol

This case study protocol is directed to a single case organisation, even though many single case organisations are studied in this research. This protocol contains instructions for the procedures and general rules to be followed with each case, which is essential in multiple-case studies. By following this case study protocol, the researcher can increase the reliability of data collection (Yin 2009).

As mentioned earlier, the purpose of this case study is to answer the latter part of the research question: *"How can organisations take these capability factors into account in their BPM initiatives?"* Case studies can also show how the BPMC artifact functions in its intended real-life environment. To find that out, the researcher uses a series of case study questions to make sure that relevant data are collected from all cases to be able to carry out cross-case comparisons and answer the research question.

The purpose of this study is to find the relevant capability factors for BPM and then transfer them into an artifact built and evaluated using the design science research method. To understand these cases, readers must be familiar with the other material presented in this research. Figure 15 (based on Yin 2009, 57) shows the process for conducting this case study.

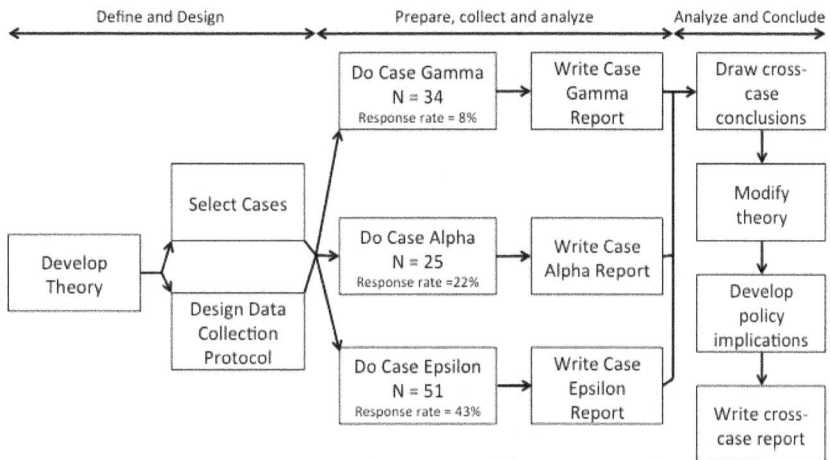

Figure 15.   Detailed process for conducting case studies in this thesis

First, the researcher developed the theory based on the first part of the research question and acquired results based on the literature review and interviews. That information was used to build the BPMC artifact, which was designed to help organisations to evaluate their capabilities to succeed in BPM initiatives. After that, the researcher designed the data collection protocol, which is presented in the following chapters, and chose appropriate cases to scrutinise.

After the planning, designing and preparation of the case study, the researcher conducted each case study separately and wrote individual case reports to be presented in this research. Those reports were used to draw cross-case conclusions, to modify theory and to develop policy implications. Finally, a cross-case report was written and presented in this research.

The process for conducting case studies is described in more detail in the following chapters and appendixes:

- Develop theory: 2 Theoretical background and 3 review ON BPM Capability literature and proposition
- Select cases: 6 Evaluating the artifact with case studies
- Design data collection protocol: 6.1 Case study protocol
- Do Case Gamma and Write Case Gamma report: 6.2 Case organisation Gamma and Appendix II
- Do Case Alpha and Write Case Alpha report: 6.3 Case organisation Alpha and Appendix III
- Do Case Epsilon and Write Case Epsilon report: 6.4 Case organisation Epsilon and Appendix IV
- Draw cross-case conclusions: 6.5 Cross-case analysis
- Modify theory: 6.5 Cross-case analysis

- Develop policy implications: 6.5 Cross-case analysis
- Write cross-case report: 6.5 Cross-case analysis

6.1.1   Data collection procedures

6.1.1.1 Data collection process

In the data collection, the researcher had to integrate real-world events with the needs of this data collection plan (Yin 2009). Figure 16 shows the steps and main format of the evidence collected by the researcher. This chapter gives description of the overall data collection process that was followed through each case. The details of cases are explained in more details in chapters 6 and appendixes describing each case separately.

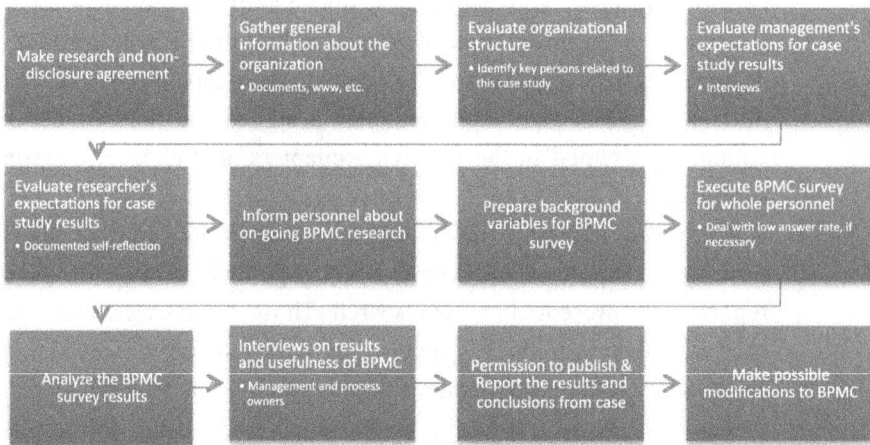

Figure 16.   Process for data collection in this thesis

Make research and non-disclosure agreement with participating organisations. The case study starts by making an agreement to protect both the researcher and the participating organisation. The person signing the agreement needs to be at a high enough level (e.g. C-level, director or equivalent) to give permission for this research. The agreement also contains information on who will have the rights to approve the public version of the case study report and what is the process for doing that. Example of this agreement can be found in Appendix VII – Case Study Research Agreement. It was key for the researcher to get a permission to publish the case studies anonymously, but still in detailed matter to be able to bring the research trail visible as required in Design Research literature (e.g. March and Smith 1995; Peffers et al. 2008). Building this artifact has been done in several stages and therefore transparency on the cases was necessary to see the iterative nature of the design process. To protect the identity of the case study companies this thesis presents only the template used with the companies.

Gather general information about the organisation. In this phase, the researcher has gathered general information about the organisation. That includes economic figures, amount of personnel, organisational structure, information on website, intranet documentation, etc. The main format of the evidence in this phase has been case specific documentation. The researcher has presented as much as possible in the case study appendixes without revealing the companies. The researcher also has interviewed general or financial management to get more specific information about the organisation where relevant. These interviews were unstructured discussion aimed to give the researcher answers to questions he had regarding the background of the organisation. The information was stored in researcher's private study diary as well as case specific file folders in researcher's computer. This information has not been made publicly available to protect the companies' identity.

Evaluate the organisational structure. The researcher has evaluated the structure of the organisation to identify the key persons related to the case study. The researcher needs to know who is able to sign the research contract, who will be the project manager for this case study from the organisation's side (coordinating their internal efforts) and what other people are involved with this research. The researcher will also find out who can help with distributing the BPMC survey to all personnel. If the organisation has a HR or internal communications department, then the researcher may work together with them to get the information and promote communication related to gathering information from the employees. The goal has been to create a relationship with key stakeholders to ensure smooth data collection. The researcher had access to all relevant information through out the study and there was no problems related to this.

Evaluate management's expectations of the case study results. This phase is for making sure that the expectations of management and the researcher are at the same level. The researcher will find out what kind of information about the organisation's BPMCs is important for the organisation and whether the BPMC tool can provide that information. This is achieved through an interview of managers after they have received the results and had have gone them through. Results of these interviews and implications of them are explained in more details in chapter 0 and in appendixes presented in chapter 0. These have been mainly one-to-one discussions between the researcher and relevant manager from the case organisation. There also has been exchange of emails and phone calls to discuss the results and what the management has been expecting from the case study. As the results will show later in thesis, the management perceived the artifact useful and giving valuable information for developing the organisation.

Evaluate the researcher's expectations of the case study results. The researcher will also evaluate his expectations of the case study results. In each case, the researcher expects at least to get information on how the BPMC tool will work in a real-life situation and to improve the designed artifact even further. Discussion of functionality of the artifact as well as improving it has been presented in chapter 0 of this study. The artifact has proven to work in 3 real-life case studies. The artifact was also refined further based on the 1st case study presented in this research.

Inform personnel about ongoing BPMC research. It is important for personnel to know that there is BPMC research going on and that they will be asked to participate in the survey. In this stage, it is important to have top management involved, so that it can share its view on how the results of the BPMC report will be used later on. Each case organisation informed personnel their own way, usually via an email by executive representative. Also the text at the beginning of the survey indicated that they are participating a scientific research. Example of that can be seen in chapter 6.1.2 Case study questions. Also appendix VI gives more information on this.

Prepare background variables for the BPMC survey. Background variables are used to categorise respondents to the BPMC survey. This information can be used to pinpoint more accurately where capabilities need to be developed. Responses were gathered using a 3-point scale to make it easy to respond (low, medium, high) for the employees. As Preston and Colman (2000) discuss in their research, 3-point scale has been perceived relatively quick and easy to answer, but it comes with the downside of less granular information. The researcher concluded that due to varying background of respondents and nature of the information need, it is an acceptable trade-off. Example of survey questions can be seen in chapter 6.1.2 Case study questions. Also appendix VI gives more information on this.

Execute the BPMC survey for all personnel. All the personnel of a case organisation are enquired for their opinions on BPMC capabilities. Before executing the survey, the researcher needs to find out how personnel are able to participate in the online survey or whether the survey be implemented with a paper and pen solution. The researcher also needs to find out when is the best time to execute the survey. The survey itself contained a welcome page, background information questions and the questions for BPMC factors. At the end of survey will be a thank you note. The unit of data collection in this survey is an individual person. These persons are categorised with the background information questions. Example of survey questions can be seen in chapter 6.1.2 Case study questions. Also appendix VI gives more information on this. Choosing the right time for the case studies proved to be a bit challenging in this study. The response rate in the first case study was fairly low due to timing of the study. This also has been explained in more details in discussion related to first case study later in this thesis.

Analyse the BPMC survey results. The researcher will analyse the results received from the BPMC survey using statistical software. In this phase, the researcher may use SPSS analytics software and other means (for example Microsoft Excel) necessary to analyse the results. This will require that the researcher's laptop (Apple MacBook Pro) is equipped with SPSS analysis software (at the time of research version 20 was the newest one available). In this phase, if it is necessary, researcher may gather more information through interviews or observations to find out more information about the possible findings in the analysed results. Such information needs are discussed in more details in each case separately. Analysis is presented in chapter 6.2, 6.3 and 6.4. Also appendixes II, II and III give more information on this.

Interviews on the results and usefulness of BPMC. The researcher will share the results with management and ask for their opinions on the accuracy of that report and the usefulness of the BPMC tool. Each case had different audience (in some organisations it was a Head of Processes in another one Head of Quality or equivalent). The target audience and their comments for each case are presented in more details in each case description. Interview results are presented in chapter 6.2, 6.3 and 6.4. Also appendixes II, II and III give more information on this.

Report the results and conclusions from the case. Finally, the researcher will report the results and conclusions from the case study. Each case company have received their own company specific case description (presented in appendixes of this study) as well as this whole research documentation. These were given to the organisation for commenting before they were published. Their specific results were discussed privately with the people mentioned in the case descriptions later in this study. Cross-case analysis is presented in chapter 6.5 and conclusions in chapter 7. Also appendixes II, II and III give more information on this. While discussing the results, the researcher was probably more in Action Research mode than in Design Science mode since the managers had a lot of detailed questions regarding suggestions to improve their business processes. It helped the researcher tremendously to have vast experience as a BPM consultant while doing that. This is also related to limitations of this study: it is one thing to use this artifact to evaluate the current capabilities of an organisation and another one to make a plan for actually improving them. This artifact does not give means to make detailed plans on how to increase the current capabilities of any specific organisation.

6.1.1.2 BPMC survey

The most important data collection method is through the BPMC survey. Appendix VI – BPMC Survey presents the BPMC survey sent to all the personnel in the case organisation to answer.

6.1.2 Case study questions

These case study questions are intended for the researcher not for interviewees. The main goal of these questions is to keep the researcher on track while collecting data from real-life events (which can easily distract the researcher). Each question is accompanied by a list of likely sources of evidence (e.g. interviewees, documents, observations, etc.). Case study questions are categorised based on levels of questions (based on Yin 2009, 87):

- Level 5: normative questions about policy recommendations and conclusions, going beyond the narrow scope of the study
- Level 4: questions asked of the entire case study
- Level 3: questions asked of the pattern of findings across multiple case organisations
- Level 2: questions asked of the individual case organisation
- Level 1: questions asked of specific interviewees (as informant about the case organisation)

'Level two' questions are the most important ones for this case study protocol, because they guide the data collection process for each case. 'Level three' and 'four' questions are important for this whole study. The researcher can use 'level five' questions to provide more general implications of this study and 'level one' questions can guide the researcher at a more detailed level. The following are the intended case questions for this research from levels five to one:

- Level 5: "What are the policy recommendations and conclusions to BPM beyond the scope of this study?" The source of evidence for this level is all the empirical findings in this study.
  - ○ Level 4: "How can organisations take BPMC factors into account in their BPM initiatives?"

- Level 3: "How do BPMC factors present themselves in the organisation?"
  - Level 2: "How do the identified BPMC factors influence the organisation at the moment?"
  - Level 2: "Does the organisation have plans for improving those capabilities that are shown to be weak?"
  - Level 2: "Does the organisation recognise their strength in those capability factors that they are strong in?"
    - Level 1: The researcher will ask relevant 'level 1' questions to interviewees depending on the situation.
- Level 4: "How does the BPMC artifact function in a real-life context for organisations?"
  - Level 3: "How did the BPMC tool perform overall?"
  - Level 3: "What in the BPMC tool was particularly useful for the organisation?"
    - Level 2: "How does the BPMC tool provide information to the organisation about its BPMCs?"
    - Level 2: "How can organisations use the BPMC tool by themselves?"
    - Level 2: "What does using the BPMC tool require from an organisation?"
      - Level 1: The researcher will ask relevant 'level 1' questions to interviewees depending on the situation.

Appendix VI – BPMC Survey presents the final BPMC survey sent to all the personnel in the case organisation to answer.

6.2   Case organisation Gamma

6.2.1   Description of case organisation Gamma

Organisation Gamma functions in the field of IT throughout Scandinavian and Baltic regions. It delivers operational solutions for improving and simplifying IT systems and processes at customer organisations and offers geographic information and business intelligence services. Gamma's head office is located in Finland and it has subsidiaries in Sweden, Norway, Denmark, Estonia, Lithuania, Latvia and Poland. The company's net sales in year 2011 were over 120 million Euros and it had over 1000 people working for it. The case is explained in more detail in Appendix II - Organisation Gamma Case Report.

Organisation Gamma was chosen to be part of this case study, since it is a management consulting company with ISO9001-certified processes. That made studying the organisation interesting, because there is readily available documentation on how it handles its business. The researcher had expectations to have easy access to information and people combined with a prior knowledge of organisation Gamma. The researcher also expected to evaluate the BPMC artifact in an environment where the use of it may be seen to be natural. The case study was limited to the offices in Finland to keep this research to a reasonable size. The net sales of organisation Gamma in Finland were over 50 million Euros and it employs over 400 people. The business in Finland focuses on information infrastructure, information and performance management, collaborative decision-making, business processes and tailor-made software solutions.

Gamma has a quality handbook, which is ISO9001-certified. This is distributed to all personnel through the intranet and it contains process maps and other guidance for handling the business at a high level. The quality manual consists of three main building blocks:

- Knowledge sharing area for employees to exchange knowledge and best practices by wiki collaboration.
- Subject area-specific guidelines.
- Quality management through common processes for management, sales, delivery and continuous development.

The overall data collection procedure for all of the cases presented in this thesis and described in chapter 6.1.1 was followed in organisation Gamma in following way:

- The quality manager and one business director signed the research agreement together with the researcher in May 2012 with consent from the CEO of the organisation Gamma. The template presented in Appendix VII – Case Study Research Agreement was used.
- General information about the organisation was gathered between May and July 2012 from the organisation's website and intranet. That information included for example annual report, financial statement and access to intranet and quality manual. Purpose of this information was to help the researcher to familiarise himself with the

case organisation from the perspective of this work. The information was stored in researcher's file system on his computer and in a research diary. Some of this information has been presented in chapter 6.2.1 and rest in Appendix II - Organisation Gamma Case Report. Also some of the general information has been omitted from this documentation to protect the identity of the organisation.

- Organisational structure was evaluated based on the internal documentation of organisation Gamma in July 2012. The key persons identified for this case study were the quality manager, head of professional services and HR assistant. Organisational structure gave also information about who to include in the BPMC survey. It was decided by the researcher to include all the employees from organisation's Finnish branch. This would give a view on a country level to the organisation. As this chapter will later discuss, this decision led to a small respondent rate since there was no strong-enough buy-in from the whole organisation for this research.

- Management's expectations for the case study results were discussed between May and June 2012. Discussions took part between the researcher, quality manager and head of professional services and were conducted through online calls. The purpose was to ensure that they understand what this research aims to do, what they can receive from it and whether they have some of their own expectations towards conducting or content of the survey. The Head of Professional Services expressed desire towards a report, which would show first overall results and then dig deeper into details of those matters that needed more attention. Researcher also discussed with two statistical research lecturers from Turku School of Economics to get advise on the wording of the BPMC survey.

- The researcher evaluated his expectations towards the case research in May 2012 and revisited them in July 2012 by reflecting the case to research questions and evaluating whether they still match. When the work progressed researcher's expectations to create a meaningful artifact that can be used for evaluating BPM capabilities became even stronger. The researcher concluded that he has successfully identified BPM capability factors and designed a practical artifact based on them. As he revisited his expectation once the survey was done, it was apparent that the artifact required new iteration round to make it useful. That has been discussed in more details later in this chapter.

- Personnel of organisation Gamma were notified about ongoing research in May 2012 by an email sent by the quality manager and later resent by the head of professional services. The purpose of these emails was to promote higher response rates, which did not work very well in case Gamma as later shown.

- Background variables that were used in surveys for case organisations (e.g. role, business unit, etc. background information about the respondent; these variables can be seen in more details in Appendix II - Organisation Gamma Case Report, chapter 1) were prepared in May 2012 by the researcher together with management assistant of organisation Gamma. The purpose of these background variables is to enable the researcher to report the results based on different categorisation options, such as department, role of the respondent, etc.

- The BPMC survey for personnel was started in May and finished in August 2012. Employees were sent to reminders to participate the survey in June 2012. Researcher should have planned the scheduling better to avoid the summer holiday season. Invitation messages were sent in Finnish, which was the native language for most of the company's employees (with few exceptions having Swedish or English as their main language). The survey was conducted through an online platform called Webropol that researcher access to through the university. This time period was expanded, because it is a common summer holiday time in Finland during June, July and early August and that affected response rates. The researcher was struggling with the response rate in this case study, because of this situation.

- The BPMC results were analysed from August until September 2012. Researcher used SPSS software for statistical analysis and Excel for additional analysis and forming graphs for reporting. The report presented in Appendix II - Organisation Gamma Case Report contains the analysis and graphs shown for the Quality and Business Managers of case Gamma.

- Interviews were executed in November and December 2012. The interviews were semi-structured face-to-face discussions based on the questions presented in Appendix VIII – Post-survey Interview Questions. Researcher interviewed Quality Manager and Business Director from Gamma and these interviews were also recorded for later use and transcription. Details of these interviews are discussed in chapter 6.2.4. These interview were not recorded to keep the situation more natural for the interviewees. The researcher made notes and later updated his research diary with notes from the interviews.

- Report of the results and conclusions from the case was written in January 2013. This report is available in Appendix II - Organisation Gamma Case Report as well as discussed further in this chapter.

6.2.2 *BPM capabilities of case organisation Gamma*

Based on the background information of 34 respondents, the survey received responses from different organisational levels of Gamma, despite a low (8%) response rate (this is discussed in more detail in chapter 6.2.4 Evaluation of the BPMC artifact in case organisation Gamma). This low response rate sets some limitations for the generalisability of these results in Organisation Gamma. Respondents have a wide background in their experience of process development. All respondents reported to have an adequate command of English to be able to understand the questions in this survey from a language perspective. The managerial level of respondents seems to evaluate their skills in process development higher than the employee level, regardless of the higher rate of formal training in process development among employees. This could potentially be affected by the ability of lower hierarchical level employees to respond to some questions that are related to managerial activities (e.g. "The organisational structure can be easily changed when needed"). The background information numbers also indicate that offering training in developing processes may raise people's own perceptions of their skills and knowledge in developing processes. More detailed analysis can be seen in appendix II.

Regarding the scoring, the underlying assumption in this thesis is that there is no predetermined level of capabilities that Gamma or any other organisation should achieve. This is different to traditional maturity models as discussed earlier in this thesis (such as Gartner's 2006, model which was also criticised by Song and Zhu 2011). Organisation Gamma needs to evaluate what will be suitable level of capabilities for their specific environment. This follows the ideas presented by Pöppelbuß and Röglinger (2011) regarding benefits of having environment specific levels.

Of the People BPMC factors, based on the case study results, Organisation Gamma should evaluate what would be an appropriate level for them to rise especially related to capabilities: BPMC6 (Managers place confidence in supervisors and their subordinates). BPMC1 (Managers share vision and information with their subordinates), BPMC2 (Managers constructively use their subordinates' ideas), BPMC4 (Top management generally supports changes in processes), BPMC8 (Top management frequently communicates with the project team and users) and BPMC14 (Management evaluates customer expectations when establishing the organisation's vision) should also be evaluated for how to improve. The rest of the People factors are at a higher level.

The overall score in the Process BPMC factors is lower than that in the People factors. There are several factors that respondents disagree with, even though they are perceived to be of medium or high importance. The organisation should evaluate how to improve the following process capabilities: BPMC17 (Everyone knows the cost of customer acquisition, the annual value of a customer and the cost of a customer complaint), BPMC28 (The organisation is able to respond to changes in markets quickly), BPMC20 (BPM concepts and methodologies are known and understood), BPMC27 (The organisation has a standard methodology for improving processes), BPMC18 (The reward system adjusts to serve employees after the changes), BPMC30 (People know the whole system they are part of), BPMC21 (The project plan for process improvement is adequate), BPMC22 (People are eager to improve the existing state of processes) and BPMC16 (The performance measurements adequately correspond to the processes and changes to them).

Technological capabilities to promote BPM success are at an average level in Organisation Gamma. The statistics show that respondents do not feel that there are big hurdles in technological support, but they do not seem to strongly agree either. Respondents are quite undecided on this matter.

Open-ended questions for each BPMC category contain relevant and interesting information from respondents. It is suggested that the people responsible for developing business processes in the case organisation should look at those comments and draw their own conclusions from them. It could be possible to do for example theme categorisation of the comments or use any other qualitative method for processing the open-ended comments further. However, in this case study there were not that many comments, so it might be enough to read them all through and make conclusions from those. In the context of this research, those open-ended comments give information that is highly specific to the situation in the organisation. To protect the identity of the organisation, researcher has modified some of the comments to remove any indications to specific people or departments. Organisation has been given the original, unmodified information also for further processing. In the context of BPMC artifact, the goal is to bring this information visible. As discussed earlier, the artifact has not been designed to give detailed suggestions on how exactly and to what level the evaluated capabilities should be raised. In similar fashion BPMC artifact brings this qualitative information out and visible, but does not give detailed explanation on how the organisation should use it. For this reason the organisation will benefit from either in-house or external help with high-level of skills in BPM consultation and improvement.

As a summary, Organisation Gamma is mainly on the positive side regarding the BPMCs measured by the BPMC artifact. There are some areas to be developed, especially around process capabilities, but people's capabilities seem to be at a good level. The technological capabilities in Organisation Gamma are not very clear, since respondents indicated that they are between undecided and positive.

6.2.3   *Future implications to organisation Gamma*

The researcher provided about 20 suggestions how to improve the capabilities of organisation Gamma. The business director reviewed the results of the BPMC report in a face-to-face meeting (and preparing for the meeting by oneself) as reliable and interesting from one's own perspective. Based on this specific business director's views, the concerned leader for the whole company should take these results as his or her own and make sure that necessary steps are taken. That leader felt that due to the nature of the suggestions, he/she could not take the responsibility solely. On the other hand, the quality manager of the company said that business directors need to receive the results and make the necessary steps in their departments: "*The ones who have profit-loss responsibility should make the decisions*". In the background questions of this survey, there was no question for the business unit, so it is not possible to compare different units. In the future, if there is a company with several departments and the whole organisation is participating in the survey, it might be better to include a question for the department of the respondent to be able to make these differences visible. More detailed analysis can be seen in appendix II.

Both the business director and the quality manager mentioned in interviews that the first thing to do regarding those capabilities that were perceived to be lower than average was to find out whether they really are true for those specific departments and what does it mean in practice for them as leaders. The business director mentioned that one reason to do this is that the survey is a study of one specific time in organisation and therefore the results may be different later when measured again. According to the business director, some BPMCs are easy to fix by increasing the flow of information, but others require a change of corporate culture and those need more discussions to be able to improve.

The business director mentioned that the psychological power of advertising higher-level BPM capabilities internally to employees is as strong influencer of thinking as discussing the lower-level ones (please note, researcher's understanding of director's implication here was that we should not focus only on the weak ones. Low- and high-level here means based on the results of they BPMC survey in that specific case study). The organisation should be happy about those capabilities that are already strong. When discussing these capabilities, the business director thinks that it is important to recognise the influencers in the organisation or department and then have them involved. The business director estimated that only 5% of people are influencers and also stated that when the overall level of capabilities in Organisation Gamma is high, then the few capabilities that are low are more emphasised in surveys and discussions.

6.2.4 Evaluation of the BPMC artifact in case organisation Gamma

Organisation Gamma was the first to participate in this BPMC research. Even though the survey and whole process were planned carefully, there were a few unanticipated problems. One was the time of survey in the organisation, which happened to overlap the summer holidays and caused a low response rate. Further, arranging the interviews with managers was found to be very challenging due to their busy schedules.

The business director could not evaluate how useful the BPMC artifact was overall, but was able to give new insights. The business director perceived the statistical information on capabilities to be interesting and useful. The quality manager, on the other hand, said: "*I think this is a good way to develop processes*". Since departments were not identified in survey, the business director was interested in making a new survey for specific departments to see the results more accurately; the quality manager did not desire that feature. Both the quality manager and the business director would also be interested in comparing the results with those of competitors.

The business director would not be able to use the BPMC tool without guidance. However, the quality manager was confident of using the tool independently. Both received the same information throughout the research, so this may be because the quality manager is already familiar with ISO9001 processes. The quality manager is interested in improving the whole organisation regarding weak capabilities, whereas the business director is more interested in specific topics. Therefore, the quality manager would like to use the tool independently, whereas the business director would like to get guidance instead. Since in organisation Gamma the quality manager's job is to support the business director, this arrangement sounds logical.

Both the business director and the quality manager were able to follow how the case study was conducted in their organisation and they both perceived the results as useful. They both agreed that it would be useful to repeat this case study once per year to monitor how actions have affected the capabilities.

Using the researcher's way to rate importance of BPM capabilities in the case company, the questions were perceived to be important in Organisation Gamma. The scale for the importance of each factor used in the survey was: Low, Medium and High. This 3-point scale was chosen to make is easier for respondents to rate the importance. Even though it is known that validity or discriminating power may be compromised with 3-point scale in some cases, it has been also said that it has use in situations where the scale needs to be simple to understand (Preston and Colman 2000). In this case the researcher estimated that asking BPM capabilities from uneducated (non-BPM professional) audience may already be confusing enough, therefore the scale should be easy to digest (low, medium and high as words).

Another thing besides the scale was to define the border values for what is perceived as low, medium or high in the reporting of results for case company. This was a difficult choice for the researcher to make. Averages are in general thought to be a good way of reporting such numbers (Rugg 2007). There are three different averages to choose from: mode, median and means (Rugg 2007). The mode is the number, which is most common on a list. It seemed that this would cause most of the BPM capabilities to be medium and it would not give a very clear picture of which capabilities are higher and which lower compared to each other. This leaves mean and median. Median was chosen over mean, because the data had extreme values that would have potentially skewed the mean for certain capabilities. Therefore, the researcher chose to use median to compare capability scores to each other. Then the researcher had to define border scores for what median is counted in which category in reporting. Since the scale was 3-point, the researcher decided to use median for evaluating importance. Whether this is the best possible score for categorizing the priorities can be debated. This was one thing that the researcher wanted to try out through the case studies and to researcher's opinion it seemed to work in those three cases presented in this thesis. None of the BPMC factors was perceived as low importance, while 40% of the factors were medium importance and about 60% high importance for the organisation based on the average median value. This indicates that the capabilities that BPMC measures are important at least for this organisation. If the rating score for the prioritisation categorisation were to be changed slightly, that would affect the percentages presented in previous phrase. That however would not change the main point of the results, which is that none of the capabilities were perceived to be unimportant (unless the score was to be made significantly closer to 1.0 which is equal to 'low' in labelling). More detailed values for the importance of each capability are available in the case appendix.

The BPM professionals interviewed had reviewed the questions of the survey (see chapter 5.4 Final artifact introduced after the building phase), but as turned out during case Gamma, respondents found them to be too difficult to understand for normal employees in a company that does not use BPM terms specifically. This caused further changes to the BPMC artifact for the next case study in Organisation Alpha. An employee, using an alias GA in this study, at Gamma showed that there is a need to make the questions simpler. Another employee named GB, commented to many questions by saying: "*I don't understand the question*" and also said: "*Hardly anyone knows what BPM actually means*". Based on the email interview of one employee GC at Gamma and one BPM researcher from researcher's own university, named BPMR, the questions were changed for future case studies in the following way (Table 8).

Table 8.   Changes to the BPMC artifact after the first case study

From (version which these case studies started with)	To (version after case organisation Gamma)
Managers share vision and information with their subordinates.	Managers share vision and information with you.
Managers place confidence in supervisors and their subordinates.	Senior management has confidence and trust in you and your managers.
Managers constructively use their subordinates' ideas.	Managers constructively use your ideas.
Top management generally has realistic expectations of process improvement projects.	Managers have realistic expectations of process changes.
Top management usually has sufficient knowledge about process improvement projects.	Managers have sufficient knowledge about process changes.
Top management frequently communicates with project team and users.	Managers frequently communicate with you.
Top management generally supports changes in processes.	Managers support changes in processes.
The organisation has empowered process owners who are responsible.	The organisation has appointed responsible people for processes.
Employees are empowered to make decisions.	You are empowered to make decisions.
There is open communication between supervisors and their subordinates.	There is open communication between you and your managers.
Teamwork between co-workers is the typical way to solve problems.	Teamwork between co-workers is the standard way to solve problems

	within this organisation.
Management evaluates customer expectations when establishing the organisation's vision.	Managers evaluate customer expectations when establishing the organisation's vision.
Performance measurements adequately correspond to the processes and changes to them.	Performance measurements adequately correspond to process changes.
Everyone knows the cost of customer acquisition, the annual value of a customer and the cost of a customer complaint.	I know the cost of customer acquisition, the annual value of a customer and the cost of a customer complaint.
The reward system adjusts to serve employees after the changes.	The bonus scheme adjusts to process changes.
There are training programs to update employees' skills.	There are training programs available to update my skills.
BPM concepts and methodologies are known and understood.	I know and understand Business Process Management (BPM) concepts and methodologies.
The project plan for process improvement is adequate.	The plans for process improvement projects are adequate.
People are eager to improve the existing state of processes.	I am eager to improve the existing state of our processes.
Business process improvement efforts are important for the organisation.	Process improvement efforts are important for the organisation.
Employees feel comfortable with the new working environment.	I feel comfortable with the new working environment after process changes.
Initiatives in the organisation respect each other and are heading in the same direction.	Initiatives in the organisation are heading in the same direction.
People know the whole system they are part of.	I know what I do within my organisation and how it affects the result
IT is integrated into the business plan of the organisation.	The business plan of the organisation also takes information technology into consideration.
There are efficient communication channels in transferring information.	There are efficient communication channels for transferring information.
Legacy information technology is reengineered if necessary.	Existing information technology is reengineered if necessary.
IT is aligned with the BPM strategy.	Information technology is aligned with the organisation's strategy.

The table above shows the version of BPMC factors that was used in the case study surveys after Gamma. The reason why this artifact was changed at this phase is that the changes make the tool more usable for others. In this way, the artifact can be both tested and improved at the same time.

6.3 Case organisation Alpha

6.3.1 Description of case organisation Alpha

Organisation Alpha functions in the field of telecommunications and IT in Finland. The real name of the organisation and IT systems have been replaced with general terms to protect the anonymity of Organisation Alpha and its employees. It delivers operational solutions for implementing IT systems both from software and from infrastructure perspective. The company's net sales in 2012 were around 40 million Euros and they had over 200 employees. Organisation Alpha was chosen for this research because it does not have quality certifications and it was possible to get the involvement of most key managers. The expectation for the researcher in this case was to see if changes to the artifact in the previous case were successful, as they turned out to be. The case is explained in more detail in Appendix III - Organisation Alpha Case Report.

The data collection procedure presented in chapter 6.1.1 was followed in organisation Alpha in the following way:

- A process manager from organisation Alpha signed a research agreement together with the researcher in November 2012. The template provided in the appendixes was used as a basis. The goal of this agreement was to protect the data of the organisation as well as to guarantee researcher permission to publish the results anonymously.

- General information about the organisation was gathered between November and January 2012 from the organisation's website, intranet and through unstructured interviews of Process and Sales Managers (who were the main sponsors of this case study in the organisation). This was used to expand researcher's understanding of the organisation. Some of this information is presented in this chapter (omitting the parts that could reveal the identity of the organisation).

- Organisational structure was evaluated by the researcher based on the internal documentation of organisation Alpha in January 2013 to decide which part of the organisation is chosen for the case study and what background variables (to categorise the data in reporting) should be used in the beginning of the BPMC survey. This information is presented later in this chapter in more details.

- Management's expectations for the case study results were discussed in January 2013. This was done through a call between the researcher and the Process manager (who's views are described in more details later in this case description). The researcher explained what the case study is supposed to do and the management approved this purpose. Their desire was to receive useful information that they can use to understand their current BPM capabilities better and especially what to improve. The purpose of these unstructured interviews was more on stakeholder management side rather than gathering data for this research.

- The researcher evaluated his expectations towards the case research in December 2012 and revisited them in January 2013. This was purely a thought exercise going through the information researcher had collected so far and included making sure that the company is suitable for the purposes of this thesis. Researcher's expectations included to test the new iteration of BPMC artifact after changed conducted based on the feedback received from case Alpha.

- The personnel of Organisation Alpha were notified about ongoing research in January 2013 by an email sent by a management assistant. This was done in hope of increasing the response rate for the survey. Communication language for the invites was Finnish even though the survey itself was in English.

- Background variables were prepared in January 2013 by the researcher together with the process manager of the case company. Background variables mean the information that is asked in the beginning of the survey to know a bit more about the respondent himself. The background variables (questions in other words) and responses are presented in more details in the case study appendix (Appendix III - Organisation Alpha Case Report.) as well as in this case description chapter. In this case Alpha, the background variables were: respondent's skills and knowledge on developing processes, their formal training on developing processes, position, business unit and command of English language.

- The BPMC survey for personnel was started and finished in January 2013. It was distributed through online survey system called Webropol. The company, pointing to the survey, emailed the invitation link to employees. No reminders were sent this time to respondents since the response rate was as high as it could be expected in these circumstances according to process manager of the organisation. Also directors of organisation Alpha wanted to receive the results as soon as possible, so the survey time was kept as short as possible. Target audience for the survey was chosen to be the whole organisation since the size of the organisation was fairly small.

- The BPMC results were analysed in January 2013 by the researcher. He used similar methods to previous case study. This included using SPSS version 20 and Excel software for the analysis and Microsoft Word for writing the report. Detailed results of this analysis are presented in the Appendix III - Organisation Alpha Case Report.

- Interviews related to the results were executed in March 2013 in the company. The interviews were semi-structured face-to-face discussions based on the questions presented in Appendix VIII – Post-survey Interview Questions. Details of the interview are presented in chapters 6.3.3 and 6.3.4. These interviews included discussions with the case study's sponsors in the company who that were namely the Process Manager and the Sales Manager. Sales Manager might not be the most natural role to be included in this kind of initiatives, but he was also part of the board of the company and very eager to participate this project, so he was included.

- The results were presented to all senior managers of the organisation in January 2013 (close to 10 persons). This was done in a face-to-face meeting in the company. Related details of the discussion are also presented in chapter 6.3.4. The results presented for the managers are available in Appendix III - Organisation Alpha Case Report.

- The report of the results and conclusions from the case were written in March 2013. This report is available in Appendix III - Organisation Alpha Case Report. Microsoft Word was used to write this report, utilising statistical information generated with SPSS and Excel.

6.3.2 BPM capabilities of case organisation Alpha

As Appendix III - Organisation Alpha Case Report shows, based on the background information of 25 respondents gathered through the case Alpha BPMC survey, we received responses from different organisational levels. This survey was concluded with a 22% response rate. Respondents have wide backgrounds in their experience in process development. All respondents reported to have an adequate command of English to be able to understand the questions in this survey. The background information presented in Appendix III (chapter 1) indicates that offering training in developing processes may raise people's own perceptions of their skills and knowledge in developing processes (as chapter 1.2 in the appendix explains). More detailed analysis is in Appendix III - Organisation Alpha Case Report.

Of the People BPMC factors, Organisation Alpha should pay close attention especially to BPMC5 (Managers have sufficient knowledge about process changes) and BPMC8 (The organisation has appointed responsible people for processes). The rest of the People factors are at a higher level. The Appendix III provides ideas on how to improve those capabilities. The suggestions are to state the processes and process responsibilities clearly and communicate a roadmap for process development for every process. People seem to have desire for BPM and Customer Expectation Management training to learn more customer-centric methods.

The overall score of the Process BPMC factors is lower than that for the People factors. Several factors respondents disagree with, even though they are perceived to be medium or high importance. The organisation should evaluate how to improve at least the following process capabilities: BPMC18 (The bonus scheme adjusts to process changes), BPMC27 (The organisation has a standard methodology for improving processes), BPMC16 (The performance measurements adequately correspond to process changes), BPMC17 (I know the cost of customer acquisition, the annual value of a customer and the cost of a customer complaint), BPMC19 (There are training programs available to update my skills), BPMC21 (The plans for process improvement projects are adequate), BPMC24 (The organisational structure can be easily changed when needed), BPMC28 (The organisation is able to respond to changes in markets quickly) and BPMC29 (Initiatives in the organisation are heading in the same direction).

The technological capabilities to promote BPM success are at an average level at Organisation Alpha. The statistics show that respondents do not feel that there are big hurdles in technological support, but they do not seem to strongly agree either. Respondents are quite undecided on this matter. However, information technology systems should be developed because Alpha should automate more processes to be efficient (many internal systems and data synchronisations are based on MS Excel).

Open-ended questions for each BPMC category contained relevant and interesting information from individual respondents, which is available for reading in Appendix III - Organisation Alpha Case Report. The people responsible for developing business processes in organisation Alpha should look at those comments and make their own conclusions from them. These comments were discussed in the post-survey interview, but this thesis does not document those discussions, because they are highly connected to this specific organisation.

As a summary, Organisation Alpha is mainly on the positive side regarding the BPMCs measured in this survey. Some areas should be developed, especially on process capabilities, but people capabilities seem to be at a good level. The technological capabilities in Organisation Alpha are not very clear, since respondents indicated that they are between undecided and positive. Organisation should take measures to strengthen negative (respondents disagree) capabilities and to increase undecided capabilities to the positive (respondents agree) side.

6.3.3   Future implications to organisation Alpha

The sales manager of organisation Alpha was interviewed regarding the research results to provide a perspective from a department that might not be traditionally regarded as a key player in the BPM arena. The researcher gave 13 suggestions for how to improve the capabilities of organisation Alpha. The sales manager confirmed that the results of the BPMC survey were accurate and also mentioned that it was nice to see from the results that the capabilities were not as low as some other managers may have predicted. According to the sales manager, the report showed that people in Alpha have good basic skills, but the leadership is weak.

The sales manager, whose native language is Finnish (not English that was used in the survey and reporting), thought that the questions in the survey were easy to understand. He also explained that some of the BPMCs are easy to see in real life. As an example, he mentioned BPMC15 (The organisation uses external consultants when needed), which was low in Alpha and also shows in real life so that the company is not very keen to get outsiders' help.

From a sales department's perspective, the sales manager mentioned that BPMC27 (The organisation has a standard methodology for improving processes) also shows as a lack of standardised ways of doing things. To change this, he says that managers need to acknowledge the problems and start to actively work on them. The sales manager says that there is a lack of motivation among top management to fix things.

Further, the organisation should consider including the identified low-level capabilities (marked as low in the case study report) found through this BPMC case study to its organisational improvement strategy. This could be done with the help of committed top management, which would draft a plan for how to increase those capabilities. This would lead to a roadmap, which would increase the BPMCs in the organisation over time.

Since organisation Alpha is currently undergoing internal disputes and problems between managers, the results of the BPMC survey, at least according to the sales manager, will not be used in the near future. For Alpha's sake, only 7% of all the factors were on the negative side, suggesting no immediate need to improve capabilities . As the case study report shows, 89% of the factors were perceived as high importance (11% on a medium level) in the organisation. Those two capabilities reported be on a low-level (BPMC18 and BPMC27) might hinder business process initiatives in the future.

6.3.4   Evaluation of the BPMC artifact in case organisation Alpha

Even though the survey and whole process were planned carefully, there were a few unanticipated problems. One was the way the survey was received by the manager's of Alpha. For some reason the results report was ignored by the leaders. In addition, arranging the interviews with managers was found to be very challenging due to their busy schedules (this might have been true or it might have been an excuse since they were not interested in the results after they came out). The case company was in a highly volatile situation when the research was conducted. The company had internal disputes amongst the leaders. Also the CEO of the company and several board members were fired shortly after this project had ended. This situation may have distracted the leaders for the sake of other, more urgent issues. Researcher was not able to study the effect of the internal conflicts to reception of this report, since the leaders were not willing to use their time on interviews.

The sales manager of Alpha would recommend also using the BPMC artifact in other companies. He thinks that the tool is great for discovering the current situation and bottlenecks. The tool is also able to give a wider view on the organisation, not limited only to management. The sales manager also said that it would be interesting to compare the opinions of employees to those of managers to see whether there is a gap.

Even though the sales manager thought that the questions were easy to understand, he does not think that the organisation could use the BPMC tool without guidance because of the lack of process knowledge and insights into how to move forward. The sales manager also thinks that it would be useful to compare the results with those of other companies in the same field.

Of the respondents, 87% indicated that the survey was very easy or easy to respond to. There was some criticism on having the survey in English in a Finnish company. One respondent commented: *"interesting survey and question layout"*. Another one said: *"Great! It is important to ask these kinds of questions"*.

The survey itself went OK from the researcher's perspective, but using the research results afterwards did not go well. Managers said that the results were presented accurately and represented Alpha well. Then, the discussion turned to how to move forward and since the managers had so differing views, the discussion could not move forward in a constructive way. This would very likely lead to a situation where the BPMC report would be ignored.

6.4 Case organisation Epsilon

6.4.1 Description of case organisation Epsilon

Organisation Epsilon provides security-related products and services in South Africa. The company is responsible for the recovery of hundreds of thousands of stolen and hijacked vehicles throughout the world. Epsilon today is a highly sophisticated technology company offering leading-edge stolen vehicle recovery and fleet monitoring solutions to both individuals and companies throughout Southern Africa. Epsilon's technology is currently installed in almost one million vehicles throughout the world.

Epsilon's four corporate values are connectedness, integrity, agility and responsibility. If you take a walk through Epsilon's head office buildings, you will notice that its values have been woven into the actual fabric of its facility – most of the walls are wallpapered and emblazoned with spectacular depictions of their customer experience and business process maps. The company has about 1000 employees in total and its revenues are around 500 Million Euros.

Epsilon does not have a quality manual or certifications. It runs processes using an ad hoc method with common values. Basically it means that they are a value-driven enterprise where decisions on details are left for empowered employees instead of strict instructions by any specific manual. The company values are the ones guiding the decisions. Lately, Epsilon has decided to enter the customer-centric arena of process optimisation and it has a wide change program in place, of goal of which is to change the whole organisation to use customer-centric strategies. This was a good time to carry out the BPMC research in Epsilon, because part of the company is already process-trained. The goal of the BPMC research was to show the current state of BPMCs in the organisation. The researcher expected to confirm the functioning of the BPMC artifact based on two previous cases.

The data collection procedure was followed in organisation Epsilon in the following way:

- The process manager signed a research agreement together with the researcher in January 2013. The template presented in Appendix VII – Case Study Research Agreement was used.

- General information about the organisation was gathered in January 2013 from the organisation's website and from the Process Manager. This was done through exchange of emails and Skype online calls (using unstructured interviews to gather the information). Researcher recorded this information into a file system on his computer as well as into a research diary. Researcher did not have access to organisation's intranet, but the Process Manager provided all the requested information with the help of his team.

- The organisational structure was evaluated based on the information received from the Process Manager in February 2012. Key persons identified for this case study were the process manager and customer centricity team. That team consisted of three persons who were responsible for customer experiences as well as overall business process management of the organisation. They were very eager to receive new information through BPMC survey. They coordinated the internal activities within Epsilon regarding this study.

- Management's expectations for the case study results were discussed in February 2012 through an online call. Discussions took part between the researcher, process manager and customer centricity team as an unstructured interview. Researcher wanted to make sure that the information BPMC would potentially produce would be of interest to the organisation. It was also discussed whether other additional information needs to be included in the survey. It was decided that the BPMC survey would be kept in its standard form for the sake of this study. The organisation could use their existing means for collecting other information if they so desired. Process manager desired that finance, acquisitions, sales, customer service and maintenance, marketing and IT departments would be included in the survey. His desire was also that the managers and other people who are related to process re-engineering are the main target group in the survey.

- The researcher evaluated his expectations towards the case research in January 2013 and revisited them in March 2013. This included ensuring that empirical data requirements related to research questions of this study would be possible to meet. Researcher also wanted to make a 'sanity check' to ensure that the BPMC survey that would be distributed does what it is designed for. Since there were done changes to artifact in case Gamma and those were evaluated in case Alpha, in this case Epsilon the purpose was to ensure that the latest version of BPMC artifact will perform properly this time.

- Participating personnel of Organisation Epsilon were notified about ongoing research in February 2013 by an email sent by the process manager of Epsilon. The purpose of this email was to promote higher response rates for the survey. The language used in the emails was English, which was the working language of the organisation. Researcher had learned through two previous case studies on how to formulate the messages and communication better to promote higher participation. This mainly involved informing Process Manager well on the intensions of this study as well as importance of high participation from the employees of organisation Epsilon.

- Background variables were prepared in February 2013 by the researcher together with process manager of Epsilon. Detailed report on background variables can be seen in Appendix IV - Organisation Epsilon Case Report (chapter 1). The background variables used in case study Epsilon were: skills and knowledge on developing processes, formal training on developing processes, position in the organisation and command of English language.

- The BPMC survey for personnel started and finished in March 2013. This was conducted through online survey system called Webropol. The system automated the invitation, survey collection and closing the survey processes. Invitation message was customised for Epsilon, though having the same standard basic message as for gamma and Alpha also. Those survey introduction and reminder messages have been omitted from this research documentation to protect the identity of the organisations. Target audience for the survey was the previously described list of departments chosen by the process manager.

- The BPMC results were analysed in March 2013. Researcher used SPSS and Excel software to do the analysis. Then reporting was composed in Microsoft Word, using the outputs produced by previously mentioned programs. Results for this analysis are available for reading in Appendix IV - Organisation Epsilon Case Report.

- Interviews of one business and one process manager were executed in March and April 2013. The interviews were semi-structured face-to-face discussions based on the questions presented in Appendix

VIII – Post-survey Interview Questions. Results of these interviews are discussed later in this case description chapter.

- The report of the results and conclusions from the case were carried out in April 2013. Results for this analysis are available for reading in Appendix IV - Organisation Epsilon Case Report. Results are also discussed in this chapter. Purpose of the report was to communicate the findings to case organisation and to give demonstration of results that can be received using BPMC artifact.

The case is explained in more detail in Appendix IV - Organisation Epsilon Case Report.

6.4.2 BPM capabilities of case organisation Epsilon

Based on the background information of 51 respondents, the survey received responses from different organisational levels, with a 43% response rate. The organisation chose 120 employees out of their total employee base. This was done since a lot of employees are working in call-centres, etc. where they might not have visibility or understanding of business process management. It was also decided together with the Process Manager that the survey would be limited to people working in their headquarters. Respondents have a wide background in their experiences of process development. All respondents reported to have an adequate command of English to be able to understand the questions in this survey. The background information numbers also indicate that offering training in developing processes may raise people's own perceptions of their skills and knowledge in developing processes.

Of the People BPMC factors, Organisation Epsilon should pay close attention to BPMC1 (Managers share vision and information with you), BPMC4 (Managers have realistic expectations of process changes) and BPMC13 (There is performance recognition among co-workers). The rest of the People factors are at a higher level, but could be improved.

Researcher used mean values to show the responses in three categories to make the reporting easier to read by the managers: Negative (<2.8), Undecided ($2.8 <= x =< 3.2$) and Positive (>3.2). This categorisation follows the same ideology as with the importance factors described earlier in this thesis. Since value 3 indicates indecisive response, researcher added 20% of 1-point scale to both directions (towards 2 and 4) from value 3 to enable categorisation of overall values for each BPMC factor. Whether 20% or some other number would be more suitable for this use can be put under debate, but at the time researcher saw this as a suitable range. For example, some organisations could decide that undecided is counted as negative value and therefore they would have only 2 categories in place. This could work for companies that want to achieve high level of BPM capabilities in their organisation. The process BPMC factors are quite high for Epsilon. The organisation should evaluate how to improve at least the following process capabilities: BPMC16 (Performance measurements adequately correspond to process changes) and BPMC28 (The organisation is able to respond to changes in markets quickly). These BPMC process factors are barely on the positive side (mean value >3.2): BPMC17 (I know the cost of customer acquisition, the annual value of a customer and the cost of a customer complaint), BPMC27 (The organisation has a standard methodology for improving processes) and BPMC29 (Initiatives in the organisation are heading in the same direction).

The technological capabilities to promote BPM success are at an average level in Organisation Epsilon. The statistics show that respondents do not feel that there are big hurdles in technological support, but they do not seem to strongly agree either. Looking at the mean values of technological capabilities, the respondents are quite undecided on this matter (in the survey scale value 3 indicated undecided). However, information technology systems should be developed because Epsilon had a below average value for IT systems being aligned with the organisation's strategy. Researcher used mean values reported as values and bad charts. It might have given more information to use Whisker boxes instead, which would have shown the extremities of answers more clearly. Since the purpose of the report was to show the BPMC factors on overall level, the bar charts were used instead. Also another options would have been to report each capability factor categorised based on the 5-point scale answers. This was not used because it would have made the report very long and harder to understand.

Open-ended questions for each BPMC category contained relevant and interesting information from respondents. The people responsible for developing business processes should look at those comments and make their own conclusions. The real names of organisation and IT systems have been replaced with general terms to protect the anonymity of Organisation Epsilon and its employees.

As a summary, Organisation Epsilon is clearly on the positive side regarding the BPMCs measured in this survey. There are some areas to be developed, especially around process and IT capabilities, but people's capabilities seem to be at a good level, even though the open-ended comments provide clear indications for the need to train managers. Technological capabilities in Organisation Epsilon are not very clear, since respondents indicated that they are between undecided and positive.

6.4.3   Future implications to organisation Epsilon

The first interview regarding the results in Epsilon was conducted with a person whose role is to interface with the Business Analysts, Business Intelligence and Technology CRM system developments to ensure projects are scoped and time-lined. This person, who we can call the business manager, coordinates all project touch points to ensure optimal work flows and common goals for Epsilon.

The researcher offered various suggestions on how to improve the capabilities of organisation Epsilon. The process manager, who was the second person interviewed, indicated that the results of the BPMC report are reliable and useful. The business manager said that the BPMC results are useful because they give insights into where Epsilon lacks internal relationships and builds a clear foundation of what it needs to do to move forward.

The business manager said that an HR representative should develop the BPMCs in Epsilon. Both the business manager and the process manager said that it is important that the results are not just discussed and forgotten about, but used, too. The business manager mentioned that the results are important for sharing the company vision and goals and ensuring everyone understands that there is a bigger picture in the company.

6.4.4   Evaluation of the BPMC artifact in case organisation Epsilon

This was the third BPMC evaluation in a real organisation. As part of these artifact iterations through cases, the researcher has learned how to use the artifact better since he conducted the research faster than previously. The process for using BPMC artifact is more standard and the artifact itself did not require changes. This process is described in chapter 6.5.3 later in this thesis. Altogether, 85% of respondents said that the survey questions were either very easy or easy to understand and the business manager agreed. In addition, the open-ended comments on the survey were mainly positive. The biggest concern respondents had was whether anything would happen based on the results (which is more related to organisation taking action than to BPMC artifact itself).

Based on the interview with the business manager, other organisations can benefit from the BPMC as not everyone takes a BPM approach. According to the business manager, companies that can benefit include governmental departments to streamline processes for public insurers, banks and large corporates in South Africa. As a best target audience for the BPMC artifact, the business manager sees large corporates that service third parties.

The business manager said that it would be beneficial to be able to compare the BPMC results with those of competitors: *"All businesses aim to do as well as others in their sector, if not better so it will definitely be useful as we would then get a clear indication as to where we need to improve and what we should be doing differently (we need to be unique) we need to understand internally what we dealing with to be able to cater for external needs."*

He also described the case study experience in the following way: *"I just feel that with BPMC it reduces human error, miscommunications, sets a tone for culture change, gets managers and stakeholders behind processes, and allows everyone to accept process outputs placing the client at the centre of everything we do. Simplifies operations and improves the entire experience."* The business manager added that *"keep things simple and don't over complicate"*, which is in conjugation with the quality measures set for this research. From the researcher's perspective, it easy to see how the BPMC report has been simplified in each of the case studies, learning on the way. Epsilon received the simplest and clearest BPMC report in this research.

6.5 Cross-case analysis

6.5.1 Short description of each case

The following table shows five highest level BPMC People factors in each case organisation with their double-digit mean values:

Organisation Gamma	Organisation Alpha	Organisation Epsilon
BPMC11 Co-workers have confidence and trust in each other (4.2)	BPMC10 There is open communication between you and your managers (4.3)	BPMC15 The organisation uses external consultants when needed (3.9)
BPMC12 Teamwork between co-workers is the standard way to solve problems within this organisation (4.2)	BPMC11 Co-workers have confidence and trust in each other (4.3)	BPMC10 There is open communication between you and your managers (3.8)
BPMC2 Senior management has confidence and trust in you and your managers (4.0)	BPMC12 Teamwork between co-workers is the standard way to solve problems within this organisation (4.2)	BPMC12 Teamwork between co-workers is the standard way to solve problems within this organisation (3.7)
BPMC10 There is open communication between you and your managers	BPMC13 There is performance recognition among co-workers (4.1)	BPMC2 Senior management has confidence and trust in

(3.9)		you and your managers (3.7)
BPMC9 You are empowered to make decisions (3.7)	BPMC6 Managers frequently communicate with you (3.9)	BPMC8 The organisation has appointed responsible people for processes (3.7)

(Likert scale: 1 = Strongly disagree 2 = Disagree, 3 = Undecided, 4 = Agree, 5 = Strongly agree)

The following table shows five highest level BPMC Process factors in each case organisation with their double-digit mean values:

Organisation Gamma	Organisation Alpha	Organisation Epsilon
BPMC23 Process improvement efforts are important for the organisation (4.0)	BPMC23 Process improvement efforts are important for the organisation (4.6)	BPMC23 Process improvement efforts are important for the organisation (4.6)
BPMC29 Initiatives in the organisation are heading in the same direction (3.6)	BPMC30 I know what I do within my organisation and how it affects the result (4.4)	BPMC22 I am eager to improve the existing state of our processes (4.5)
BPMC25 No one has to be concerned about losing his or her job because of process changes (3.4)	BPMC22 I am eager to improve the existing state of our processes (4.3)	BPMC30 I know what I do within my organisation and how it affects the result (4.3)
BPMC19 There are training programs available to update my skills (3.3)	BPMC26 I feel comfortable with the new working environment after process changes (4.0)	BPMC26 I feel comfortable with the new working environment after process changes (3.8)
BPMC28 The organisation is able to respond to changes in markets quickly (3.2)	BPMC25 No one has to be concerned about losing his or her job because of process changes (3.9)	BPMC20 I know and understand Business Process Management (BPM) concepts and methodologies (3.8)

142

(Likert scale: 1 = Strongly disagree, 2 = Disagree, 3 = Undecided, 4 = Agree, 5 = Strongly agree)

The following table shows five highest level BPMC Technical factors in each case organisation with their double-digit mean values:

Organisation Gamma	Organisation Alpha	Organisation Epsilon
BPMC31 The business plan of the organisation also takes information technology systems into consideration (3.3)	BPMC32 The organisation extensively uses information technology systems (4.0)	BPMC31 The business plan of the organisation also takes information technology systems into consideration (3.6)
BPMC33 There are efficient communication channels for transferring information (3.3)	BPMC34 Existing information technology systems are reengineered if necessary (3.7)	BPMC32 The organisation extensively uses information technology systems (3.2)
BPMC32 The organisation extensively uses information technology systems (3.2)	BPMC33 There are efficient communication channels for transferring information (3.7)	BPMC34 Existing information technology systems are reengineered if necessary (3.2)
BPMC35 Information technology systems are aligned with the organisation's strategy (3.0)	BPMC31 The business plan of the organisation also takes information technology systems into consideration (3.7)	BPMC33 There are efficient communication channels for transferring information (3.1)
BPMC34 Existing information technology systems are reengineered if necessary (2.9)	BPMC35 Information technology systems are aligned with the organisation's strategy (3.0)	BPMC35 Information technology systems are aligned with the organisation's strategy (2.8)

(Likert scale: 1 = Strongly disagree, 2 = Disagree, 3 = Undecided, 4 = Agree, 5 = Strongly agree)

6.5.2 Cross-case conclusions

The three case organisations showed that the BPMC artifact in its final version performs well. The artifact is able to produce useful information regarding an organisation's BPMCs. Also it was seen that response rates and engagement with the artifact grew as the artifact was iterated further in each organisation.

The response rates improved along with the researcher's skills to conduct BPMC surveys. In addition, the importance of each BPMC factor rose in each case as the response increased. None of the case organisations indicated that any of the factors would be of low importance. Most of them are highly important (71%) and some medium (29%) based on the criteria set by the researcher. The importance of BPMC factors was measured on a scale: Low,

Medium and High. The median values for importance of each BPMC factor show that we can divide the responses into three categories: Low, Medium and High. The researcher decided these thresholds for different categories. This same categorisation was used for all cases. Figure 17 shows the importance of each BPMC factor in all three cases in order of importance (valid listwise N=38, for individuals factors N varies between 53 and 93). As the picture will show, none of the capability factors presented in the artifact were perceived to be of low importance by the respondents, which is important from the validity perspective for this research. The figure 17 also is related to research question *"Which capability factors are related to the success and failure of BPM?"* showing that these factors are important for the matter.

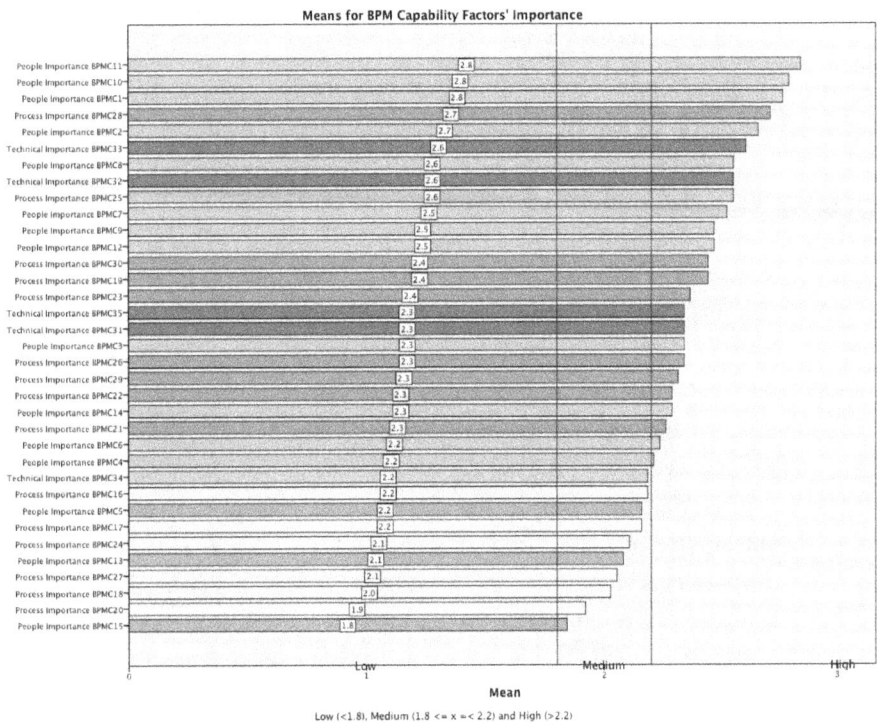

Figure 17.   Importance of each BPMC factor

Based on the figure above, the top 10 most important BPMCs found in this research are in order of importance as follows:

    1. BPMC11 (People) Co-workers have confidence and trust in each other.

2. BPMC10 (People) There is open communication between you and your managers.
3. BPMC1 (People) Managers share vision and information with you.
4. BPMC28 (Process) The organisation is able to respond to changes in markets quickly.
5. BPMC2 (People) Senior management has confidence and trust in you and your managers.
6. BPMC33 (Technology) There are efficient communication channels for transferring information.
7. BPMC8 (People) The organisation has appointed responsible people for processes.
8. BPMC32 (Technology) The organisation extensively uses information technology systems.
9. BPMC25 (Process) No one has to be concerned about losing his or her job because of process changes.
10. BPMC7 (People) Managers support changes in processes.

The interview results for each case organisation validated that managers find the information produced by the BPMC artifact to be useful. At the same time, both employees responding to the surveys as well as managers are concerned that the results will not be put into use. It seems that the organisations are quite happy to continue as they are even though they would receive useful information on how to improve the organisation. This may indicate that it is important to get the commitment of top management to change the organisation in the early phases of using the artifact.

The easiness of the survey questions was perceived as lower in the first case study (Gamma) than in the others. This caused the researcher to change the questions and add one more question to the survey to ask how easy respondents thought the questions were. This was reported by response category (5-point scale). After two cases, 93% of respondents felt that the questions were easy or very easy. This still leaves 7% of respondents who found it difficult to answer the questions. It is left for future research to find out which questions exactly are those that are difficult to understand. Figure 18 shows the total for easiness based on these two case studies (Alpha and Epsilon, valid N listwise = 67).

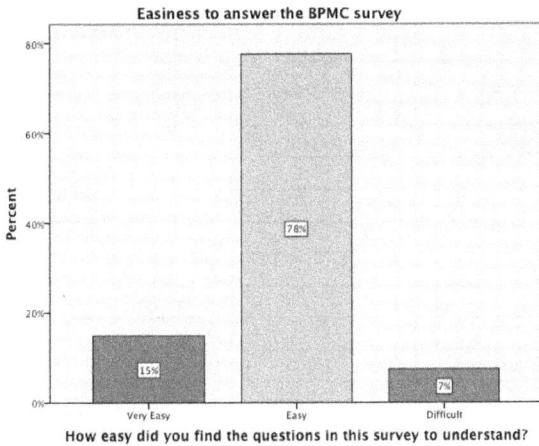

Figure 18.   Easiness to answer the BPMC survey

The easiness could be evaluated also from the perspective that which BPMC factors have most missing values. The table below shows the missing values for each case and the total.

Table 11.   Missing values

BPMC Factor	Gamma N=34	Alpha N=25	Epsilon N=51	Sum N=110
BPMC1	0	0	0	0
BPMC2	2	1	2	5
BPMC3	2	0	2	4
BPMC4	8	1	1	10
BPMC5	7	1	1	9
BPMC6	2	0	1	3
BPMC7	6	1	2	9
BPMC8	8	1	3	12
BPMC9	4	0	2	6
BPMC10	0	0	1	1
BPMC11	0	0	1	1
BPMC12	0	0	1	1
BPMC13	3	0	2	5
BPMC14	9	1	2	12
BPMC15	7	1	3	11
BPMC16	7	2	4	13
BPMC17	3	1	3	7
BPMC18	5	3	--	8
BPMC19	2	0	0	2
BPMC20	9	1	0	10
BPMC21	12	5	1	18
BPMC22	5	0	0	5

BPMC23	4	0	1	8
BPMC24	5	1	2	8
BPMC25	8	0	1	9
BPMC26	6	0	2	8
BPMC27	12	4	3	19
BPMC28	6	0	2	8
BPMC29	9	2	2	13
BPMC30	4	0	0	4
BPMC31	3	3	1	7
BPMC32	2	1	0	3
BPMC33	1	0	0	1
BPMC34	10	0	0	10
BPMC35	10	1	1	12

The numbers in table above indicate the absolute amount of missing answers per BPMC factor. Based on the table above the most missing answers are in BPMC factors: BPMC27 (19), BPMC21 (18), BPMC16 (13), BPMC29 (13), BPMC8 (12), BPMC14 (12) and BPMC35 (12). These questions would require future research to find out if these missing values correlate to difficultness to answer. This may have implications to easiness of use for survey respondents. The current data collect by the researcher is not able to answer that question and is left for the future research.

The final version of the BPMC artifact factors based on these three case studies is as follows:

BPMC People

BPMC1 Managers share vision and information with you.

BPMC2 Senior management has confidence and trust in you and your managers.

BPMC3 Managers constructively use your ideas.

BPMC4 Managers have realistic expectations of process changes.

BPMC5 Managers have sufficient knowledge about process changes.

BPMC6 Managers frequently communicate with you.

BPMC7 Managers support changes in processes.

BPMC8 The organisation has appointed responsible people for processes.

BPMC9 You are empowered to make decisions.

BPMC10 There is open communication between you and your managers.

BPMC11 Co-workers have confidence and trust in each other.

BPMC12 Teamwork between co-workers is the standard way to solve problems within this organisation.

BPMC13 There is performance recognition among co-workers.

BPMC14 Managers evaluate customer expectations when establishing the organisation's vision.

BPMC15 The organisation uses external consultants when needed.

BPMC Process

BPMC16 Performance measurements adequately correspond to process changes.

BPMC17 I know the cost of customer acquisition, the annual value of a customer and the cost of a customer complaint.

BPMC18 The bonus scheme adjusts to process changes.

BPMC19 There are training programs available to update my skills.

BPMC20 I know and understand Business Process Management (BPM) concepts and methodologies.

BPMC21 The plans for process improvement projects are adequate.

BPMC22 I am eager to improve the existing state of our processes.

BPMC23 Process improvement efforts are important for the organisation.

BPMC24 The organisational structure can be easily changed when needed.

BPMC25 No one has to be concerned about losing his or her job because of process changes.

BPMC26 I feel comfortable with the new working environment after process changes.

BPMC27 The organisation has a standard methodology for improving processes.

BPMC28 The organisation is able to respond to changes in markets quickly.

BPMC29 Initiatives in the organisation are heading in the same direction.

BPMC30 I know what I do within my organisation and how it affects the result.

BPMC Technology

BPMC31 The business plan of the organisation also takes information technology systems into consideration.

BPMC32 The organisation extensively uses information technology systems.

BPMC33 There are efficient communication channels for transferring information.

BPMC34 Existing information technology systems are reengineered if necessary.

BPMC35 Information technology systems are aligned with the organisation's strategy.

The purpose of using cases in this study was to evaluate the ease of use, practical usefulness, completeness, simplicity, elegance and understandability of the built artifact (March and Smith 1995). Based on these three cases, we can see that ease of use happened partially. The BPMC artifact is fairly easy to use for those who have prior knowledge of BPM, but for others it may not be as clear. Practical usefulness has been proven through post-case study interviews where the managers of the participating companies confirmed the usefulness of the information provided by the BPMC artifact. From a completeness perspective, the research was able to show that the 35 chosen capability factors are important for organisations, but it could not show what is still missing. As an artifact, the BPMC tool is quite simple, it consists of 35 capability factors and a process to use them. If 35 factors are too many for a target organisation's purposes, it is possible to choose the most important BPMC categories and exclude others. Another option for shortening the number of factors is to use only high importance ones and exclude the medium ones. The elegance and understandability of the BPMC artifact is left for the reader to decide. The researcher thinks that the tool is elegant and understandable. It reveals information about the organisation's capabilities with quite little effort and can produce useful information.

6.5.3   *Artifact in practical use*

To use BPMC artifact, there are some things to consider. These are suggestions on how to use the artifact based on the researcher's perceptions during the three case studies presented in this theses. Business process management changes are rarely easy to implement, because for example top management support, a dedicated process team and the alignment of financial incentives each contribute to the likelihood that the change will succeed (Paulus 2008; Manfreda et al. 2014).

Top management's commitment to using the BPMC artifact, especially to fix the issues identified, is very important from the beginning. It is possible to conduct the survey and analyse the results without the support (as in case Alpha), but it would not be useful unless the organisation learns from the results and improves the capabilities identified.

Respondents need to be able to read and write good enough English to be able to answer the questionnaire and read the report. Translating the questions and writing the report in the target language could overcome this issue. In this research, English was used in all cases. That affected the case Alpha, a Finnish company, based on the open-ended comments in the BPMC survey.

It is possible to think of each question category as modules, which can be chosen to be included in the survey or not. In some cases, it might make sense only to survey People or Process factors, whereas in some cases we could leave the Technology section out. This would make the survey shorter and easier for respondents to participate. In this regard, it is important first to evaluate which section could be left out.

Moreover, adjusting individual questions for the organisation's situation may be needed in some cases. For example, in Epsilon there are big process changes under way and for political reasons managers did not want to expose employees to questions that might upset them.

The latter part of the research question in this study was *"How can organisations take these capability factors into account in their BPM initiatives?"*. The process chart in Figure 19 is a part of the answer to that question. It is based on the research process used in this thesis.

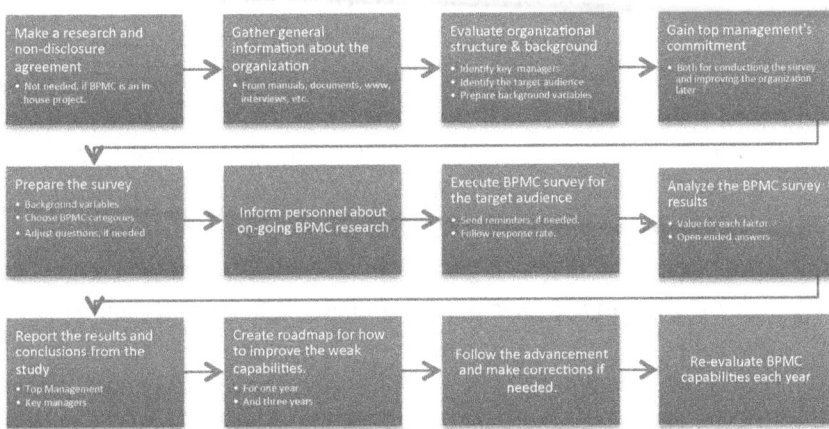

Figure 19.   Process for using the BPMC artifact

This process is based on the interview results from the cases and the researcher's experience while conducting the case studies. Each phase in the process map above is designed to support using the BPMC artifact in a reliable way. Preparation for the survey is as important as conducting the actual survey. In addition, gaining commitment from top management is important for getting the improvement roadmap in place and moving the organisation forward.

Make a research and non-disclosure agreement. This might not be a necessary step when research is conducted in-house. In case external researcher is used, the process for using the BPMC artifact should start by making an agreement to protect both the researcher and the participating organisation. The person signing the agreement needs to be at a high enough level (e.g. C-level, director or equivalent) to give permission for the research. The agreement should also contains information on who will have the rights to approve the public version of the case study report and what is the process for doing that. Example of such an agreement can be found in Appendix VII – Case Study Research Agreement.

Gather general information about the organisation. In this phase, the researcher should gather relevant, general information about the organisation. That includes economic figures, amount of personnel, organisational structure, information on website, intranet documentation, etc. If the artifact is used in-house, this should be fairly easy phase to complete.

Evaluate the organisational structure and background. The researcher should evaluate the structure of the organisation to identify the key persons related to the use of BPMC artifact. The researcher needs to know who is able to sign the research contract, who will be the project manager for the initiative study from the organisation's side (coordinating their internal efforts) and what other people are involved with this research. The researcher will also find out who can help with distributing the BPMC survey to all personnel. If the organisation has a HR or internal communications department, then the researcher may work together with them to get the information and promote communication related to gathering information from the employees.

Gain top management's commitment. This is important to get support for the project.

Prepare the survey. This includes preparing background variables for the BPMC survey. Background variables are used to categorise responses while reporting. This information can be used to pinpoint more accurately where capabilities need to be developed. Also questions in the BPMC artifact may need adjusting for the organisation's environment. Depending whether the artifact is used in project or organisational scope, this may affect preparation of the survey.

Inform personnel about ongoing BPMC research. It is important for personnel to know that there is BPMC research going on and that they will be asked to participate in the survey. In this stage, it is important to have top management involved, so that it can share its view on how the results of the BPMC report will be used later on.

Execute the BPMC survey for the target audience. Chosen personnel, if limited scope for the use of artifact (or potentially all if organisational scope), from the organisation are enquired for their opinions on BPM capabilities. Before executing the survey, the researcher needs to find out how personnel are able to participate in the online survey or whether the survey be implemented with a paper and pen solution. The researcher also needs to find out when is the best time to execute the survey. The survey itself should contain a welcome page, background information questions and the questions for BPMC factors. At the end of survey there should be a polite thank you note.

Analyse the BPMC survey results. The researcher will analyse the results received from the BPMC survey using statistical software. In this phase, the researcher may use SPSS analytics software and other means (for example Microsoft Excel) necessary to analyse the results. In this phase, if it is necessary, researcher may gather more information through interviews or observations to find out more information about the possible findings in the analysed results.

Report the results and conclusions from the study. Finally, the researcher will report the results and conclusions from the study. There should be an executive summary for top management and key managers. The results should be discussed with them and clarify any questions they might have. If new information needs arise that can be satisfied, the researcher should address those desires.

Create roadmap for how to improve the weak capabilities. This requires BPM knowledge. Receiving the insights will not change the organisation by itself. It is required that the organisation will take actions to improve weak capabilities on purpose. Since building capabilities may take considerably much time, it is suggested to have one year and potentially 3 years plans. However, such timescales should be determined based on the organisation's current situation, environment and capability to change.

Follow the advancement and make corrections if needed. Change of capabilities should be observed and adjustments made when necessary.

Re-evaluate BPMC capabilities each year. As a general suggestion, it is recommended to use BPMC artifact once a year. However, again it is highly recommendable to make such decisions based on the organisations situation, environment and appetite for change.

7   CONCLUSIONS

In this thesis, the researcher challenged the dominant maturity model perspective on BPM development and suggested an alternative approach in a form of a BPMC artifact. The researcher conceptualised business process management as a dynamic capability, which implies that BPM capabilities should be developed in a way that a fit with the organisational environment and market is achieved (aligned to ideas presented in Niehaves et al. 2014). Based on this understanding, the researcher argued that existing BPM capability development and maturity models are limited at presenting a practical tool for organisations to use to understand their current capabilities. As Niehaves et al. (2014) have stated, *"striving for the most sophisticated BPM capability according to existing maturity models will not necessarily lead to an environment-BPM-fit"*. As they say, instead, *"when determining the right level of BPM capability, contingency factors like environmental variables or organizational characteristics have to be taken into account"*. BPMC artifact helps organisations to thrive towards this goal, even though it might not be able to provide the whole roadmap by itself. The researcher suggests in this work that organisations do not have to take prescribed paths shown by maturity models, but rather aim for continuous improvement through aligning their BPM capabilities with operational environment and market situation.

The objective of this thesis was to build an artifact for evaluating business process management capabilities (BPMC) in an organisation, using design science and case studies research methods. To meet this objective, the thesis commenced with an introduction and then discussed theoretical background of business process management and capability factors. Then literature review and proposition for the first version of the BPMC artifact based on the literature was presented. Next, the methodological choices were presented, which discussed how the empirical data was collected and analysed to determine how the artifact will function in case organisations. Then the artifact was built further based on expert interviews. Once that was concluded, the researcher evaluated the artifact with case studies. It was necessary to iterate the artifact once more after the first case study. Then the artifact was tested in two more organisations. The outcomes and findings of this research were then presented. A key finding is that whilst there exists several models for business process management capabilities, there are also points of uniqueness namely in the way the capabilities are measured and used to improve organisations. Also there is uniqueness in the identified capability factors themselves as presented later in this chapter.

7.1   A summary of the results

This research started from the personal interest of the researcher in BPM. He found a lot of research on the success and failure factors of BPM, but this information had not been put to use in the best possible way. This led to an idea to gather important factors and to create a BPMC artifact. This research focused on *which capability factors are related to the success and failure of BPM and how organisations can take these capability factors into account in their BPM initiatives*. The contributions of this work were divided into theoretical and practical sections, which are described in later chapters. However, it can be stated here that this research has been able to use design science to produce a unique BPMC artifact, which helps organisations to evaluate their business process management capabilities in different way than with the traditional BPM maturity models.

The biggest difference between this study and the others described in the literature review is that the previous studies mainly observed factors that affected BPM success and failure and reported them. This study has used that information combined with real-life cases to build an artifact, which may be used as a tool in evaluating organisations. It can be combined with the knowledge and skills of person doing the evaluation to suggest how to improve the organisations. Until now, it has been job of those people to accumulate the information from the literature (or from existing maturity models) and use it as they best see. The BPMC artifact has created a systematic method, which can be used for organisation's benefit without going through all that work. Evaluation of BPMC artifact has shown that the information it produces is useful for participating organisations (see case descriptions for evidence).

This research combines an extensive literature review with design science method. The goal of the research was to create an artifact that enables organisations to evaluate their BPMC factors. For the empirical data collection, researcher used interviews, surveys and case studies. The artifact was developed based on the literature review combined with expert interviews and one case study. Then, the artifact was evaluated in its natural environment through two case studies. The advantage of using design science as a research method was to produce an artifact that can be practically used in organisations. This study did not use action design science (Sein et al. 2011), because the researcher concluded that traditional design science was more suitable for the research question (as discussed in previous chapters in this thesis).

Based on the case study findings, it is important for organisations to be able to measure their process improvement capabilities. Processes are effectively part of everything that is done in an organisation and they need to be developed due to changing business environments. The case studies conducted in this research showed that all recognised BPMC factors are important for case organisations. The confirmatory artifact review interviews, concluded as part of case studies, indicated that organisations perceived the information received through the BPMC artifact as useful and important. It was also found that the organisations might not be able to use the BPMC tool without process expertise. Another concern presented by the participating organisations was related to the actual implementation of the results of using the BPMC artifact. The organisations expressed that support from top management is crucial for increasing the BPMC's of an organisation.

This study had some limitations, which are discussed in mode details in chapter 1.8. One is that this research is not able to show why the BPMC factors discovered are important. The research is also not able to compare different industries or cultures. Since the focus of this research was on a practical approach to developing the BPMC artifact, some parts of the theory could be researched deeper. For example, it is important to discover how those chosen capability factors are related. Another limitation concerns the use of the BPMC artifact. Only process professionals who have enough knowledge to adjust to the use of a tool to suit the target organisation may be able use it.

Hevner et al. (2004) provide a set of seven guidelines to help researchers conduct, evaluate and present design science research. These seven guidelines address design as an artifact, problem relevance, design evaluation, research contributions, research rigor, design as search process and research communication. This research has followed these guidelines as well as maintained high quality for interviews, surveys and case studies. Some criteria set for this study by the research were usefulness and easiness. The empirical data showed that the case organisation perceived the information provided by the BPMC artifact to be useful and interesting. In addition, ease of answering the BPMC survey was high, but analysing the survey results without statistical and process expertise may not be possible. The contributions of this thesis are explained in the following chapters.

The final BPMC artifact is explained in more details in chapter 6.5.2 Cross-case conclusions. This research has born from different need than traditional BPM maturity models (e.g. Fisher 2004; Rosemann and de Bruinn 2005; Rosemann et al. 2006; Hammer 2007; Lee et al. 2007; Rohloff 2009; Weber et al. 2008). The idea was not to build yet another maturity model to tell the organisation at what level they are (following BPM maturity critique presented in Niehaves et al. (2014) as well as Pöppelbuß and Röglinger (2011)), but rather to have a tool for easily and clearly understanding what capability factors should be in place to promote BPM success in companies. The BPM field has not been very organised in giving practical guidance on capabilities. The main motivation to carry out this research was to find out which capability factors are related to the success and failure of BPM and how organisations can take them practically into account in their BPM initiatives. The basis of the research comes from theory, and that knowledge is then practically used by building an artifact, which is also evaluated. The researcher found maturity models to be impractical in his consulting work and this has been expressed also by Niehaves et al. (2014, p.91) in their research. This has inspired the researcher to design a practical artifact, which can be used to understand current level of BPM capabilities in organizations in their respective environment. The list below shows the final version of the designed artifact.

People

BPMC1 Managers share vision and information with you.
BPMC2 Senior management has confidence and trust in you and your managers.
BPMC3 Managers constructively use your ideas.
BPMC4 Managers have realistic expectations of process changes.
BPMC5 Managers have sufficient knowledge about process changes.
BPMC6 Managers frequently communicate with you.
BPMC7 Managers support changes in processes.
BPMC8 The organisation has appointed responsible people for processes.
BPMC9 You are empowered to make decisions.
BPMC10 There is open communication between you and your managers.
BPMC11 Co-workers have confidence and trust in each other.
BPMC12 Teamwork between co-workers is the standard way to solve problems within this organisation.
BPMC13 There is performance recognition among co-workers.
BPMC14 Managers evaluate customer expectations when establishing the organisation's vision.
BPMC15 The organisation uses external consultants when needed.

Process

BPMC16 Performance measurements adequately correspond to process changes.
BPMC17 I know the cost of customer acquisition, the annual value of a customer and the cost of a customer complaint
BPMC18 The bonus scheme adjusts to process changes.
BPMC19 There are training programs available to update my skills.
BPMC20 I know and understand Business Process Management (BPM) concepts and methodologies.
BPMC21 The plans for process improvement projects are adequate.
BPMC22 I am eager to improve the existing state of our processes.
BPMC23 Process improvement efforts are important for the organisation.
BPMC24 The organisational structure can be easily changed when needed.
BPMC25 No one has to be concerned about losing his or her job because of process changes.
BPMC26 I feel comfortable with the new working environment after process changes.
BPMC27 The organisation has a standard methodology for improving processes.
BPMC28 The organisation is able to respond to changes in markets quickly.
BPMC29 Initiatives in the organisation are heading in the same direction.
BPMC30 I know what I do within my organisation and how it affects the result.

Technology

BPMC31 The business plan of the organisation also takes information systems into consideration.
BPMC32 The organisation extensively uses information systems.
BPMC33 There are efficient communication channels for transferring information.
BPMC34 Existing information systems are reengineered if necessary.
BPMC35 Information systems are aligned with the organisation's strategy.

Comparing the BPM capability factors list to Rosemann and de Bruin (2006) BPM Maturity Framework shows that this work is different to it. Mathiesen et al. (2011, chapter 3.1) have a summary figure of factors and capability areas of Rosemann and de Bruin (2006). It is evident that some parts of these two models are similar, which validates both studies, but there are also differences due to different perspectives. For example, where this work has 3 categories for these factors, Rosemann and de Bruin (2006) have 6. From those 2 are similar (people and technology) and one is different (process). Wording of capability areas are mostly different. Also Rosemann and de Bruin (2006) model suggests for organisations to achieve a specific maturity level, when BPMC artifact is more for understanding current level of capabilities and then designing a desired level of capabilities based on the organisational context and operating environment. Other differences to relevant maturity and capability models are discussed further later in this chapter.

Škrinjar et al. (2010) have also done similar kind of work as presented in the list above. They did research in Slovenian and Croatian organisations looking for statistically significant differences in factors related to process-orientation. This thesis is different to this work since the goal has been to create a practical tool, which can be used by organisations to evaluate their current BPM capabilities. In Škrinjar et al. (2010) the goal has been to find statistically significant factors as a scientific exercise. Also they write, *"the main goal of our study was to determine whether there are differences in BPO adoption between Croatian and Slovenian companies"*, when goal of this work has been to create a global tool using design science method for practical use. Similar between these two works has been the attempt to propose a framework for understanding business process management capabilities and relevant elements. Differences are in the end-results where Škrinjar et al. (2010) have fewer elements and they also did not present any practical method for using their findings. Their *"results have many practical implications for managers of the Slovenian, but especially of the Croatian companies"* when this research has more global view.

Lifecycle of the BPMC artifact is shown in the picture below with main stages to build the artifact into its final form through iterations. Boxes with solid line are different versions of the artifact and boxes with dashed line are main events shaping the next iteration of the artifact.

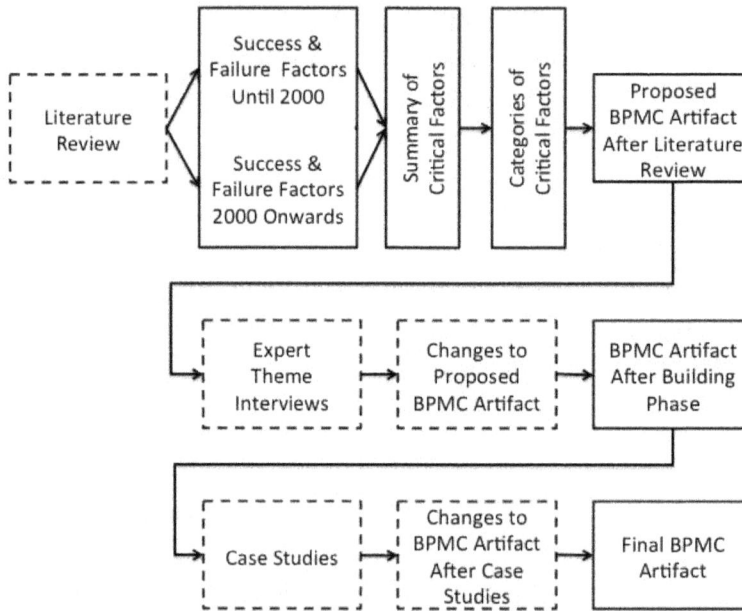

Figure 26.   The lifecycle of BPMC artifact

7.2   Theoretical contribution

One purpose of this thesis was to follow the idea presented by Peffers et al. (2008) on creating a thing that will serve human purposes. This thesis has presented a combination of design science method with expert theme interviews, surveys and case studies in the BPM field. The researcher was able to use all these methods successfully to build and evaluate the BPMC artifact. The findings in this research are significant for academics, since the BPMC artifact can be used as basis for other studies and as a further study to research why these capabilities are important. Researcher also found out that controlling the design science process as well as articulating clearly what is done is important for the study to be successful. Peffers et al. (2008, p.49) have written that it is important for the research to produce an artifact that is created to address a problem. This thesis has presented a solution to practical problem of having a non-staged (unlike most of the BPM maturity models), relatively easy-to-use tool for understanding the current level of BPM capabilities in an organisation. Creating the BPMC artifact has been a search process that draws from existing theories and literature (as suggested in Peffers et al. 2008).

As the empirical part of this thesis has shown, all the capability factors identified as part of the BPMC artifact were perceived to be mainly highly important for the case organisations, with some medium importance, but none were seen as low importance. Also, this research identified the top 10 most important BPMC factors based on three case studies presented in this study. Those are presented in chapter 6.5.2 Cross-case conclusions. This information can be used by academics to focus efforts in their own studies.

The researcher answered the research question of *"Which capability factors are related to the success and failure of BPM?"* in chapter 5.4 Final artifact introduced after the building phase and as refined in chapter 6.5.2 Cross-case conclusions. The list of relevant capability factors contains 35 aspects categorised in three themes. Peffers et al. (2008) have written, design science *"is of importance in a discipline oriented to the creation of successful artifacts"*. In this thesis design science has been used to create a successful artifact (evaluated with 3 case studies) that will help the academics to understand capabilities contributing to BPM initiatives better. This work has been able to satisfy the demands presented by March and Smith (1995), Hevner et al. (2004) and Peffers et al. (2008) for design science. The following table compares BPMC artifact with other capability and maturity models to bring the uniqueness of this artifact more visible.

Table 12. Comparing BPMC artifact with other business process management capability and maturity models.

Model and Categories		Description	Capabilities
Rosemann and de Bruin (2006)	Strategic Alignment	Alignment to corporate strategy & mission	Strategic Focus; Process Management; Communication; Leadership; Negotiation
	Governance	Organisational implementation of BPM and responsibilities for assigned tasks	Process Management; Leadership; Project Management
	Methods	Methods for all BPM relevant tasks	Process Modelling; Process Frameworks; Process training; Process Model development; Workshop facilitation; Stakeholder interviews
	Information Technology	Technology which supports & enables BPM	Software Skills; Process Modelling; Process Management; Project Management
	People	Competencies of	Process expertise;

		people involved in BPM	Process Management; Process qualifications; Communication; Leadership; Negotiation; Communication; Collaboration
	Culture	Common values towards BPM & process change	Adaptable to change; Process thinking; Leadership; Communication; Collaboration
BPTrends Pyramid (Harmon 2007)	Enterprise Level	Organisational strategic alignment and governance	Strategy, Process Architecture, Process management, Program/project management
	Business Process Level	Process design and improvement	Process analysis, Process improvement, Methodologies, Process modelling and documentation
	Implementation Level	Process execution via technical, human and infrastructure resources	Knowledge Management, BPMS knowledge, Role definitions, Employee skill development, Software development
Public Administra-tion BPM Maturity Model for the 48-h-service promise (Zwicker et al. 2010)	Strategy	Definition and communication of the model as a strategic objective and a measure	Definition of objective, Definition of objective values
	Design	Designing the model	Process documentation, definition of basic parameters, definition of actions, definition of roles and responsibilities, information technology of design
	Implementation	Implementing the model	Resource planning and allocation, management enforcement, implementation of actions

	Controlling	Controlling the model	Definition of measures, use of measures, information technology for controlling
	People and culture	Factors in the model	Knowledge and competencies, willingness to implement
Business Process Maturity Model (Fisher 2004)	Strategy	Strategic understanding of the role, positioning and focus for enterprise-wide decision-making in support of overall company objectives	Siloed, Tactically integrated, Process driven, Optimised enterprise, Intelligent operating network
	Controls	The governance model for the management, administration, and evaluation of initiatives, with a strong focus on the appropriate metrics applied for measurement	Siloed, Tactically integrated, Process driven, Optimised enterprise, Intelligent operating network
	People	The human resource environment, including skills, organizational culture, and organizational structure	Siloed, Tactically integrated, Process driven, Optimised enterprise, Intelligent operating network
	Technology	Enabling information systems, applications, tools, and infrastructure	Siloed, Tactically integrated, Process driven, Optimised enterprise, Intelligent operating network
	Process	Operating methods and practices, including policies and procedures, which determine the way activities are performed	Siloed, Tactically integrated, Process driven, Optimised enterprise, Intelligent operating network
OMG Business Process Maturity Model (Weber, Curtis, and Gardiner 2008)	Initial	Wherein business processes are performed in inconsistent sometimes ad hoc ways with results that	A multitude of action fields.

		are difficult to predict.	
	Managed	Wherein management stabilizes the work within local work units to ensure that it can be performed in a repeatable way that satisfies the workgroup's primary commitments. However, work units performing similar tasks may use different procedures.	A multitude of action fields.
	Standardised	Wherein common, standard processes are synthesized from best practices identified in the work groups and tailoring guidelines are provided for supporting different business needs. Standard processes provide an economy of scale and a foundation for learning from common measures and experience.	A multitude of action fields.
	Predictable	Wherein the capabilities enabled by standard processes are exploited and provided back into the work units. Process performance is managed statistically throughout the workflow to understand and control variation so that process outcomes can be predicted from intermediate states.	A multitude of action fields.
	Innovating	Wherein both proactive and opportunistic improvement actions seek innovations that	A multitude of action fields.

		can close gaps between the organization's current capability and the capability required to achieve its business objectives.	
Process and Enterprise Maturity Model (Hammer 2007)	Leadership	The company's senior executives must be committed to the business process approach.	Awareness, Alignment, Behaviour, Style
	Culture	Organizations whose cultures value customers, teamwork, personal accountability, and a willingness to change will find it possible to move forward with process-led change projects.	Teamwork, Customer focus, Responsibility, Attitude towards change
	Expertise	Businesses must have some people with skills in, and knowledge of, process redesign.	People, Methodology
	Governance	Enterprises must be sure to have ways of governing projects and change initiatives.	Process model, Accountability, Integration
BPMC artifact (this thesis)	People	People impacting the success of BPM initiatives	Sharing information, Management trust, Knowledge, Support, Empowerment, Confidence, Teamwork, Customers, Consultants
	Process	Process related capabilities	Measurements, Rewards, Plans, Prioritisation, Job security, Standard methods, Change responsiveness
	Technology	Supports and enables BPM initiatives	Alignment to business plan, Using IT extensively, Communications, Reengineering,

			Alignment to strategy

This table is adapted from Mathiesen et al. (2011) and Niehaves et al. (2013) and expanded with the BPMC artifact.

Niehaves et al. (2013) describe four common elements of extant BPM capability (or maturity) models. First is that those models have a number of stages (usually four or five), through which an organization proceeds to the most beneficial BPM. Niehaves et al. (2013) wrote, *"divergence theory appears to be better able to inform decision makers for building dynamic capabilities than maturity models"*. BPMC artifact does not present a maturity model with desirable stages, but rather functions as a practical tool for understanding the level of current capabilities, which then enables organisation to define their desired stage based on their environment and other variables (requiring help from BPM professional). Second point they presented is that most models are very practitioner-oriented and seldom refer to any body of theoretical knowledge. BPMC artifact is also very practitioner-oriented, but its basis has been solidly built on BPM literature (presented in literature review and 1st version of BPMC artifact in this thesis). Third point by Niehaves et al. (2013) is that models propose developing BPM capabilities until the highest level is achieved, following a prescribed sequential developmental path. BPMC artifact makes no such proposition. Instead it is proposed to achieve an organisation-specific appropriate level, determined by someone capable of using BPMC tool as well as determining what is a suitable level for that organisation. This follows what Niehaves et al. (2013) have said, *"an ideal state does not exist and organizations should develop only specific dynamic capabilities"*. Lastly, Niehaves et al. (2013) present that the original area of application and focus of the majority of capability assessment models is the private sector. BPMC artifact is not limited to private sector, but includes also literature targeting public sector as discussed in chapter 3.4.4. The researcher could have done case studies in public sector also as part of this thesis, but due to time constraints it was not possible this time. It is suggested in future to conduct BPMC case studies also in public sector to make it possible to evaluate the artifact in that environment.

As a theoretical contribution, based on the Niehaves et al. (2011) research, the existing BPM framework capabilities are missing evaluation of leadership attention to processes. BPMC artifact has addressed this issue in people capabilities evaluation, especially with capabilities BPMC4, BPMC5 and BPMC 7.

Bandara et al. (2009) mention in their research that many BPM capability studies are predominantly focused at an overarching organizational level and do not explain factors and issues related to success at the level of individual projects. BPMC artifact can be used both on organisational and on individual project level by adjusting the scope where the artifact is used. Manfreda et al. (2014) discuss about radicalness of change imposed to organisations. When organisations are chasing increasing BPM maturity model levels (as suggested by traditional BPM maturity models), increasing the organisation from one level to another may be radical for the organisation. Contrary to that, BPMC artifact enables organisations to understand the current level they are at and then to choose the level they want to be regardless of any pre-defined maturity levels. Using BPMC artifact instead, organisations are able to control the level of radicalness imposed to organisation.

Gartner (2006) maturity model is not included in the previous table or discussed in more details here since it is already widely criticised in work by Song and Zhu (2011). The following lengthy quote from Pöppelbuß and Röglinger (2011) describes the ideology of this thesis well:

> *Since their provenance, maturity models have been subject to criticism. For instance, they have been characterized as "step-by-step recipes" that oversimplify reality and lack empirical foundation (Benbasat et al. 1984, de Bruin et al. 2005, King and Kraemer 1984, McCormack et al. 2009). Moreover, maturity models tend to neglect the potential existence of multiple equally advantageous paths (Teo and King 1997). According to Mettler and Rohner (2009), maturity models should be configurable because internal and external characteristics (e.g., the technology at hand, intellectual property, customer base, relationships with suppliers) may constrain a maturity model's applicability in its standardized version (Iversen et al. 1999). King and Kraemer (1984) postulate that maturity models should not focus on a sequence of levels toward a predefined "end state", but on factors driving evolution and change.*

Following the ideas of the quote above, the focus of BPMC artifact has been to identify factors that drive positive evolution and change in an organisation. The artifact has been designed to be a practical tool for such use. According to Curtis and Alden (2007), a majority of maturity models contain only a set of capability areas and descriptions of capability and maturity levels, and leave the identification of improvement measures to the model user. BPMC artifact has been designed to round that problem by giving instructions on how to do the improvement measurement using the artifact. Appendixes also give examples of suggestions on how to improve BPM capabilities in each case organisation.

7.3 Practical contribution

The researcher was able to answer the latter part of the research question of *"How can organisations take these capability factors into account in their BPM initiatives?"* through the three case studies presented in this study. The practical application of the BPMC artifact is described in chapter "6.5.3 Artifact in practical use". Even though each of the capability factors in BPMC artifact are independent of the others, the overall desired outcome is a positive organisational impact and success of the BPM initiative (deBruin et al. 2005; Mathiesen et al. 2011).

As a practical contribution of this research, the researcher has built and evaluated the BPMC artifact and created a process that can be followed to use the artifact in real life. Mathiessen et al. (2011) describe the differences between Business Analyst (BA) and BPM practitioner roles. BPMC artifact can help both of those roles to evaluate the current BPM capabilities of the organisation. BA might use the artifact more from business value perspective, focusing on the people capabilities while BPM practitioner might put more emphasis on process and IT capabilities. Researcher created the artifact more from the BPM practitioner perspective. As an example, two consulting companies are using this artifact as part of their consulting efforts. They use the artifact to evaluate BPM capabilities in their client organisation and then offer consulting services for improving low-level capabilities to the required level. That level for each capability is determined by the consulting companies, using market research, etc. means to understand the environment the client organisation is functioning in. The findings in this research are significant for practitioners, because the BPMC artifact can be used to first evaluate current BPM capabilities of an organisation and then to make a roadmap to improve them.

This research identified some important BPMC factors that organisations can use to evaluate their current capabilities. One of the goals of this thesis was to see whether it is possible to build an artifact that uses BPMC factors in a practical way. The final version of the BPMC artifact is presented in chapter 6.5.2 Cross-case conclusions.

As an artifact, BPMC enables different stakeholders to discuss business process management and organisation's capabilities from different perspectives. While the artifact will give information from various perspectives, depending on the target audience of the survey, it can be also discussed between various stakeholders to design the best course of action for the organisation to take. The information provided by the BPMC artifact may be utilised by both Business Analysts and BPM professionals. As Mathiesen et al. (2011), discusses in their research, whilst there exists a high degree of correlation between the previously mentioned professions, there are also points of uniqueness namely in the knowledge areas of process strategy, governance and general organisational process awareness. BPMC gives insight in to the level of such matters in organisation's unique environment.

7.4 Suggestions for future research

One future research suggestion is to find out why the BPMC factors discovered in this research are important. Further, comparing different departments within the organisation, between individual employees or industries and cultures from a BPMC perspective might be interesting. It might also be important to discover how BPMC factors are related. The dependencies between factors may help group and explain them better. Also it could be interesting to research potential configurations of different capabilities (which capabilities need to be on high-level, medium, etc. depending on the situation of the organisation). That could potentially research further what those two consulting companies mentioned earlier are already doing.

Another suggestion is to discover possible new capability factors related to BPM (see Table 7). The researcher suggests carrying out another study of the new capability factors presented in this research to see how relevant they are.

This research is a kind of snapshot of the case organisations, not spanning over long period of time and recurring use of the artifact. This decision was done to keep the length of building and evaluating the artifact sensible for the researcher. It might be beneficial to revisit these organisations after a year (or in other more suitable timeframe) to reevaluate how their BPMCs have developed. Naturally, this is more useful for those case organisations that are going to purposefully improve their BPMCs in the future.

An interesting future research topic might also be to find out how organisations can be motivated to improve their BPMCs. The case studies in this research showed that the actual implementation of changes after the BPMC artifact has been able to identify the bottlenecks is lacking. Perhaps suitable approach for doing this could be action research.

The current research has shown that approximately 7% of respondents found the survey difficult to answer. This research is not able to show, which questions they mean and how those questions are difficult. It is also left for future research to find out whether the difficultness is related to language skills or understanding the context under enquiry. It is left for future research to find out these matters.

As Niehaves et al. (2013) have stated in their work, "*it remains unclear to a large degree why certain BPM capabilities should be developed and what (positive) effects can be expected as a consequence*". This is left for future research to explore. As part of this also creating a system for benchmarking the level of BPM capabilities between companies, industries, countries, etc. might be of interest to practitioners.

Schmiedel et al. (2012) write about organisational culture and BPM. Following their ideas, BPMC artifact could potentially be expanded to provide practitioners with an analysis and benchmarking tool that could be used to examine the extent to which their organizational culture facilitates improving their BPM capabilities.

It is suggested to research long- and short-term economic effects of business process management capability development decisions. One should also have a look at the repeated strengthening and cutting of capabilities in order to adapt to a dynamic environment.

As part of the different levels of the case study questions (evaluating the artifact) presented in chapter 6.1.2, it is suggested in future research to look more deeply into these levels and to extract more information for example regarding the findings of artifacts across organisations.

As part of future research, it is suggested to evaluate what scale would be most powerful in evaluating the BPM capabilities in an organisation. In this study both 3- and 5-point scales were used. It remains under debate whether these or some other scales would be more suitable.

REFERENCES

Abdolvand, N. – Albadvi, A. – Ferdowsi, Z. (2008) Assessing readiness for business process reengineering. *Business Process Management Journal*, 14 (4), 497–511.

Ahadi, H. R. (2004) An Examination of the role of Organizational Enablers in Business Process Reengineering and the Impact of Information Technology. *Information Resource Management Journal*, 17 (4), 1-19.

Ahmad, H. – Francis, A. – Zairi, M. (2007) Business process reengineering: critical success factors in higher education. *Business Process Management Journal*, 13 (3), 451–469.

Alasuutari, P. (1994) *Laadullinen tutkimus*. Tampere, Finland: Vastapaino.

Alavi, M. – Yoo, Y. (1995) Productivity gains of BPR: achieving success where others have failed. *Informations Systems Management*, 4, 43–47.

Aler, R. – Borrajo, D. – Camacho, D. – Sierra-Alonso, A. (2002) A knowledge-based approach for business process reengineering. *Knowledge-Based Systems*, 15, 473–483.

Al-hudhaif, S. A. (2009) Process redesign: reenggineering core process at computer department - a case of SWCC. *Business Process Management Journal*, 15 (2), 184–200.

Al-Mashari, M. – Zairi, M. (1999) BPR implementation process: an analysis of key success and failure factors. *Business Process Management Journal*, 5 (1), 87–112.

Al-Mashari, M. – Irani, Z. – Zairi, M. (2001) Business process reengineering: a survey of international experience. *Business Process Management Journal*, 7 (5), 437–455.

Alibabaei, A. – Bandara, W. – Aghdasi, M. (2009) Means of achieving Business Process Management sucess factor. Paper presented at the *4th Mediterranean Conference on Information Systems*, Athens University of Economics and Business.

Alvesson, M. – Sköldberg, K. (2000) *Reflexive Methodology. New Vistas for Qualitative Research*. Sage publications, London, UK.

Anthony, N. – Dearden, J. – Vancil, R. (1972) *Management Control Systems*. Homewood: Richard D. Irwin.

Antonucci, Y. L. – Goeke, R. J. (2010) Identification of appropriate responsibilities and positions for Business Process Management success: Seeking a valid and reliable framework. *Business Process Management Journal.*

Anyanwu, K. – Sheth, A. – Cardoso, J. – Miller, J. – Kochut, K. (2003) Healthcare enterprise process development and integration. *Journal of Research and Practice in Information Technology*, 35 (2), 83-98.

Ardhaldjian, R. – Fahner, M. (1994) Using simulation in the business process re-engineering effort. *Industrial Engineering, 26* (27), 60–61.

Ariyachandra, T. R. – Frolick, M. N. (2008) Critical Success Factors in Business Performance Management—Striving for Success. *Information Systems Management*, 25 (2), 113–120.

Attaran, M. (2004) Exploring the relationship between information technology and business process reengineering. *Information and Management*, 41 (5), 585–596.

Attaran, M. – Wood, G. G. (1999) How to succeed at reengineering. *Management Decision, 37* (10), 752–757.

Babbie, E. (1998) *The Practice of Social Research.* Wadsworth publishing company, Belmont, CA, USA.

Bala, H. – Venkatesh, V. (2007) Assimilation of Interorganizational Business Process Standards. *Information Systems Research*, 18 (3), 340–362.

Bandara, W. – Alibabaei, A. – Aghdasi, M. (2009) Means of achieving Business Process Management success factors. In: *Proceedings of the 4th Mediterranean Conference on Information Systems*, 25-27, Athens University of Economics and Business, Athens.

Bandara, W. – Chand, D. R. – Chircu, A. M. – Hintringer, S. – Karagiannis, D. – Recker, J. – van Rensburg, A. – Usoff, C. – Welke, R. J. (2010) Business Process Education in Academia: Status, Challenges, and Recommendations. *Communications of the Association for Information Systems*, 27 (41).

Malcolm Baldrige National Quality Program. (2009) *Criteria for Performance Excellence.* National Institute of Standards and Technology, Gaithersburg, MD.

Bandara, W. – Indulska, M. – Chong, S. – Sadiq, S. (2007) *Major issues in business process management: An expert perspective.* BPTrends, 1–8.

Bandara, W. – Gable, G. G. – Rosemann, M. (2005) Factors and measures of business process modelling: model building through a multiple case study. *European Journal of Information Systems*, 14, 347–360.

Bandara, W. – Alibabaei, A. – Aghdasi, M. (2009) Means of achieving Business Process Management success factors. In: *Proceedings of the 4th Mediterranean Conference on Information Systems*, 25-27 Athens University of Economics and Business, Athens.

Bartlett C. A. – Ghoshal S. (1995) Rebuilding Behavioral Context: Turn Process Reengineering into People Rejuvenation, *Sloan Management Review*, Fall 1995, 1-23.

Bartram, P. (1994) Re-engineering revisited. *Management Today*, 7, 61–63.

Becker, J. – Niehaves, B. – Pöppelbuß, J. – Simons, A. (2010) Maturity models in IS research, *Proceedings of the European Conference on Information Systems (ECIS)*, Pretoria, South Africa.

Bell, J. (1993) *Doing your research project - a guide for first-time researchers in education and social science.* Buckingham, U.K., Open University Press.

Benbasat, I. – Dexter, A. S. – Drury, D. H. – Goldstein, R. C. (1984), A critique of the stage hypothesis: theory and empirical evidence. *Communications of the ACM*, 27 (5), 476–485.

Biehl, M. (2007) Success Factors for Implementing Global Information Systems. *Communications of the ACM*, 50 (1).

Bleistein, S. J. – Cox, K. – Verner, J. – Phalp, K. T. (2006) B-SCP: A requirements analysis framework for validating strategic alignment of organizational IT based on strategy, context, and process. *Information and Software Technology*, 48, 846–868.

Bouckaert, G. – Halachmi, A. (1995) Reengineering in the public sector. *International Review of Administrative Sciences*, 61 (3), 329–342.

Bowers, J. – Button, G. – Sharrock, W. (1995) Workflow from within and without: technology and cooperative work on the print industry shopfloor. *In Marmolin, H., Sunblad, Y. and Schmidt, K. (Ed.), Proceedings of European Conference on Computer- Supported Cooperative Work*, 51-66, Kluwer, Stockholm.

BPTrends (2010) Executive Overview: The State of Business Process Management – 2010. A BPTrends BPM Market Survey Report. A BPTrends BPM Market Survey Report. Fetched from BPTrends.org website 2nd of December 2014 at http://www.bptrends.com/publicationfiles/03-01-10-Executive%20Overview%20Survey-2010.doc-FINAL.pdf.

Bund, B. (2005) *The Outside-In Corporation: How to Build a Customer-centric Organization for Breakthrough Results.* McGraw-Hill.

172

Burlton, R. (2001) *Business Process Management: Profiting from Process.* Indiana: Sams Publishing.

Carmines, E.G. – Zeller, R.A. (1979) *Reliability and Validity Assessment.* Sage publications, California, USA.

Caron R. – Jarvenpaa S. – Stoddard D. (1994) Business Reengineering at CIGNA Corporation: Experiences and Lesssons Learned From the First Five Years. *MIS Quarterly,* September 1994, 233-250

Carr, D. K. – Johansson, H. J. (1995) *Best Practices in Reengineering: What Works and What Doesn't in the Reengineering Process.* McGraw-Hill, New York, 1995.

Chabrow, E. – Sullivan, L. (2004) Billions to Save. *Information Week,* July 12th 2004, 18-19.

Chalmers, A. F. (1999) *What is this thing called science?* 3rd edition, Open University Press, Buckingham.

Chan, Y. – Sabherwal, R. – Thatcher, J. (2006) Antecedents and Outcomes of Strategic IS Alignment: An Empirical Investigation. *IEEE Transactions on Engineering Management,* 53.

Choi, C. F. – Chan, S. L. (1997) Business process re-engineering: evocation, elucidation and exploration. *Business Process Management Journal,* 3 (1), 39–63.

Clemons E.K. – Thatcher M.E. – Row M.C. (1995) Identifying Sources of Reengineering Failures: A Study of the Behavioral Factors Contributing to Reengineering Risks. *Journal of Management Information Systems,* 12 (2), 9-36.

Coffey, A. – Holbrook, B. – Atkinson, P. (1996) Qualitative Data Analysis: Technologies and Representations. Sociological Research Online 1 (1). Paper available at www.socresonline.org.uk/1/1/4.html.

Collins Cobuild English language dictionary (1987) The University of Michigan.

Cook, T.D. – Campbell, D.T. (1979) *Quasi-experimentation: Design and Analysis Issues for Field Settings.* Rand McNally College publishing Company, Chicago, USA.

Cooper, R.B. (1994) The inertial impact of culture on IT implementation. *Information & Management,* 27, 17–31.

Creswell, J.W. (1988) *Qualitative Inquiry and Research Design: Choosing Among Five Traditions.* Sage publications, Thousand Oaks, CA, USA.

Crowne, T. – Fong, P. – Zayas-Castro, J. (2002) Quantative risk level estimation of business process reengineering efforts. *Business Process Management Journal,* 8 (5), 490–511.

Curtis, B. – Alden, J. (2007) Maturity Model du Jour: A Recipe for Side Dishes. Retrieved from http://www.bptrends.com/publicationfiles/10-07-COL-maturitymodeldujour- CurtisAldenfinal.pdf

Danesh, A. – Kock, N. (2005) An experimental study of process representation approaches and their impact on perceived modeling quality and redesign success. *Business Process Management Journal*, 11 (6), 724–735.

Daniel, R. (1961) Management information crisis. *Harvard Business Review*, *39* (5), 111–121.

Day, G.S. – Moorman, C. (2010) *Strategy from the Outside In: Profiting from Customer Value*. 1st edition (23 July 2010), McGraw-Hill, ASIN: B0041842UG.

Davenport, T. – Short, J. (1990) The new industrial engineering: information technology and business process redesign. *Sloan Management Review*, 30 (4), 11–27.

Davenport T. (1993) *Process Innovation: Re-engineering work through information technology*. Cambridge, MA, Harvard Business School Press.

Davenport, T. – Stoddard, D. (1994) Reengineering business change of mythic proportions? *MIS Quarterly*, 121–127.

Davenport, T. (2013) Process Innovation: Reengineering Work Through Information Technology. *Harvard Business Press*, 30 Dec 2013.

Davidson, M. – Holt, R. (2008) Failure Points: Where BPM Projects Tend To Falter. *Business Performance Management*, 18 Dec 2008.

Davidson, W. (1993) Beyond re-engineering: the three phases of business transformation. *IBM Systems Journal*, 32 (1), 65–79.

de Bruin, T. – Rosemann, M. – Freeze, R. – Kulkarni, U. (2005) Understanding the main phases of developing a maturity assessment model. *In Proceedings of the Australasian Conference on Information Systems (ACIS)*, Sydney.

Dennis, A. – Carte, T. – Kelly, G. (2003) Breaking the rules: success and failure in groupware-supported business process reengineering. *Decision Support Systems*, 36, 31–47.

DeToro, I. and McCabe, T. (1997) How to stay flexible and elude fads. *Quality Progress*, *30* (3), 55–60.

Dishaw, M. T. – Strong, D. M. (1999) Extending the technology acceptance model with task-technology fit constructs. *Information and Management*, 36, 9–21.

Drucker, P. (1954) *The Practice of Management*. Harper Business.

Eardley, A. – Shah, H. – Radman, A. (2008) A model for improving the role of IT in BPR. *Business Process Management Journal*, 14 (5), 629–653.

Earl, M. – Khan, B. (1994) How new is business process redesign? *European Management Journal*, 12 (1), 20-30.

Eckerson, W. (2006) *Performance dashboards: Measuring, monitoring, and managing your business*. New Jersey: John Wiley and Sons, Inc.

Egnell, P.-O. – Klefsjö, B. (1995) Experiences from Process Management in Swedish Organisations. In *People for quality – Quality for people*, 141–147, Lausanne: Proceedings from the 39th EOQ Annual Congress.

Eisenhardt, K. M. – Martin, J. A. (2000) Dynamic capabilities: what are they? *Strategic Management Journal*, 21, 1105–1121.

Elzinga, D. – Horak, T. – Lee, C. – Bruner, C. (1995) Business process management: survey and methodology. *IEEE Transactions on Engineering Management*, 42, 119–128.

Eriksson, P. – Kovalainen, A. (2008) *Qualitative Methods in Business Research*. London: Sage.

Feltes, P. – Karuppan, C. (1995) Re-engineering: getting down to the business of doing business. *Industrial Management*, 37 (4), 3–6.

Fettke, P. – Houy, C. – Loos, P. (2010) On the Relevance of Design Knowledge for Design-Oriented Business and Information Systems Engineering. *Business and Information Systems Engineering*, 2, 347–358.

Fiedler, F. E. (1964) *A contingency model of leadership effectiveness. In Advances in experimental social psychology*, 1, 149–190, New York: Academic Press.

Fisher, D. M. (2004) The Business Process Maturity Model A Practical Approach for Identifying Opportunities for Optimization. Fetched from Business Process Trends 9(4): http://www.bptrends.com

Flick, U. – Kvale, S. – Angrosino, M. – Barbour, R. – Banks, M. – Gibbs, G. (2007) *Doing Interviews*. London: Sage Publications Ltd.

Forsberg, T. – Nilsson, L. – Antoni, M. (1999) Process orientation: the Swedish experience. *Total Quality Management*, 10 (4–5), 540–547.

Forstner, E. – Kamprath, N. – Röglinger. M. (2013) Capability development with process maturity models - Decision framework and economic analysis. *Journal of Decision Systems*, 23 (2), 127-150.

Fowler, F. (1984) *Survey Research Methods*. Beverly Hills, California: Sage Publications.

Francis, A. – MacIntosh, R. (1997) The market, technological and industry context of business process re-engineering in the UK. *International Journal of Operations and Production Management*, 17 (4), 344–364.

Frolick, M. – Ariyachandra, T. R. (2006) Business performance management: One truth. *Information Systems Management*, 23 (1), 41–48.

Fui-Hoon, F. – Nah, K. – Zuckweiler, M. (2002) ERP Implementation: Chief Information Officers' Perceptions of Critical Success Factors. *International Journal of Human Computer Interactions*, 16 (1), 5–22.

Gartner Group (2009) Meeting the Challenge: The 2009 CIO Agenda. *EXP Premier Report January 2009*, Gartner Inc., Stamford, Connecticut.

Gartner Group (2010) IT Spending 2010: CIO Agenda. 2010, January 21st. Fetched from http://www.gartner.com/newsroom/id/1283413 on 2nd of December 2014.

Garvare, R. (2001) Process Management in Small Organisations - Experiences of a Swedish Study. *Quality Improvement*, Saint Petersburg: The 6th TQM World Congress, 124–130.

Ghauri, P. – Grønhaug, K. (2002) *Research methods in business studies: a practical guide.*

Gill, J. – Johnson, P. (1991) *Research methods for Managers.* London.

Glaser B.G. – Straus A.L. (1967) *The Discovery of Grounded Theory: Strategies for Qualitative Research.* ISBN 978-0-202-30260-7.

Goll, E. – Cordovano, M. (1993) Construction time again. *CIO*, 7 (2), 32–36.

Goodhue, D. – Thompson, R. (1995) Task–technology fit and individual performance. *MIS Quarterly*, 19 (2), 213–236.

Grant, D. (2002) A wider view of business process reengineering. *Communicatoins of the ACM*, 45 (2), 84–92.

Griffin, J. (2004) Information Strategy: Overcoming Political Challenges in Corporate Performance Management. *DM Review*, January.

Grover, V. – Jeong, S. – Kettinger, W. – Teng, J. (1995) The implementation of business process re-engineering. *Journal of Management Information Systems*, 12 (1), 109–144.

Gruman, G. (2004) CPM software: an elegant way to measure business indicators. *InfoWorld*, October.

Grönfors, M. (1982) *Kvalitatiiviset kenttätyömenetelmät.* Werner Söderström, Juva.

Gubrium, J. – Holstein, J. (2002) *Handbook of interview research: context and method.* London: Sage.

Guha, S. – Kettinger, W. (1993) Business process reengineering. *Information Systems Management*, 10 (3), 13–22.

Guimaraes, T. (1999) Field testing of the proposed predictors of BPR success in manufacturing firms. *Journal of Manufacturing Systems*, 18 (1), 53–65.

Guimaraes, T. – Bond, W. (1996) Empirically assessing the impact of BPR on manufacturing firms. *International Journal of Operations and Production Management*, 16 (8), 5–28.

Gulledge, Jr – Sommer, J. A. (2002) Business process management: public sector implications, *Business Process Management Journal*, 8 (4), 364 – 376.

Gummesson, E. (2000) *Qualitative Methods in Management Research.* 2nd Edition ed., Thousand Oaks, CA: Sage Publications.

Gummesson, E. (2003) All research is interpretive! *Journal of Business and Industrial Marketing,* 18(6/7), 482-492.

Gunasekaran, A. – Chung, W. W. – Kan, K. (2000) Business process reengineering in a British company: a case study. *Logistics Information Management*, 13 (5), 271–285.

Halachmi, A. (1996) Business process re-engineering in the public sector: trying to get another frog to fly? *National Productivity Review*, 15 (3), 9–18.

Hall, G. – Rosenthal, J. – Wade, J. (1993) How to make re-engineering really work. *Harvard Business Review*, November, 119–131.

Hammer, M. (1990) Reengineering work: don't automate, obliterate. *Harvard Business Review*, July-August, 104–112.

Hammer, M. (2007) The process audit. *Harvard Business Review*, 85 (4), 111–123.

Hammer, M. – Stanton, S. (1999) How process enterprises really work. *Harvard Business Review*, November-December, 108–118.

Hammer, M. – Champy, J. (1993) *Re-engineering the corporation: a manifesto for business revolution.* New York: Harper Business.

Hanson, N. R. (1958) *Patterns of Discovery.* Cambridge University Press, Cambridge, UK.

Harmon, P. (2007) *Business Process Change.* 2nd Edition, Morgan Kaufman Publishers.

Harmon, P. – Wolf, C. (2010) *The State of Business Process Management 2010.*

Hartlen, B. (2004) Playing Politics: Debunking the Myths That Blosk a Successful BPM Implementation. *Business Performance Management.* June.

Havenstein, H. (2006) Data governance, Exec buy-in are keys to BI adoption. *Computerworld*, 40 (40).

Helfat, C. – Peteraf, M. (2003) The dynamic resourcebased view: Capability lifecycles. *Strategic Management Journal*, 24 (10), 997–1010.

Herzig, S. E. – Jimmieson, N. (2006) Middle managers' uncertainty management during organizational change. *Leadership and Organization Development Journal*, *27* (8), 628–645.

Hevner, A. – March, S. – Park, J. – Ram, S. (2004) Design Science in Information Systems Research. *MIS Quarterly*, *28* (1), 75–105.

Hill, J. – Pezzini, M. – Natis, Y. (2008) *Findings: confusion remains regarding BPM terminologies.* Stamford, CT: Gartner Research.

Hill, J. B. – McCoy, D. W. (2011) *Key Issues for Business Process Management 2011*, Gartner Inc., Stamford, CT.

Hirschheim, R. – Sabherwal, R. (2001) Detours in the path to strategic information systems alignment. *California Management Review*, 44 (1), 87–108.

Holland, D. – Kumar, S. (1995) Getting past the obstacles to successful re-engineering. *Business Horizons*, May-June, 79–86.

Houghton Mifflin Company. (2000) *The American Heritage Dictionary of the English Language.* Fourth Edition.

Houy, C. – Fettke, P. – Loos, P. (2011) On Theoretical Foundations of Empirical Business Process Management Research. *In (Eds.):* BPM 2011 Workshops, Part I, LNBIP 99, 320–332.

Hunt, V. (1996) *Process Mapping; How to Reengineer Your Business Processes.* New York: Wiley.

Hutton, G. (1996) Business Process re-engineering - a public sector view. In C. Armistead and P. Rowland, *Managing Business Processes - BPR and beyond.* Chichester: John Woley and Sons.

Hyde, A. (1995) A primer on process re-engineering. *The Public Manager*, 24 (1), 55–68.

Irani, Z. – Hlupic, V. – Baldwin, L. – Love, P. (2000) Re-engineering manufacturing processes through simulation modelling. *Journal of Logistics and Information Management*, 13 (1), 7–13.

ITIL (2007) OGC. London: TSO.

Ives, B. – Olson, M. H. (1984) User involvement and MIS success: A review of research. *Management Science*, 30 (5), 586–603.

Järvinen, P. (1999) *On Research Methods.* Tampere, Finland: Tampereen Yliopistopaino Oy.

Jensen, A. – Sage, A. (2000) A Systems Management Approach for Improvement of Organizational Performance Measurement Systems. *Information Knowledge Systems Management*, 2 (1).

Johnson, P. – Harris, D. (2002) Qualitative and quantitative issues in research design. Teoksessa D. Partington, *Essential skills for management research,* 99–116, London: Sage.

Johnson, S. (1993) Re-engineering: what works, what doesn't? *Retail Business Review*, *61* (5), 28–30.

Jurisch, M. C. – Palka, W. – Wolf, P. – Krcmar, H. (2014) Which capabilities matter for successful business process change? *Business Process Management Journal,* 20 (1), 47-67.

Karimi, J. – Somers, T. – Bhattacherjee, A. (2007) The impact of ERP implementation on business process outcomes: A factor-based study. *Journal of Management Information Systems*, 24 (1), 101–134.

Kasanen, E. – Lukka, K. – Siitonen, A. (1993) The constructive approach in management accounting research. *Journal of Management Accounting Research,* 5, 243–264.

Keen, P. (1997) *The process edge.* Boston: Harvard Business School Press.

Kemsley, S. (2006) BPM Implementation Pitfalls. *AIIM E-Doc Magazine*, 20 (2), 35.

Kerlinger, F. (1988) *Foundation of behavioral research.* New York: Holt Rinehart and Winston Inc.

Kern, T. – Willcocks, L.P. (2002) Exploring relationships in information technology outsourcing: the interaction approach, *European Journal of Information Systems*, 11 (1), 17.

Kiely, T. J. (1995) Managing change: why re-engineering projects fail". *Harvard Business Review*, 73 (2), 15.

King, J.L. – Kraemer, K.L. (1984) Evolution and organizational information systems: an assessment of Nolan's stage model, *Communications of the ACM*, 27 (5), 466-475.

Kirk, J. – Miller, M.L. (1986) *Reliability and Validity in Qualitative Research.* Sage publications, Beverly Hills, CA, USA.

Kirschmer, M. (2009) *High performance through process excellence.* Berlin: Springer.

Klein, M. (1994) Re-engineering methodologies and tools: a prescription for enhancing success. *Information Systems Management*, 11 (2), 30–35.

Ko, R. – Lee, S. – Lee, E. (2009) Business process management (BPM) standards: a survey. *Business Process Management Journal*, 15 (5), 744–791.

Kohlbacher, M. (2010) The effects of process orientation: a literature review. *Business Process Management Journal*, 16 (1), 135–152.

Korogodsky, A. (2004) Moving toward alignment. *Best's Review*, *104* (9), 67.

Kotter, J. (1995) Leading change: why information efforts fail? *Harvard Business Review*, 73 (2), 59–67.

Kovacic, A. (2001) Business renovation projects in Slovenia. *Business Process Management Journal*, 7 (5), 409–419.

Kumar, M. – Antony, J. – Cho, B. R. (2009) Project selection and its impact on the successful deployment of Six Sigma. *Business Process Management Journal*, 15 (5), 669–686.

Kuwaiti, M. (2004) Performance measurement process: definition and ownership *International Journal of Operations and Production Management*, 24 (1), 55–78.

Kvale, S. (1983) The qualitative research interview - A phenomenical and a hermeneutical mode of understanding. *Journal of Phenomenical Psychology*, 14 (2), 171–196.

Laamanen, K. – Tinnilä, M. (2009) *Terms and concepts in business process management - Prosessijohtamisen käsitteet.* 4th revised edition ed., Espoo: Teknologiainfo Teknova Oy.

Larsen M. A. – Myers M. D. (1997) BPR Success or Failure? A Business Process Reengineering Project in The Financial Services Industry. *In the Proceedings of the Eighteenth International Conference on Information Systems*, Atlanta, Georgia, December 15-17, 1997, 367-382.

Lee, G. – Pai, J. (2003) Effects of organizational context and inter-group behavior on the success of strategic information systems planning: an empirical study. *Behavioral and Information Technology*, 22 (4).

Lee, L. L. (2005) Balancing business process with business practice for organizational advantage. *Journal of Knowledge Management*, 9 (1), 29–41.

Lee, R. – Dale, B. (1998) Business process management: a review and evaluation. B*usiness Process Re-engineering and Management Journal*, 4 (13), 214–225.

Lee, J. – Lee, D. – Sungwon, K. (2007) An overview of the Business Process Maturity Model (BPMM). *In Proceedings of the International Workshop on Process Aware Information Systems (PAIS 2007)*, 384-395, Huang Shan (Yellow Mountain), China.

Leith, S. (1994) Critical success factors for re-engineering business processes. *National Productivity Review*, 13 (4), 559–568.

180

Ligeti, M. (1994) Corporate re-engineering should not stop at the factory door. *Industrial Engineering*, 26 (8), 14–15.

Lincoln, Y. – Guba, E. (1985) *Naturalistic inquiry.* Sage, Beverly Hills, CA, USA.

Linden, R. (1993) Busines Process Reengineering: newest fad, or revolution in government. *Public Management*, 75 (11), 8–12.

Lindsay, A. – Downs, D. – Lunn, K. (2003) Business process – attempt to find a definition. *Information and Software Technology*, 45(15), 1015-1019

Lopez, J. (2011) Executive Advisory: In Comparing Gartner's Board, CEO and CIO Surveys, CIOs Take Last Year's Challenge and Build for Growth, *Gartner Inc.*, Stamford, CT.

Lu, X.-H. – Huang, L.-H. – Heng, M. S. (2006) Critical success factors of inter-organizational information systems—A case study of Cisco and Xiao Tong in China. *Information and Management*, 43 (3), 395–408.

Mabin, V. – Forgeson, S. – Green, L. (2001) Harnessing resistance: using the theory of constraints to assist change management. *Journal of European Industrial Training*, 25 (2–4), 168–191.

Magal, S. R. – H. H. Carr (1988) Critical Success Factors for Information Center Managers. *MIS Quarterly*, 12 (3), 413- 425.

Manfreda, A. – Kovačič, A. – Indihar Štemberger, M. –Trkman, P. (2014) Absorptive Capacity as a Precondition for Business Process Improvement. *Journal of Computer Information Systems*, 54 (2), 35-43.

Manning, H. – Bodine, K. (2012) *Outside In: The Power of Putting Customers at the Center of Your Business.* Amazon Publishing (28 Aug 2012). ISBN-13: 978-1477800089

March, S. T. – Smith, G. F. (1995) Design and natural science research on information technology. *Decision Support Systems*, 15, 251–266.

Mathiesen, P. – Bandara, W. – Delavari, H. – Harmon, P. – Brennan, K. (2011) A Comparative Analysis Of Business Analysis (Ba) And Business Process Management (BPM) Capabilities. *ECIS 2011 Proceedings*, Paper 26.

Matthews, R. (1995) Does re-engineering really work? *Progressive Grocer*, 74 (2), 29–38.

Maul, R. – Weaver, A. – Childe, S. – Smart, P. – Bennett, J. (1995) Current issues in business process re-engineering. *International Journal of Operations and Production Management*, 15 (11), 37–52.

Maull, R. – Tranfield, D. – Maull, W. (2003) Factors characterising the maturity of BPR programmes. *International Journal of Operations and Production Management*, 23 (6), 596–624.

McAdam, R. (1996) An integrated business improvement methodology to refocus business improvement efforts. *Business Process Re-engineering and Management Journal*, 2 (1), 63–71.

McAdam, R. – Donaghy, J. (1999) Business process re-engineering in the public sector - A study of staff perceptions and critical success factors. *Business Process Management Journal*, 5 (1), 33–49.

McCormack, K. – Willems, J. – van den Bergh, J. – Deschoolmeester, D. – Willaert, P. – Stemberger, M. I. – Skrinjar, R. – Trkman, P. – Ladeira, M. B. – Valadares de Oliveira, M. P. – Vuksic, V. B. – Vlahovic, N. (2009) A global investigation of key turning points in business process maturity. *Business Process Management Journal*, 15 (5), 792-815.

McKeen, J. – Smith, H. (2003) *Making IT Happen: Critical Issues in IT Management.* Chichester: Wiley.

Melão, N. – Pidd, M. (2000) A conceptual framework for understanding business processes and business process modelling. *Information Systems Journal*, 10 (2), 105–129.

Meredith, J. (1993) Theory building through conceptual methods. *International Journal of Operation & Production Management*, 13 (5), 3-11.

Mettler, T. – Rohner, P. (2009) Situational Maturity Models as Instrumental Artifacts for Organizational Design. *In Proceedings of the DESRIST'09.*

Mingers, J. (2003) The paucity of multimethod research: a review of the information systems literature, *Information Systems Journal*, 13 (3), 233-249.

Morris, D. – Brandon, J. (1993) *Re-engineering your business.* New York, NY, U.S., McGraw-Hill.

Morton, N. A. – Qing, H. (2008) Implications of the fit between organizational structure and ERP: A structural contingency theory perspective. *International Journal of Information Management*, 28, 391–402.

Motwani, J. – Subramanian, R. – Gopalakrishna, P. (2005) Critical factors for successful ERP implementation: exploratory findings from four case studies. *Computers in Industry*, 56, 529–544.

Myers, M. – Newman, M. (2007) The qualitative interview in IS research: Examining the craft. *Information and Organization*, 17 (1), 2–26.

Möller, K. – Halinen, A. (1999) Business relationships and networks: managerial challenges of network era. *Industrial Marketing Management,* 28 (5), 413-427.

Møller, C. – Maack, C. – Tan, R. (2008) What is business process management: A two stage literature review of an emerging field. Springer, City, 2008. *In Research and Practical Issues of Enterprise Information Systems II.* DOI 10.1007/978-0-387-75902-9_3.

Nah, F. – Lau, J. – Kuang, J. (2001) Critical factors for successful implementation of enterprise systems. *Business Process Management Journal,* 7, 285–296.

Niehaves, B. – Henser, J. (2011) Boundary spanning practices in BPM: a dynamic capability perspective, *Proceedings of the AMCIS,* 1-11.

Niehaves B. – Plattfaut R. – Becker J. (2013) *Business process management capabilities in local governments: A multi-method study.* Elsevier.

Niehaves, B. – Poeppelbuss, J. – Plattfaut, R. – Becker, J. (2014) BPM capability development – a matter of contingencies, *Business Process Management Journal,* 20 (1), 90 – 106.

Ohtonen, J. – Lainema, T. (2011) Critical Success factors in Business Process Management – A literature review. *In T. L. (Ed.; Toim.), Proceedings of IRIS 2011,* 15, 572–585. Turku: Turku Centre for Computer Science.

Ongaro, E. (2004) Process management in the public sector - The experience of one-stop shops in Italy. *The International Journal of Public Sector Management,* 17 (1), 81–107.

Oracle. (2008) *State of the Business Process Management Market 2008.* An Oracle White Paper Updated August 2008. U.S.A.: Oracle.

Ortbach, K. – Plattfaut, R. – Pöppelbuß, J. – Niehaves, B. (2012) A Dynamic Capability-based Framework for Business Process Management: Theorizing and Empirical Application. *Proceedings of the 45th Hawaii International Conference on System Sciences,* Maui.

Packwood, T. – Pollitt, C. – Roberts, S. (1998) Good medicine? A case study of business reengineering in a hospital. *Policy and Politics,* 26 (4), 401–415.

Palmberg, K. (2009) *Beyond process management - Exploring organizational applications and complex adaptive systems.* Dissertation thesis for Luleå University of Technology, Department of Business Administration and Social Sciences. Record ID lulea:63877790-4448-11de-83dd-000ea68e967b. Downloaded from http://www.mementor.se/wp-content/beyond-process-management-palmberg.pdf December 2nd, 2014.

Paper, D. J. – Rodger, J. A. – Pendharkar, P. C. (2001) A BPR case study at Honeywell. *Business Process Management Journal*, 7 (2), 85–99.

Parberry, I. (1989) A guide for new referees in theoretical computer science. *SIGACT News*, 20 (4), 92–109.

Paulus, R.A. – Davis, K. – Steele, G.D. (2008) Continuous innovation in health care: Implications of the Geisinger experience, *Health Aff*, 27 (5), 1235-1245.

Pavlou, P. A. – El Sawy, O. A. (2011) Understanding the Elusive Black Box of Dynamic Capabilities. *Decision Sciences*, 42 (1), 239-273.

Peffers K. – Tuunanen T. – Rothenberger M. – Chatterjee S. (2008) A Design Science Research Methodology for Information Systems Research. *Journal of Management Information Systems*, 24 (3), Winter 2007-8, 45-78.

Peirce, C. S. (1931-1958) *Collected Papers 1-8*. Harvard University Press and Philadelphia: Open University Press, Cambridge, UK.

Perry, C. (1998) Process of case study methodology for postgraduate research in marketing. European Journal of Marketing, 32 (9/10), 785-802.

Peshkin, A. (1993) The goodness of qualitative research. *Educational Researcher*, 22 (2), 24-30.

Peter, J.P. (1981) Construct Validity. A Review of Basic Issues and Marketing Practices. *Journal of Marketing Research,* 58 (May), 133-145.

Pinsonneault, A. – Kraemer, K. L. (1993) Survey Research Methodology in Management Information Systems: An Assessment. *Journal of Management Information Systems*, 10 (2), 75–105.

Plattfaut, R. – Niehaves, B. – Pöppelbuß, J. – Becker, J. (2011) Development Of BPM Capabilities – Is Maturity The Right Path? *ECIS 2011 Proceedings*. Paper 27.

Politano, T. (2007) *Master data management: A key enabler for CPM.* Retrieved 2010 from http://www.tdwi.org/ info.aspx?id=33659

Poon, P. – Wagner, C. (2001) Critical success factors revisited: success and failure cases of information systems for senior executives. *Decision Support Systems*, 30 (1), 393–418.

Prananto, A. – Mckay, J. – Marshall, P. (2003) A Study of the Progression of E-Business Maturity in Australian SMEs: Some Evidence of the Applicability of the Stages of Growth for E-Business Model. *In Proceedings of the Pasific Asia Conference on Information Systems (PACIS)*, Adelaide.

Preston, C.C. – Colman, A.M. (2000) Optimal number of response categories in rating scales: reliability, validity, discriminating power, and respondent preferences. *Acta Psychologica*, 104 (2000), 1-15.

184

Pritchard, J.-P. – Armistead, C. (1999) Business process management—lessons from European business. *Business Process Management Journal*, 5 (1), 10–32.

Pöppelbuß, J. – Röglinger, M. (2011) What Makes A Useful Maturity Model? A Framework Of General Design Principles For Maturity Models And Its Demonstration In Business Process Management. Fetched from http://is2.lse.ac.uk/asp/aspecis/20110028.pdf on December, 2nd, 2014.

Quinton, S. – Smallbone, T. (2006) *Postgraduate research in business: a critical guide.*

Ranganathan, C. – Dhaliwal, J. (2001) A survey of business process reengineering practices in Singapore. *Information and Management*, 39, 125–134.

Ray, G. – Muhanna, W.A. – Barney, J.B. (2005) Information technology and the performance of the customer service process: a resource-based analysis, *MIS Quarterly*, 29 (4), 625-652.

Reich, B. – Benbasat, I. (2000) An Empirical Investigation of Factors Influencing the Success of Customer-Oriented Strategic Systems. *Information Systems Research*, 1 (3).

Reijers, H. (2006) Implementing BPM systems: the role of process orientation. *Business Process Management Journal*, 12 (4), 389–409.

Reijers, H. – Mansal, S. (2005) Best practices in business process redesign: an overview and qualitative evaluation of successful redesign heuristics. *Omega, 33* (4), 283–306.

Remenyi, D. – Williams, B. (1996) The nature of research: qualitative or quantitative, narrative or paradigmatic?. *Information Systems Journal*, 6 (2), 131-146.

Rentzhog, O. (1996) *Core process management.* Division of Quality and Technology, Department of Mechanical Engineering. Linköping: Linköping University. Issue 542 of Linköping studies in science and technology: Thesis. ISBNS: 9178716780, 978917871678

Robb, D. J. (1995) Business Process Innovation: Re-engineering for Operations Renewal, *Operations Management Review,* 10 (3), 12-15.

Rockart, J. (1979) Chief executives define their own data needs. *Harvard Business Review*, 57 (2), 81–93.

Rogers, P. R. – Miller, A. – Judge, W. Q. (1999) Using information-processing theory to understand planning/performance relationships in the context of strategy. *Strategic Management Journal*, 20 (6), 567–577.

Rohloff, M. (2009) *Case study and maturity model for business process management implementation.* Springer, City, 2009. In 7th International Conference, BPM 2009, Ulm, Germany, September 8-10, 2009. Proceedings. DOI: 10.1007/978-3-642-03848-8_10.

Rosemann, M. – de Bruinn, T. (2005) *Application of a Holistic Model for Determining BPM Maturity.* BPTrends February 2005. Fetched from http://www.bptrends.com/publicationfiles/02-05%20WP%20Application%20of%20a%20Holistic%20Model-%20Rosemann-Bruin%20-%E2%80%A6.pdf on December 2nd, 2014.

Rosemann, M. – De Bruin, T. – and Power, B. (2006) A model to measure business process management maturity and improve performance. In J. Jeston and J. Nelis (Eds.), *Business Process Management,* 299-315, Burlington, MA: Butterworth Heinemann.

Rosemann, M. (2010) The service portfolio of a BPM center of excellence, in Vom Brocke, J. and Rosemann, M. (Eds), *Handbook on Business Process Management 2*, Springer, Berlin, 267-284.

Rothwell. (1995) Human resource management: restructuring and re-engineering organisations. *Manager Update*, 6 (4), 23–31.

Rugg, G. (2007) *Using Statistics: A Gentle Introduction.* Open University Press. New York.

Rummler, G.A. – Brache A.P. (2012) *Improving Performance: How to Manage the White Space on the Organization Chart*

Ruusuvuori, J. – Nikander, P. (2010) *Haastattelun analyysi.* (M. Hyvärinen, Toim.) Tampere, Finland: Vastapaino.

Ruusuvuori, J. – Tiittula, L. (2005) *Haastattelu - Tutkimus, tilanteet ja vuorovaikutus.* Tampere, Finland: Vastapaino.

Sandhu, M. A. – Gunasekaran, A. (2004) Business process development in project-based industry. *Business Process Management Journal*, 10 (6), 673–690.

Sarker S. – Lee A.S., (1998) Using a Positivist Case Research Methodology to Test a Theory about IT-Enabled Business Process Redesign. *In the Proceedings of the Nineteenth International Conference on Information Systems*, Helsinki, Finland, December 13-16, 1998, 237-252.

Saunders, M. – Thornhill, A. – Lewis, P. (2007) *Research Methods for Business Students.* Prentice Hall.

Savolainen, T. I. (1999) Cycles of continuous improvement: Realizing competitive advantages through quality. *International Journal of Operations and Production Management*, 19 (1), 1203–1222.

Schmiedel, T. – vom Brocke, J. – Recker, J. (2012) Development and validation of an instrument to measure organizational cultures' support of Business Process Management. *Information & Management,* 51 (2014), 43–56. http://dx.doi.org/10.1016/j.im.2013.08.005

Schiff, C. (2006) A Key Ingredient for BPM Success. *DM Review,* 16 (5), 56.

Schiff, C. (2005) Five BPM Mistakes to Avoid, Part 1. *DM Review,* 15 (2), 29.

Schiff, C. (2008) Watch Your Step: The Potentially Perilous Route to BPM in 2008. *Business Performance Management,* 21–24.

Seddon, P. B. – Staples, S. (1999) Dimensions of information systems success. *Communications of the Association for Information Systems,* 2(3).

Seidel, J. (1991) Method and Madness in the Application of Computer Technology in Qualitative Research. In: Denzin N. and Lincoln Y. (eds). *Handbook of Qualitative Research.* Sage publications, Thousand Oaks, CA, USA.

Sein, M. – Henfridsson, O. – Purao, S. – Rossi, M. – Lindgren R. (2011) Action Design Research. *MIS Quarterly,* 35 (1), 37-56.

Sentanin, O. – Santos, F. C. – Jabbour, C. J. (2008) Business process management in a Brazilian public research centre. *Business Process Management Journal,* 14 (4), 483–496.

Seuring, S. – M. Muller (2008) From a literature review to a conceptual framework for sustainable supply chain management, *Journal of Cleaner Production,* 16 (15), 1699-1710.

Shewhart, W. (1931) *Economic Control of Quality of Manufactured Products.* New York: D. van Nostrand Company.

Shin, B. (2003) An exploratory investigation of system success factors in data warehousing. *Journal of the Association for Information Systems,* 4, 141–168.

Shin, N. – Jemella, D. (2002) Business process reengineering and performance improvement. *Business Process Management Journal,* 8 (4), 351–363.

Siha, S. M. – Saad, G. H. (2008) Business process improvement: empirical assessment and extensions. *Business Process Management Journal,* 14 (6), 778–802.

Simon, H. (1980) The behavioral and social sciences. *Science* (209), 72–78.

Simonsson, M. – Johnson, P. – Wijkström, H. (2007) Model-based IT Governance Maturity Assessment with CobiT. *In Proceedings of the European Conference on Information Systems (ECIS),* St. Gallen, Switzerland.

Škrinjar R. – Vukšić V.B. – Štemberger M.I. (2010) Adoption of Business Process Orientation Practices: Slovenian and Croatian Survey. *Business Systems Research*, 1 (1-2), 1-50.

Škrinjar, R. – Bosilj-Vuksic, V. – Indihar-Štemberger, M. (2008) The impact of business process orientation on financial and non-financial performance. *Business Process Management Journal*, 14 (5), 738–75

Smith, B. (1994) Business process re-engineering: more than a buzzword. *Human Resources Focus*, 7 (1), 17–18.

Smith, H. – Fingar, P. (2003) *IT does not matter, business processes do.* Tampa, Florida: Meghan-Kiffer Press.

Smith, M. (2003) Business process design: correlates of success and failure. *The Quality Management Journal*, 10 (2), 38–49.

Sobo, E.J. – de Munck, V.C. (1998) The Forest of Methods. *In: de Munck V.C. and Sobo E.J. (eds) Using Methods in the Field. A Practical Introduction and Casebook.* Altamira press, Walnut Creek, CA, USA.

Song, N. – Zhu, J. (2011) Evaluating Business Process Management Maturity - A case study on a Chinese electronic company. *Dissertation in Strategic Management and Leadership*, 1st June 2011.

Sousa, R. – Voss, C. A. (2008) Contingency research in operations management practices. *Journal of Operations Management*, 26, 697–713.

Spanyi, A. (2003) *Business Process Management (BPM) is a Team Sport: Play it to Win!*, Anclote Press.

Stiffler, M. A. (2006) Move from managing to driving performance. *Performance Improvement*, 45 (9), 17–20.

Strnadl, C. (2006) Aligning business and it: The process-driven architecture model. *Information Systems Management*, 23 (4), 67–77.

Subramoniam, S. – Tounsi, M. – Krishnankutty, K. (2009) The role of BPR in the implementation of ERP systems. *Business Process Management Journal*, 15 (5), 653–668.

Tanur, J. (1982) Advances in methods for large-scale surveys and experiments. In *Behavioral and social science research: A national resource*. N. Smelser and D. Treiman, Washington, D.C., National Academy Press.

Teece, D. – Pisano, G. – Shuen, A. (1997) Dynamic capabilities and strategic management. *Strategic Management Journal*, 18 (7), 509–533.

Teo, T. S. H. – King, W. R. (1997) Integration between Business Planning and Information Systems Planning: An Evolutionary-Contingency

Perspective. *Journal of Management Information Systems*, 14 (1), 185-214.

Terziovski, M. – Fitzpatrick, P. – O'Neill, P. (2003) Successful predictors of business process reengineering (BPR) in financial services. *International Journal of Production Economics*, 84, 35–50.

Tonnessen, T. (2000) Process improvement and the human factor. *Total Quality Management*, 11 (4/5), 773–778.

Trkman, P. (2010) The critical success factors of business process management. *International Journal of Information Management*, 30, 125–134.

Tucker, S. – Dimon, R. (June 2009) Design to Align: A Key Component in BPM Success. *Business Performance Management Magazine*, 7.

van Looy, A. – de Backer, M. – Poels, G. (2011) Defining Business Process Maturity: A Journey towards Excellence. *Total Quality Management & Business Excellence*, 22 (11), 1119-1137.

Vessel, D. (2005) Bridging the IT and business needs gap. *InfoWorld*, 27 (22), 27–30.

vom Brocke, J. – Rosemann, M. (2010) *Handbook on business process management 1: Introduction, methods, and information systems.* Springer, Heidelberg, 2010.

Watson, H. J. (2006) Three targets for data warehousing. *Business Intelligence Journal*, 11 (4), 4–7.

Weber, C. V. – Curtis, B. – Gardiner, T. (2008) Business process maturity model (BPMM), version 1.0. Retrieved from http://www.omg.org/spec/BPMM/1.0/

Wellins, R. – Murphy, J. (1995) Re-engineering: plug into the human factor. *Training and Development*, 49 (1), 33–37.

Wernerfelt, B. (1984) A resource-based view of the firm. *Strategic Management Journal*, 5(2), 171- 180.

Whitley, R. (1984) The scientific status of management research as a practically-oriented social science. *Journal of Management Studies*, 21(4), 369–390.

Willaert, P. – van den Bergh, J. – Willems, J. – Deschoolmeester, D. (2007) The process-oriented organization: a holistic view. *In P. Dadam Alonso and M. Rosemann, BPM 2007*, 1–15, Berlin: Springer.

Willcocks, L. P. – Currie, W. – Jackson, S. (1997) In pursuit of the reengineering agenda in public administration. *Public Administration*, 75, 617–649.

Willmott, H. (1994) Business process re-engineering and human resource management. *Personnel Review*, 23 (3), 34–46.

Wixom, B. – Watson, H. (2001) An Empirical Investigation of the Factors Affecting Data Warehousing Success. *MIS Quarterly*, 25 (1), 17–41.

Woolfe, R. (1993) The path of strategic alignment. *Information Strategy: The Executives Journal*, 10 (2), 13–23.

Yin, R.K. (2003), *Case Study Research: Design and Methods*, 3rd ed., Sage, Thousand Oaks, CA.

Yin, R. K. (2009) *Case Study Research - Design and Methods* (4th ed.). California: Sage Publications Inc.

Zairi, M. (1997) Business Process Management: a Boundaryless Approach to Modern Competitiveness. *Business Process Management Journal*, 3 (1), 64–80.

Zairi, M. – Sinclair, D. (1995) Business process re-engineering and process management: a survey of current practise and future trends in integrated management. *Management Decision*, 33 (3), 3–16.

Zeid, A. (2006) Your BI competency center: A blueprint for successful deployment. *Business Intelligence Journal*, 11 (3), 14–20.

Zinser, S. – Baumgartner, A. – Walliser, F. (1998) Best practise in reengineering: a successful example of the Porsche research and development center. *Business Process Management Journal*, 4 (2), 154–167.

APPENDIXES

7.5   APPENDIX I - Descriptions of Expert Interviews

7.5.1   Description of Respondent A's interview

Respondent A sees business process management as: *"... all the activities conducted systematically within the organization to continuously monitor, analyze and improve its business processes (from) regardless of whether its manufacturing or services or whatever..."* and continues, *"...it is about some deliberate efforts to improve business processes".* Respondent A sees everything that is done to improve business processes as BPM.

Respondent stated concern about having same capability factors twice in success and failure side with following comment: *"...whether it makes sense to divide it into critical success and critical failure factors, because you know it does feel like they are just reverse..."* and continues with an example *"...F1, you have top management is not committed to process improvement, you know, this is just a reverse question of top management is committed".* According to respondent, these two lists of success and failure factors could be combined into a one list: *"I would even maybe remove those failure factors and just if there is something new, something that is not, critical success factors, umm, just put them among success factors."* Respondent A says, failure factors should be such factors that if they realize, then BPM project will fail for sure. He sees those failure factors more as project ender than just minor annoyances: *"if you don't have this you will fail, then you consider this really is a failure factor".*

Researcher was interested in how such strong failure factors can be identified and respondent suggested using literacy and doing case studies. Researcher continued with asking that what kind of risks does it pose to this study, if those failure factors are joined with success factors. The response was: *"I don't think there is a risk, I think its more a lot risky but more inconvenient if you have both."* This response indicates that respondent thinks the risk of loosing something joining these two lists together is smaller than inconvenience caused by having the two lists. Respondent suggests moving failure factors to success factors side.

Respondent A says that purpose of BPM project affects what success factors are important. Respondent says: *"The purpose of BPM influence is which the most important success factors are. So that is maybe something that should be recognized in the tool".* Respondent suggests that the BPMC tool should be built so that it is possible to see what factors are more important for which kind of business process management project doing it by this way: *"Potential wise would be to prepare a kind of a matrix or a table where you could listen the literature, identify the typical types of projects, documentation improvement, maybe, IT support is another one, and then say ok, maybe for this type of project, these critical success factors are the most important"*. But respondent is also hesitating that what kind of table it should be. Respondent feels that importance of success factor per BPM project type would be needed at least. Respondent says that it is possible to make overall BPM success factor tool, with slightly different answers depending on BPM project type. To find out those connections between capability factors and BPM project types, respondent suggests using literature, survey and case studies.

When researcher asked respondent: *"when you were reading those success factors, were there some that you can really say that you have seen these based on your experience and that it is important factor"*, the answer was, *"top management support is important, there is no doubt, I think they are all important in a way, so top management support is definitely something you cannot do without, because process orientation and process improvement obviously requires that"*. Respondent says also that it is not enough for top management just to support change in the processes, but they need to get involved in whole BPM project.

Respondent thinks that success factors should have factor for internal expertise of an organization for BPM: *"I think I've noticed that maybe it's not included in the success factors is some kind of internal expertise within the organization, so whether they have, not necessarily department, but they have people who are kind of expert in the process management"*. Respondent says that failure factor F14 is not enough, because it talks about the organization in whole, but it should say more clearly that organization needs BPM personnel.

Respondent A also suggests new failure factor to add: internal power struggle between BPM team and the IT. Respondent said: *"it's the kind of internal power struggle between the BPM team and the IT. Basically, they somehow don't personally like each other in a way that both directors are almost not speaking to each other. I exaggerated a bit but not a lot. Obviously that means that whatever the BPM team would like to change they will not be able to do so, because it would obviously require some IT changes and IT support and since they are not working together well, the project or the BPM is kind of bound to fail"*.

Respondent says that S16 does not belong under ITA category: *"S16, does everyone know the cost of customer acquisition then it will vary value of customer and cost of customer complain this definitely would not long belong to IT and architecture because this is a kind of customer orientation"*. As an answer to researcher's question *"Where would you put it?"* respondent suggests putting S16 under collaboration & communication category.

Respondent A says that these success factors may change over time when BPM project evolves: *"IT does change a bit, slower you know, legacy information systems or the alignment between IT that can really change relatively slowly but the thing is, from my experience I can say that the top management's attitude can really change for better or for worse".*

Respondent made also a remark that different people from organization can give different answers to these questions on BPMC artifact. Therefore, researcher asked: *"who do you think we should ask these questions from?"* and received an answer saying BPMC questions should be asked from everyone in an organization to get wide opinion about the situation. Respondent also reminded that *"some of the questions are maybe not so applicable, for example, I don't think normal employee judge the state of legacy information systems or so"*, which means people may not be able to answer all the questions that BPMC tool has for them. Respondent also suggests using Likert scale for asking BPMC questions in a survey.

From research itself respondent reminds that there are already tools measuring process orientation and gives an advice: *"you should obviously be careful to somehow show how your tool is different than the others"*. Respondent also comments on limitations of this study by saying: *"regardless of what you will do will have obviously some limitations and there is nothing wrong with it. Not ... Of all the limitations as long as you are aware of them, it is ok"*.

As an idea to widen the BPMC artifact respondent suggests besides measuring BPMC, there could be also given suggestions how to fix the situation: *"interesting, as a manager probably would be to identify the state, but then also to maybe suggest some actions, that should be done"*. Respondent also suggests benchmarking BPMC results to other similar organizations to show on what level that organization is compared to others: *"if you have enough data collected from different organizations then you can benchmark each individual organization and tell them, show them where they are worse than the rest"*.

Respondent A analyses usefulness of BPMC artifact in following way: *"maybe you could get the tool basically to identify which are the weaknesses in the organization"*. Respondent also says that it is not possible to 100% validate the model produced with Design Science. Respondent says that if BPMC research is cited or used by other people, then it will show its value as a *"test of time"*.

7.5.2 Description of Respondent B's interview

During the interview of respondent B, there was very much background noise in the Skype call at the respondent's end. It was not possible to get rid of the noise, so the call was recorded, but because poor quality of audio, it was not transcribed. Analysis of respondent B interview is done based on notes written by researcher during the call and using the audio recording directly without transcription.

Respondent B combines BPM with process improvement, process modeling and performance management using Lean 6Sigma approach and scorecards for process performance management. Respondent calls this approach process excellence instead of business process management. In recent years respondent has added more customer orientation to this combination. Respondent B uses following BPM methods in projects: Outside–In thinking, Supply Chain Operations Reference (SCOR) and Capability Maturity Model Integration (CMMI) combined together to get the best results.

Respondent said that in 'management and leadership' category key success factors are capturing processes, and sharing and using those materials. Respondent B sees modeling processes as important part in BPM success. For respondent, process modeling and linking helps to find out causes and effects of processes. Respondent also says that cascading those process models from head office to other offices is important, too. In those process models respondent focuses on Outside-In concepts like Moment of Truth, Breakpoints and Rules. Respondent says that constant success factors are S1-S3 (managers share vision and information with their subordinates, managers place confidence between supervisors and their subordinates and managers constructively use their subordinates' ideas). Other factors in 'management and leadership' category change depending on the phase of the BPM project. Respondent B gives an advice to "*keep senior management on sight all the time*".

Respondent commented about 'IT and architecture' category that communication is important (for example to "*have intranets for linking everything to target audience*"). Also technology is important, but not the only thing to keep in mind. Respondent B reminds to keep process first and then technology as second. Respondent says that BPM helps to analyze success factor S16 (Does everyone know the cost of customer acquisition, the annual value of a customer and the cost of a customer complaint?) and continues saying: "*its all good stuff S11-S16*". Respondent suggests getting IT people on board very early in the BPM project and states that we need to get rid of legacy systems to have standardized systems.

Respondent B commented that 'change management' needs to be strategic and continuous. For respondent process excellence model is key tool for change management. Organization needs process excellence, process management, project management and change management to be on the same level. Also process champions are needed on senior level and frequent communication is important. Respondent B says that people are never happy with change. Stakeholder analysis is crucial to get right people on board in early stage.

For collaboration and communication respondent presented question, *"What is the process design you try to achieve?"* We have to build processes on cause and effect. We have to also let the customer know what you are doing or improving in organization. Respondent suggests having communication plan for external customers.

Respondent B also commented measuring process improvement and said that we need to ask, *"Did we get revenue we wanted?"* and measure with lead indicators.

Researcher asked, *"is (BPMC) tool useful?"* and the response was: *"yes"* and then respondent gave an advice to *"avoid absorbing all the things in different models"*. He also warned that *"message has to be accurate in factors"*, which means not to have too much in the beginning.

For question about limitations of BPMC artifact respondent commented: *"BPM is a journey, not one big project"* and continued that you need to plan a path to walk on towards the set goals. Respondent also said that it is impossible to make BPM as one project.

Respondent B suggests two new success factors: *"know why you need BPM and process modeling and such"* and *"have a BPM roadmap for next upcoming years"*.

To question about success vs. failure factors respondent gave list of three things: *"keep the board engaged and interested in getting forward"*, *"turn process improvement into a habit"* and *"you need a good sponsor/champion"*.

7.5.3 Description of Respondent C's interview

Respondent C sees that there are two schools of BPM: the other focuses more on *"improving single processes with the use of tools such as lean and six sigma"* and the other one focuses on BPM from more managerial perspective, leading the organization as a whole, which respondent calls *"the CEO version of business process management"*. Respondent says that there are not enough tools for more holistic BPM, because most of the tools focus on single processes.

Respondent C says that one missing success factor is how organizations choose process owners: what is their background and knowledge on BPM. Respondent suggest adding competence and experience of process owners to change management category. Respondent also says that the power relationship between process owner and line managers is important: *"how the process owners are organized if they are part of line organization, or if they are part of a quality organization ... because the process owners need to have some kind of access to the agenda of the management".*

Respondent says that process owners have the responsibility over the processes, but they do not have budget or personnel to fulfill that responsibility, which causes frustration in them. Respondent C also continues: *"And by my experience that's a good frustration, because if the organization has a possibility of creating a positive dynamic where the process owner has the process perspective ... They have to kind of set the two different perspectives every time, that can create a positive development dynamic, but if it's not managed right, it's just a conflict".* Respondent says that it can be also a good thing to have this tension between process owner and line manager, if that relationship works well. Then there will be two different perspectives balancing each other. But if that relationship does not work well, then it will cause problems.

Second success factor respondent talked about was that organizations can go wrong when they map their processes only from internal perspective and they do not include their customers in it: *"that's the worst case scenario when you see someone's process map and there isn't a client, it's just the internal relations between different departments and you can't see what the customer needs or you can't see the customer in the process because even though business process management can be fantastic you shouldn't do it because of internal perspectives, you should do it to perform even better for your clients".* Respondent C thinks that S26, which is *"Customer expectations are considered in discussions about organizations business",* is too weak to express that. Respondent says that it is not enough to be customer considerate, but the organization has to be customer focused.

Respondent says even internal support processes have to have a ground on customer needs: *"all processes, even support processes have to have a ground or a basis in customer need".* Reason for this is that if processes focus more on customer experience, then they will get also more attention from top management *"if the process work can show that you have focus on the customers and that the process work can be a tool for improving customer experience then it is getting the attention from the top management".* Respondent says: *"you have to be focused on the client and then when you have a basis with a customer focus, then you can go to work on your internal processes".*

Respondent says that BPM systems can be useful but the challenge is to keep it up-to-date and have responsible people for ownership, here is an example described by the respondent: *"the process system itself was good, but they didn't have access to update their maps once they had done it and that really complicated to work with continuous improvements for the processes*". According to respondent C, organizations need to both upgrade and maintain their process systems all the time.

When discussing about categorization of capability factors, the respondent suggested: "*maybe you should have a fifth one with customer headline, and then S16 would fit in that box*". Researcher suggested also moving S26 into that new category, which respondent agreed on.

Respondent says that it could be possible to combine 'change management' and 'management and leadership' categories, but it is not really necessary: "*there are several of those that you could combine, but I don't know if there is need for that*".

Respondent C says that success and failure capability factors are two sides of the same coin. Respondent thinks that it is more fun to think about positive things than negative: "*I would be looking at the success factors and talking about the success factors with clients*". According to respondent different audiences might be interested in different topics: "*the failure factors are interesting, but that's from a more academic perspective, from a practical perspective, the success factors are the interesting part*".

When using BPMC tool in practical environment, respondent C suggests using self-assessment as a tool to evaluate organization's capabilities. Respondent would use scale 1-10. Respondent continues saying: "*I would use that kind of tool more for when you are starting off a BPM project, I would use such a survey tool more to identify areas where the organization is weak, like we need to focus on the IT perspective because everything else was quite okay, or we need to focus on the knowledge part because no one, everyone is enthusiastic but no one knows anything. You use it for identifying areas for improvement*". Respondent says that benchmarking is not necessarily needed, but if there is a benchmark, it could be general. There is no need for industry specific benchmark because BPM is quite industry unspecific: "*it could be interesting to be able to compare yourself with other organizations. I don't know if it has to be from different types of organizations or maybe it could be a general index, I don't know if different industries have to have, like finance industry or pharmaceutical industries, I think the work with business process management is rather industry unspecific*".

Respondent C says that there is a risk when using BPMC tool that if only BPM professionals are asked, then other perspectives are not included in: "*if you had such a tool, that you also asked ordinary people, not business process professionals, there is a risk of too much of process internal perspective of you and me as process nerds, talking to each other and you talking to other process nerds and then if you would use such a tool for the process professionals, if you call people like us that, I think you have to have a, let's call the others ordinary people, ordinary managers and maybe you should also ask clients, because there is risk of both in academic and as the practitioner of having people with the same focus into each other and kind of complaining about others not seeing the great things that we see, and that could be a risk of such of a tool*". So, when using BPMC tool for example through surveys, respondent says that it is important to get different stakeholders to be involved.

Respondent says that there should not be put too much emphasis on developing the tool itself only, but also into process how it is used: "*there is always a risk of putting too much emphasis on developing the tool and less emphasis on the process where the tool should be used*", and continued, "*if we are talking about a survey, how many responders do you need to make a proper conclusion and when you get a result from such a survey what should you use it for? Who should listen to the results? What should you do with the results? Because just having the scores doesn't change anything*".

Respondent suggests creating an online tool to use for BPMC evaluation: "*online tool kind of generates the survey and emails it, like the technical part of the distribution and getting an index and getting the benchmark, but also that it should be simple. As I said there has to be fewer factors than 26, you have to index the numbers or factors*". Respondent says that 15 factors is suitable amount.

7.5.4 Description of Respondent D's interview

Respondent D describes BPM in following way: "*It's mind-set or it's a management approach, like how to, manage a company from a process perspective. It's more viewing the organization or the company as a system where each part is working very integrated rather than separated in their more traditional functional specialism silos and with a focus on the customer outcome, which is either a product or a service or a combination of both*".

Respondent D says that top management's commitment is more complex issue than presented in factor F1. It is more about how able that top management is to handle BPM matters: "*it's more of how able or are your top management to adopt into a BPM*". Respondent has notice that top management may be committed, but they are not ready to go deep enough into BPM to get the benefits: "*it's still a matter of degree how far are they willing when they can say we are going to do this and you are doing things but, they are not ready to do it deep enough to actually get real benefits*". Based on respondent's comments, "*it's the degree of commitment*" that top management is willing to show for process improvement that affects the level of success in BPM project.

Respondent describes problems related to funding BPM projects: *"They [i.e. top management] are not prepared to abandon their functional silo thinking and that is also dominant when it comes to financing initiatives or the organization, how you fund things, which is a huge, to call it hurdle or hinder, when it comes to working with the BPM because the way projects are funded are mainly in functional areas and there is no one that is prepared to, even though they see own benefits they are not prepared to take costs across and if you go higher in the management it still becomes a matter of you have to pull the resources from with under"*. What respondent explains is that budget should reflect more processes rather than internal, functional areas. According to respondent, organizations should put more power to processes owners than what is done today: *"often it's the functionally unit manager that have the funding ... so it's where the money goes, that is important I think"*. Money distribution affects where the power is in an organization and at the moment process owners *"do what they can with what they have"*.

To question about categorization of BPM capability factors respondent said: *"in this context I think it works well"* but continued by saying *"one category that I am thinking of when I see this, which is, there is not so much emphasis on, is what drives the process which is the customer need, the questions around that"*. Respondent D suggests that there should be success factor for organizing work based on customer needs and how organization addresses those needs. To solve that respondent suggests asking, *"Who's responsible for customer interactions"*. Here respondent is talking about category and factors little bit mixed, but the main point is that customer needs should be more visible in BPMC.

Respondent says that everyone in an organization should focus more on customer needs: *"when the rest of the organization work with process improvements they are not considering the customer or when they talk about the customers"*. Respondent says that not all departments are attached enough to delivering against customer needs. They do not necessarily understand that everyone has to be connected to the reason why organization exists.

Respondent comments on success and failure factors, *"you might want to mix it, making more random"*. Respondent feels that having one list of success factors and another one for failure factors puts too much attention to those positive and negative perspectives: *"maybe you want to put the questions a little more randomly so it doesn't become so apparent that's it a positive and a negative"*.

Respondent says that BPMC tool *"from a consultant point of view (it) would be a good tool to find areas for improvement. And well, from a project point of view it's the same thing"*.

7.5.5 Description of Respondent E's interview

Due to time difference and technical difficulties, respondent E was interviewed with Word –document. Research sent word document with questions for respondent to fill in. The good side of this method was that researcher was able to get respondent's perspective, but the downside is loosing that interactive relationship that you can have in a call. Respondent E describes BPM as such: *"the management and improvement of essential business activities to meet an organization's objectives"*.

Respondent E commented on BPM capability factors list in following way: *"The items on the list are all very relevant. They are very complementary to business models I have seen around organizational maturity.   I would consider including an additional success factor under the Collaboration and Communication category that address the requirement for understanding motivational factors of all workers. And in the Management and Leadership category, I would include a factor that considers whether management have evaluated customer expectations when establishing the organization's vision."*

Importance of BPM factors respondent commented writing: *"The most important factors that I see are around leadership and communication. In particular, the sharing of vision and the empowerment of employees"*, and continued, *"The factors that I consistently see as lacking are those around leadership. In particular, the definition and sharing of vision, and the collaboration between top and middle management."*

Respondent had suggestion on reorganizing the categories differently: *"The breakup into the four areas of ML, ITA, CM and CC is logical. I would personally shift the ITA factors to the bottom of the list to lower their importance below the other (human) factors."*

Respondent was very positive towards usefulness of BPMC: *"These factors provide a relevant evaluation of an organization's capacity to achieve success within a BPM program. I expect that when coupled with supporting research, they could be used in ultimately providing a benchmark for an organization's readiness to undertake a BPM initiative."*

Respondent was not very keen on failure factors: *"To be honest, they appear to be confused. Some factors I perceive as positives rather than negatives.   For example, setting an expectation on benefits (F2), understanding BPM concepts (F14), having standard methods for improvement (F15), and having a well-defined scope and objectives (F16), are all positives in my experience. I may have completely miss-understood the context of how these may be used, but having a failure list to complement the success list doesn't seems somewhat redundant."*

Respondent explains own experiences on these failure factors: *"The factors that I've seen (and in some instances actually experienced) in the past include the lack of integrated IS (F8), the lack of culture, skepticism among employees (F12), methodology or tools for renewal (F19) and the lack of consideration of customer expectations (F26)."*

To question *"Which failure factors you have not noticed in your work and why?"* respondent gave following answer: *"Out of all the work environments that I've either been employed in or consulted to, the only failure factor that you have listed that I haven't actually seen is F22 – several corporate initiatives going on. I expect that this is because most organizations differentiate between "business as usual" and change initiatives, whereas change itself should be considered normal, especially given the rate of change of significant factors influencing almost all businesses."* and continued, *"I'd still prefer to see the focus on success factors rather than failure factors. Many of the failure factors have corresponding positive factors. In that regard, I don't see a great distinction from the success factors."*

Respondent E suggested following scaling for measuring organization's current state with BPMC: *"An arbitrary scale of 1 to 5, or 1 to 7. In many instances, the responses will be subjective, ranging between "not at all", to "sometimes" and "always". Placing these against a numbered scale will quantify the responses and allow for some analysis."* Respondent gave following comments on analyzing results received with previously described scale: *"The results would need to be weighted to give priority to different factors based on their expected impact on the success of a BPM initiative. Not all factors will contribute in the same way or to the same degree on the success or failure of a BPM initiative. Weighting each factor on a low/med/high basis would be a way to accommodate this recognition. Identifying the correct weighting for each factor would require further research."*

Future potential of BPMC was commented in following: *"In both an academic and practical application, this tool would raise the awareness of the influencing factors impacting on the success or failure of a BPM initiative."* And respondent continued by describing possible limitations of this tool: *"The obvious limitation that I see from a practical point of view is one of acceptance. Like a BPM initiative itself, or any strategic initiative for that matter, its success or failure, acceptance or rejection, is predominantly dependent on leadership and whether or not it is driven from top management.*"

7.5.6 Description of Respondent F's interview

Respondent F sees BPM as a way to run an organization: "*I define it as one of many ways to run a company, run an organization. It is ...well, it is just one way to manage your organization*", and continues by saying, "*processes are just one way of doing it and a company that runs real processes management is a company that actually cares about the customers*".

Respondent F is worried about that no one knows how to measure what is implemented in BPM and other organizational improvement methods such as Lean or ITIL and poses an important questions: "*How do you measure that it is implemented? What is the success? What is the success of BPM?*" And continues by describing that BPM cannot be measured as a success or failure, but it needs to be measured as maturity: "*The whole nature of BPM is that it is a process in itself. No, you cannot say that now we have succeeded or now we have failed. You know, it's baby steps all the time. And then you tune into a certain maturity and you always want to become more and more mature.*"

Respondent says that it is important to know why organization wants to have BPM at all and describes the core reason as: "*Why does the company want to have BPM? Because as I said in the beginning, you should care about your customers.*"

When asked about most important success factors, the responded named S8: "*Basically, it is S8 that the organization has empowered process owners who are responsible. For me that's the No. 1*" and continued, "*Turning to a process organization can be very threatening to the people in management. Because you start to see what is not working and you start to hold people accountable for and you are creating a transparency of what is not working. And it's about letting people who actually do the work to have something to say about it. And this is not time for management to tell them what to do. This is the time actual time for business, for people who actually work in the business to say what's not working.*"

Also S9 is important from respondent's opinion: "*S9, performance measurements adequately corresponds to the process and changes in to them, that's to create credibility for the processes. I have experienced when you create measurements for the processes, but at the same time the management creates a different organization and creates different measurements for the success or failure, or how they should be measured. So, you have a conflicting way of measuring the business, one through processes and one through different organizational measurements."*

Respondent F suggests adding new success factor for having a process organization. This could be joined with current S8: *"It is important to have a process organization and it that you have people who are committed and dedicated to the process work. I mean it's not something that somebody should do part time. You need to have an own organization that does this. And it should be well defined and well communicated to the organization that these are the people who are responsible for the processes".*

Respondent says that S15 is not critical, but nice to have factor: *"I have never experienced that. So I don't know if it's a critical success. More rather than I would love to have it that way, sorry that is not a critical success. That would be nice. For BPM to be successful you need to have done it through management and IT can come later on. You need to have structure in the business before you can start messing with IT".*

Respondent F thinks that knowing BPM concepts and methodologies is very important: *"It doesn't really need to be the best BPM method... You just have to have a method that is good enough and that you stick to it and don't change it all the time. And of course as you go along the way, you can change the method once in a while. But, it needs to be manageable. You cannot just change it for every project or anything like that. It's important that you have the concepts and methodologies and that they are agreed upon and known".*

Respondent says that S26 is the core of BPM: *"For me that factor is the core of BPM. I have met so many people who actually think that they have the perfect processes. But they have not even thought of the customer. And when you start mentioning the customer, 'Is that good for the customer?' people just have a big question mark. And I've also been noting that there are some companies out there, who do not really care about the customer. They are getting their money; they are getting out their products and services. But, there is this trend that you stop concerning about the customers or the customer value. You are just out for increasing your market share."*

Respondent says that F1, F3 and F11 are important failure factors. But respondent F also says that if IT falls BPM, then organization has bigger problems than IT: *"I just skipped IT because if you have an IT and that makes the BPM fall, then that's a bigger problem".*

Respondent says that F19 and F22 are important also and explains more about F22: *"And I would say that F22 is critical if there are counterproductive initiatives. I have experienced that you have BMP initiatives and it's going very well and then you have new initiatives where there is a new organization, it comes and have conflicting agendas. So you can have several initiatives as long as they respect each other and are heading in the same direction."*

Respondent says that failure factors are more like critical showstoppers while success factors are more like good things to have: "*I think that's its somewhere maybe the failure is that if you have anything of these, don't even try to start it... You are probably fine just the way you are. And while the success factors are more like this is what experienced people tell you, if you really want to be good, do this.*"

Usefulness of BPMC artifact respondent F commented in following way: "*These factors make management start to think what is it I want and why do I want it? And also, what's the path I am getting into? Because people say I want this to go perfectly and I want everybody to be happy. I want to have control of my costs or I want to have happy customers. But you need to know that to get there, it's going to be a bumpy road. And you need to know that there is commitment, not to expect too much from the first start, there will be conflicts and you have to start to think before you start to control or manage. What roads are we going in for, what are the problems we will run into? What will it take form us to actually succeed and actually get over those bumps.*"

When asked how respondent would use BPMC artifact, the following answer is given: "*I would have it and I would use it for them to be aware. I would also use it to show that it's not scary, but it's also very in line with what process is about. It's about transparency. So, this is the way of showing the problems. And showing also a good way or best practice. That's what we are actually going into here. To take away some of the misunderstandings and also expectation management.*"

Respondent says that the BPMC tool could be used more as a checklist than a survey tool: "*it should be like a checklist before you start with the BPM. These are things that you need to be aware of or handle*".

Respondent says that change management and collaboration-communication are not easy to understand what they mean as categories. As a solution, respondent suggests changing category 'Change Management' into 'Transformation Management' and changing category 'Collaboration and communication" into 'Culture'. Respondent F thinks also that 'IT and Architecture' category is not directly related to BPM maturity.

7.5.7 Description of Respondent G's interview

Researcher sent respondent document containing the interview questions as planned. However, respondent decided to write in the answers and send them to researcher before the agreed Skype call, so that researcher has time to review the answer and ask more detailed questions. Thus, this interview is a combination of email and phone call interviews.

The respondent indicated that following factors are important for success in BPM based on respondent's experience: Managers share vision with their subordinates; top management usually has sufficient knowledge about the projects (*"this applies only to small organizations"*); top management generally supports changes in processes; the performance measurements adequately correspond to the processes and changes into them; information technology is integrated in business plan of the organization; the organization extensively uses the information systems; There are efficient communication channels in transferring information; Legacy information systems are reengineered if necessary; IT is aligned with business process management strategy; BPM concepts and methodologies are known and understood (*"only applies to people in charge of BPM"*); the project plan for reengineering processes is adequate; There is open communication between supervisors and their subordinates (*"but in an environment where BPM is transparent, subordinates typically have a very good understanding what is going on"*); Customer expectations are considered in discussions about organization's business.

Respondent commented on factor 'S17, the reward system adjusts to serve the employees after the changes': *"People are lucky to have a job. There is no need for reward system."*

Respondent suggested adding following success factor: *"Do you have the ability to choose the right BPMS system (list of vendors, BPMS, etc.) that best suits your meets? And if you don't, do you consider using consultants?"*

For failure factors respondent suggested removing factor: 'F2 Top management expects to get benefits of < 30%, 30%-50%, >50% from BPM' with comment *"the scale for percentages depends on organization"*. Respondent also said that 'F6 It is hard to change organizational structure' is not relevant, because *"probably not necessary to change organizational structure in many cases, we need functional silos, staff simply have to come out of these silos to do work and then they can go return to their silos"*, and continued, *"Horizontal functional structures (projects), like in aerospace they need those. They don't try to replicate for example legal stuff in every silo, but use legal department for it. If you have BPM in case management environment, that's good for the case to have people doing different phases"*. For failure factor 'F14 Organization knows and understands BPM concepts and methodologies' respondent commented, *"only a few need to know"*, meaning that not everyone in organization needs to know BPM. Respondent also commented factor 'F16 Organization has well-defined scope and objectives for process improvement efforts': *"ROIs take care of this"*, so according to respondent it is not a relevant issue.

For scaling respondent suggest using 0 = not relevant and 1-5 from not very important to very important. When asked more details about scaling, respondent explained that 1-10 is too large scale (generates un-useful data points).

To question *"What do you think about having both, success and failure factors?"* responded answered, *"You have to be consistent with success and failure factors. There are same questions for both, so it is tricky to answer. Put them together to one set and remove reverse questions. It would be good to combine these two sets"*.

7.5.8   *Description of Respondent H's interview*

BPM for respondent H is identifying, registering or documenting, purely or fully understanding and continuously improving all the processes within the organization. Respondent H says that leader of BPM initiative should have certain capabilities like *"be intelligent enough, have excellent personal skills because he/she is just about to change a culture"*. Those people *"should have a very well and very clear understanding of BPM concept"*. Respondent H says that training BPM people is important.

Respondent H says, *"We can divide the experiences (BPM people need) into 3 different levels. We can call them people skills, technical skills and process skills. We can have elements of knowledge from each one of these. So have it like a set, like a checklist of things that they know or they don't know"*.

Respondent H suggest not talking about success or failure factors, but rather from facts that are related to previously mentioned three categories: *"So, maybe the set of factors that you have collected there, instead of calling them success or failure, just forgetting about positive impact or negative impact, lets look at them as facts"*. The reason is that success or failure means different things to different people: *"People can disagree with you in [what is] success or failure, so you could tell them that for example, top management's support is the success factor. Other people would tell you it wasn't important. It wasn't a success factor. So, you have allowed a margin being unsure in terms of where its gradation between one or the other"*.

Respondent H describes one possible limitation for this thesis in following way: *"As I said, the main feeling I got through this right away is that I could see these coming from academic articles ... So very old critical success factors that have been out there since the 70's-80's? And now that we have a new domain called BPM, just because they have been out there for so long, it is quite difficult to find someone who would disagree with you on that"*.

Respondent H feels that critical factors for BPM have been around so long time that they have become sort of 'de facto'.

For scaling respondent suggest using "*scale 1-7*" and converting the items in BPMC artifact into survey items before doing the survey.

7.5.9   Description of Respondent I's interview

Respondent I was interviewed through email, since there was a big time difference with the researcher. Respondent describes BPM in following way: "*BPM is a discipline that brings measurements, analysis and improvements in organization's Business Processes. BPM is also termed as a structured approach employing methods, policies metrics, management practices and software tools to manage and continuously optimize an organization's activities and processes*".

The respondent mentioned that following success factors are the most critical to respondent's opinion: S8, S9, S15, S21 and S26. And following failure factors: F1, F3, F4, F5, F6, F10, F12, F18, F19, F24, F25 and F26. The respondent has not noticed factors S3, S5, S10, F2, F14, F15 and F16 in his line of BPM work, so these are not important factors according to respondent.

Respondent I shared following general comments on success capability factors: "*I believe IT is only required initially at the BPM toolset level, which is extremely necessary, other than this, it is not necessary to have underlying applications to support the process in order to implement a BPM practice.*" This perspective is similar to other respondent's that IT is very important capability in BPM.

Categorization of factors respondent suggest adjusting in following way: "*The categorization is fine, expect that the Collaboration and Communication (CC) should be there within ML, IT & CM and should not be a category on its own.*"

Failure factors respondent I comments in following: "*I did not find either of the factors listed under ITA as a contributing factors to the BPM failure, in fact, these are the factors that encourage adoption of a BPM discipline.*" This suggests that the line between failure and success factors is not clear.

For measuring BPMC factors, respondent suggested following: "*I would suggest a ranking in terms of importance High, Medium and low. Response would highlight the importance given to these factors as perceived by the survey target segment. The perception could vary from segment to segment. An ideal combination of target segments could be various employee levels in an organization. This analysis would seriously contribute towards devising a customized changed management methodology to suit the organization.*"

7.6   Appendix II - Organization Gamma Case Report

Analyzed 18th – 20th of September 2012 with SPSS19 and Webropol Professional Statistics by BPM researcher Janne Ohtonen (University of Turku).

7.6.1   *Executive summary*

Based on background information of 34 respondents, we can state that the survey has been able to receive responses from different organizational levels, despite of low 8% respond rate. This low response rate sets some limitations for generalizability of these results in Organization Gamma. Respondents have wide background in their experience in process development. All respondents had adequate command of English to be able to understand the questions in this survey. Managerial level of respondents seem to evaluate their skills in process development higher than employee level, regardless of higher rate of formal training in process development amongst employees. Background information numbers also indicate, that offering training in developing processes may raise people's own perception on their skills and knowledge in developing processes.

In People BPMC factors, Organization Gamma should turn close attention especially to BPMC6 (Managers place confidence between supervisors and their subordinates). Also BPMC1 (Managers share vision and information with their subordinates), BPMC2 (Managers constructively use their subordinates' ideas), BPMC4 (Top management generally supports changes in processes), BPMC8 (Top management frequently communicates with project team and users) and BPMC14 (Management evaluates customer expectations when establishing the organization's vision) should be evaluated how to improve. Rest of the People factors are on a higher level.

Overall score in Process BPMC factors is lower than in People factors. There are several factors that respondents disagree with, even though they are perceived to be medium or high importance. Organization should evaluate how to improve at least following process capabilities: BPMC17 (Everyone knows the cost of customer acquisition, the annual value of a customer and the cost of a customer complaint), BPMC28 (Organization is able to respond to changes in markets quickly), BPMC20 (BPM concepts and methodologies are known and understood), BPMC27 (Organization has standard methodology for improving processes), BPMC18 (The reward system adjusts to serve the employees after the changes), BPMC30 (People know the whole system they are part of), BPMC21 (The project plan for process improvement is adequate),

BPMC22 (People are eager to improve the existing state of processes) and BPMC16 (The performance measurements adequately correspond to the processes and changes into them).

Technological capabilities to promote BPM success are on average level in Organization Gamma. The statistics show that respondents do not feel that there are big hurdles in technological support, but they do not seem to strongly agree either. Respondents are quite undecided in this matter.

Open-ended questions for each BPMC category contain relevant and interesting information from individual respondents. People responsible for developing business processes should take a look at those comments and make their own conclusions from them. Real name of organization and IT systems have been replaced with general terms to protect the anonymity of Organization Gamma and its employees.

As a summary, Organization Gamma is mainly on positive side regarding BPM capabilities measured in this survey. There are some areas to be developed especially on process capabilities, but people capabilities seem to be on a good level. Technological capabilities in Organization Gamma are not very clear, since respondents indicated that they are something between undecided and positive. Organization should take measures to strengthen negative (respondents disagree) capabilities and to increase undecided capabilities to positive (respondents agree) side.

7.6.2 Suggestions for actions to improve BPM Capabilities in Organization Gamma

These suggestions for actions are in order of importance based on the importance found through analyzing the survey responses. These are explained in more detail for each BPMC category later in this research.

Based on background information, the suggestion is to train more people on process development to possibly raise the people's perception to be able to participate the process projects in organization more.

BPMC6 indicates that there is a need for having more trust between supervisors and their subordinates. Organization Gamma should evaluate further how this trust could be build (for example using trust based management).

BPMC1 (Managers share vision and information with their subordinates) may be improved by having discussions between managers and subordinates about the ways in which they would like to receive information, how often and in what format. After that appropriate ideas from those discussions may be taken in use.

BPMC4 (Top management generally supports changes in processes) could be improved by clearer support from top management towards process changes. Top management should evaluate their views on process management and tell subordinates what are the ways they are willing to show support for changes in processes.

BPMC8 (Top management frequently communicates with project team and users) could be improved by having more good quality communication between top management and project teams. Respondents would like to get more frequently communication from top management.

Respondents would like to management to evaluate customer expectations when establishing the organization's vision (BPMC14). Top management should look for methods that help them to identify and measure customer expectations when forming vision for Organization Gamma.

Respondents have indicated that top management generally should have more realistic expectations of the process improvement projects (BPMC7). Top management could re-evaluate the ways they set and measure expectations towards process improvement projects.

BPMC17 (Everyone knows the cost of customer acquisition, the annual value of a customer and the cost of a customer complaint.) Employees do not know these measurements, but they think it would be important to know them. Organization should develop a way to let everyone know what are the values of these measurements.

BPMC28 (Organization is able to respond to changes in markets quickly.) Organization is working on process improvement, but slowly. Management should look into ways to make this process faster.

BPMC20 (BPM concepts and methodologies are known and understood.) Background information shows that, only 29% of employees have received formal training for business process development. This indicates that management should consider training people on BPM more.

BPMC27 (Organization has standard methodology for improving processes.) Management should consider adopting some standard method for process development in organization and teaching it to employees.

Based on this survey the respondents disagree that reward system adjusts to serve the employees after the changes (BPMC18). This indicates that the way reward system is adjusted is not as flexible as process changes would require. Revisiting reward system from process perspective may improve this capability.

BPMC30 (People know the whole system they are part of.) Management should find ways to bring more visibility to people's work in relation to whole system they are part of. Possibly this could be achieved through standardized process management, which people have access to.

BPMC21 (The project plan for process improvement is adequate.) This may tell that process improvement should be planned better and it may also mean that employees are not aware of project plans for process improvements.

Management should get people more involved with process improvement projects to improve BPMC22 (People are eager to improve the existing state of processes).

Process factor BPMC16 (The performance measurements adequately correspond to the processes and changes into them.) Organization Gamma should look into their performance measurements to see which parts of them are not adequately corresponding to processes.

BPMC35 (IT is aligned with business process management strategy.) Organization could make it more clear that how IT systems support business processes. This matter might also be linked to lack of standardized process management system, which would make the links more visible. Organization should look into possibilities how to evaluate whether IT systems are aligned with BPM.

BPMC32 (The organization extensively uses the information systems.) Respondents slightly agree on this statement and they think it is important to use information systems. Organization should evaluate where in processes there are places to use information systems more efficiently.

BPMC34 (Legacy information systems are reengineered if necessary.) Respondents slightly disagree with this statement. Organization should evaluate which legacy information systems may be in a need of reengineering.

7.6.3   Background information

Background information shows what kind of respondents this survey had. All 34 respondents gave an answer to these background questions, so there were no missing values to handle.

7.6.3.1 General description

BPMC survey in Organization gamma was able to receive 34 responses. Target audience was 415 people, so 34 responses gives 8% response rate. This low response rate sets some limitations to generalizability of these results. The survey was done during summer 2012, which has caused response rate to be low. Many employees were on summer holiday during the survey. The survey was published in intranet news once and emailed to employees two times. Some employees indicated that they have not received invitation to participate the survey, so it is also possible that not all employees were able to receive it (however, there is no sensible way to find out who received the invitations and who not). Having the survey earlier was not possible since the survey was not ready and the Organization Gamma is very busy right after summer holidays, so that limited also time of having the survey. Postponing the survey to later in year 2012 would have caused the researcher's thesis to delay. So, the schedule for having the survey was compromise of situations and resulted in low response rate. Quality Manager and one Business Unit Manager promoted answering to survey.

Anonymity of respondents was assured through general invitation that was sent in email to all employees in Organization Gamma and pronouncing the survey in intranet. So, no respondents can be traced back and this was mentioned in invitation letter.

How would you describe your skills and knowledge on developing processes? ■ None ■ Beginner □ Advanced ■ Professional 9% 6% 35% 50%	In organization gamma 56% of respondents indicate that they are either beginners in developing processes or they do not have skills in it at all. That leaves 44% respondents who feel that they are either advanced or professionals in process development.
Have you received any formal training or certifications for developing processes? ■ No □ Yes 29% 71%	29% of respondents have received some kind of formal training or certifications in developing processes. 71% of respondents have not received any official training.

32% of respondents are junior level employees. 38% are on senior level. That leaves 30% respondents into managerial role. Organization has 415 employees, which of 45 belong to top management, middle management or are team leaders. That leaves 11 % of employees on managerial level. Since 30% respondents in this survey are on managerial level, it indicates that managerial level people were little bit more active on this survey compared to rest of the organization.

None of respondents indicated that they have poor skills in English language. 100% respondents indicated they have either good or excellent skills in English. None of the respondents are native in English. Based on these language skills, we can suppose that respondents have been able to understand the survey questions correctly language-wise.

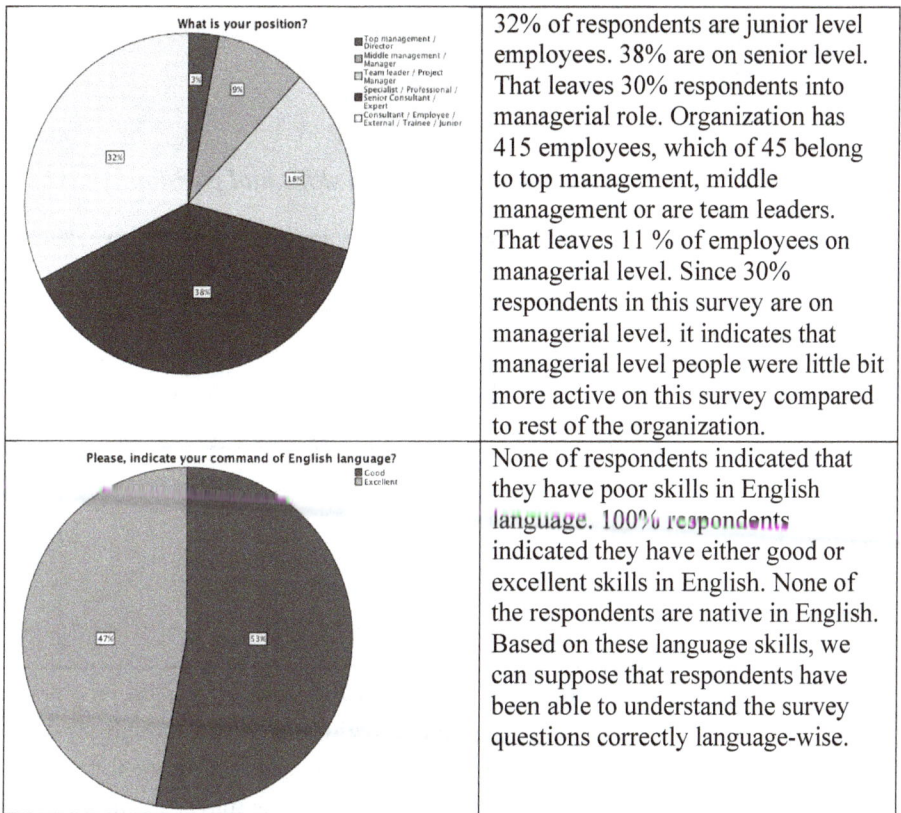

7.6.3.2 Relationship between process skills and formal training

		Have you received any formal training or certifications for developing processes?		
		No	Yes	Total
How would you describe your skills and knowledge on developing processes?	None	2 (6%)	0 (0%)	2
	Beginner	14 (41%)	3 (9%)	17
	Advanced	7 (21%)	5 (15%)	12
	Professional	1 (3%)	2 (5%)	3
Total		24	10	34

Background information shows 44% of respondents feel that they are either advanced or professionals in process development, but only 29% of respondents have received some kind of formal training or certifications in developing processes. Table above shows that only 16% of people who are on beginner level or lower have received training. On the other hand 47% of advanced or professional people have received process training. These numbers indicate, that offering training in developing processes may raise people's own perception on their skills and knowledge on developing processes.

7.6.3.3 Relationship between process skills and position

		What is your position?					
		Top management / Director	Middle management / Manager	Team leader / Project Manager	Specialist / Professional / Senior Consultant / Expert	Consultant / Employee / External / Trainee / Junior	Total
How would you describe your skills and knowledge on developing processes?	None	0	0	0	1	1	2
	Beginner	0	1	2	7	7	17
	Advanced	0	1	3	5	3	12
	Professional	1	1	1	0	0	3
Total		1	3	6	13	11	34

Table above shows that the higher the position person has, the better skills in developing processes they perceive to have even though table below shows that actually junior level employees have received more formal training. This indicates that management level employees have acquired their skills in process development through practical work rather than through official training. This data is not enough to show the causalities behind this finding.

		Have you received any formal training or certifications for developing processes?		Total
		No	Yes	
What is your position?	Top management / Director	0	1	1
	Middle management / Manager	2	1	3
	Team leader / Project Manager	5	1	6
	Specialist / Professional / Senior Consultant / Expert	11	2	13
	Consultant / Employee / External / Trainee / Junior	6	5	11
Total		24	10	34

7.6.3.4 Summary of background information

Based on background information of 34 respondents, we can state that the survey has been able to receive responses from different organizational levels, despite of low 8% respond rate. Respondents have wide background in their experience in process development. All respondents had adequate command of English to be able to understand the questions in this survey. Managerial level of respondents seem to evaluate their skills in process development higher than employee level, regardless of higher rate of formal training in process development amongst employees. Background information numbers also indicate, that offering training in developing processes may raise people's own perception on their skills and knowledge in developing processes. Since level of trained people in Organization Gamma is quite low (29%), it is suggested to train more people for process development.

7.6.4   BPMC – People factors

BPMC Survey people factors contain BPMC factors from BPMC1 until BPMC15:
BPMC1 Managers share vision and information with their subordinates.
BPMC2 Managers constructively use their subordinates' ideas.
BPMC3 Top management usually has sufficient knowledge about the process improvement projects.
BPMC4 Top management generally supports changes in processes.
BPMC5 The employees are empowered to make decisions.
BPMC6 Managers place confidence between supervisors and their subordinates.
BPMC7 Top management generally has realistic expectations of the process improvement projects.
BPMC8 Top management frequently communicates with project team and users.
BPMC9 Organization has empowered process owners, who are responsible.
BPMC10 Co-workers have confidence and trust in each other.
BPMC11 There is performance recognition among coworkers.
BPMC12 Organization uses external consultants when needed.
BPMC13 Teamwork between coworkers is the typical way to solve problems.
BPMC14 Management evaluates customer expectations when establishing the organization's vision.
BPMC15 Organization uses external consultants when needed.

These factors were measured from two perspectives: how do respondents feel these statements apply to Organization Gamma (value) and how important they think each statement is (importance).

7.6.4.1 BPMC People Value

People value describes how respondents valued Organization Gamma in BPMC factors 1-15. This was measured by asking them how much do they agree or disagree with statements regarding this organization.

Value questions were measured with Likert scale: 1 = Strongly disagree, 2 = Disagree, 3 = Undecided, 4 = Agree, 5 = Strongly agree

Means table and graph

Variables	count	average	unique (number of values)	median	standard_deviation	
People Value: BPMC1	34	3.4	5		4.0	
People Value: BPMC2	32	4.0	5		4.0	0.8032193
People Value: BPMC3	32	3.3	5		3.0	0.8654432
People Value: BPMC4	26	3.1	5		3.0	0.863802
People Value: BPMC5	27	2.9	5		3.0	0.9167637
People Value: BPMC6	32	2.5	5		2.0	1.077164
People Value: BPMC7	28	3.3	5		3.0	0.9048663
People Value: BPMC8	26	3.0	6		3.5	1.21592
People Value: BPMC9	30	3.7	6		4.0	0.8366601
People	34	3.9	5		4.0	0.9650764

Value: BPMC10						
People Value: BPMC11	34	4.2	4		4.0	0.6866437
People Value: BPMC12	34	4.2	4		4.0	0.7164976
People Value: BPMC13	31	3.4	5		3.0	0.843699
People Value: BPMC14	25	2.9	5		3.0	0.8812869
People Value: BPMC15	27	2.9	5		3.0	

People Value

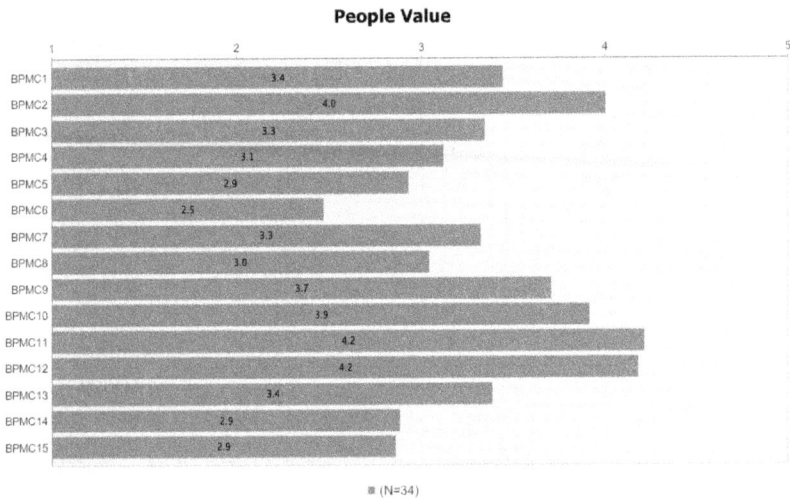

■ (N=34)

These mean values show that we can divide the responses into three categories: Negative (<2.9), Undecided (2.9 <= x =< 3.1) and Positive (>3.1). The researcher decided these thresholds for different categories. The thought pattern behind is that values close to 3 mean that respondents are undecided whether to have positive or negative standing. So, this undecided mean value is given +/- 0.1 units to sway on both negative and positive side. Any mean value differentiating more than 0.1 units from 3 are regarded either as negative (respondents disagree with statement) or positive (respondents agree with statement). This same logic is used also later on Process and Technology categories. Using the means values from above factors go into these categories in the following way:

Negative	Undecided	Positive
BPMC6 Managers place	BPMC14 Management	BPMC1 Managers share

confidence between supervisors and their subordinates.	evaluates customer expectations when establishing the organization's vision.	vision and information with their subordinates.
	BPMC15 Organization uses external consultants when needed.	BPMC2 Managers constructively use their subordinates' ideas.
	BPMC5 The employees are empowered to make decisions.	BPMC3 Top management usually has sufficient knowledge about the process improvement projects.
	BPMC8 Top management frequently communicates with project team and users.	BPMC7 Top management generally has realistic expectations of the process improvement projects.
	BPMC4 Top management generally supports changes in processes.	BPMC9 Organization has empowered process owners, who are responsible.
		BPMC10 Co-workers have confidence and trust in each other.
		BPMC11 There is performance recognition among coworkers.
		BPMC12 Organization uses external consultants when needed.
		BPMC13 Teamwork between coworkers is the typical way to solve problems.
TOTAL NEGATIVE: 1 (7%)	**TOTAL UNDECIDED: 5 (33%)**	**TOTAL POSITIVE: 9 (60%)**

As table above shows, 60% of people value factors are positive in Organization Gamma. There is only one people factor that clearly needs improvement, but there are 5 factors that require attention also to move them from undecided to positive side.

R (Pearson) Correlations for people value

In this report, correlation values 0.50 or above are considered as correlating for BPMC People value factors. Correlations below 0.50 are regarded as uncorrelated. Please, see the table below for correlated values:

People	

Value: BPMC1	P-value: 0.002
People Value: BPMC6	Correlation: 0.52
People Value: BPMC2	P-value: 0.003
People Value: BPMC6	Correlation: 0.53
People Value: BPMC4	P-value: 0.000
People Value: BPMC5	Correlation: 0.68
People Value: BPMC6	P-value: 0.004
People Value: BPMC8	Correlation: 0.54
People Value: BPMC7	P-value: 0.003
People Value: BPMC13	Correlation: 0.56
People Value: BPMC9	P-value: 0.000
People Value: BPMC10	Correlation: 0.70
People Value: BPMC14	P-value: 0.019
People Value: BPMC4	Correlation: 0.52
People Value: BPMC6	P-value: 0.022
People Value: BPMC4	Correlation: 0.52

This information may be used to evaluate how change in certain people value may affect other people values also. However, this does not mean that another one causes one value. For example there is quite strong correlation between BPMC9 (Organization has empowered process owners, who are responsible) and BPMC10 (Co-workers have confidence and trust in each other) factors. Since several People factors correlate each other, this indicates that these factors are related to each other and therefore they belong to this same category.

7.6.4.2 BPMC People Factors' Importance

People factors' importance describes, how important respondents think BPMC factors 1-15 are. This was measured by asking them how important they think each statement is.

Importance of these people factors was measured with scale: 1 = Low, 2 = Medium, 3 = High

Means for BPMC people factors' importance

Variab-les	count	Avera-ge	unique (num-ber of values)	Me-dian	Standard deviation	
People Imp.: BPMC1	32	2.7	3		3.0	
People Imp.: BPMC2	31	2.6	3		3.0	0.5641627

People Imp.: BPMC3	30	2.4	3		2.0	0.504007
People Imp.: BPMC4	30	2.3	3		2.0	0.7396799
People Imp.: BPMC5	30	2.2	3		2.0	0.5683208
People Imp.: BPMC6	30	2.2	3		2.0	0.6260623
People Imp.: BPMC7	30	2.5	3		3.0	0.5723515
People Imp.: BPMC8	28	2.4	3		2.0	0.4879501
People Imp.: BPMC9	29	2.6	3		3.0	0.5061201
People Imp.: BPMC10	31	2.7	3		3.0	0.4448028
People Imp.: BPMC11	31	2.7	3		3.0	0.4614144
People Imp.: BPMC12	31	2.6	3		3.0	0.6204403
People Imp.: BPMC13	31	2.0	3		2.0	0.4069293
People Imp.: BPMC14	31	2.3	3		2.0	0.5287437
People Imp.: BPMC15	28	1.8	3		2.0	

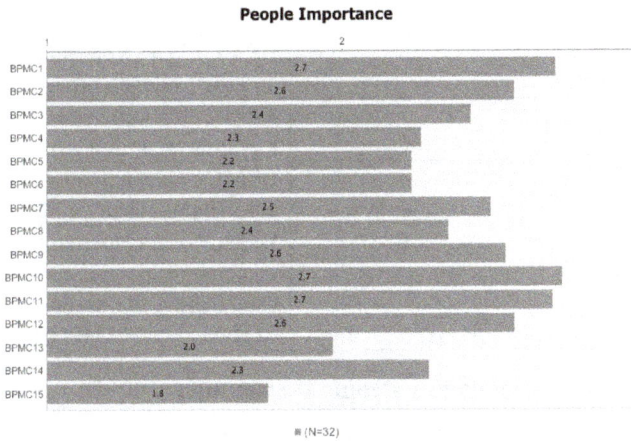

People Importance

These mean values show that we can divide the responses into three categories: Low (<1.8), Medium (1.8 <= x =< 2.2) and Positive (>2.2). The researcher decided these thresholds for different categories. The thought pattern behind is that values close to 2 mean that respondents think the statement is medium importance. So, this medium mean value is given +/- 0.2 units to sway on both low and high side. Any mean value differentiating more than 0.2 units from 2 are regarded either as low or high. This same categorization is used later also on Process and Technology importances.

Based on mean values of importance in above table and graph we can conclude that respondents indicate that these people BPMC factors are important for organization. None of the factors were regarded as low importance (mean value below 1.8). Following People BPMC factors are regarded as medium or high importance:

Medium importance (1.8 <= x =< 2.2)	High importance (>2.2)
BPMC5 The employees are empowered to make decisions.	BPMC1 Managers share vision and information with their subordinates.
BPMC6 Managers place confidence between supervisors and their subordinates.	BPMC2 Managers constructively use their subordinates' ideas.
BPMC13 Teamwork between coworkers is the typical way to solve problems.	BPMC3 Top management usually has sufficient knowledge about the process improvement projects.
BPMC15 Organization uses external consultants when needed.	BPMC4 Top management generally supports changes in processes.
	BPMC7 Top management generally has realistic expectations of the process improvement projects.
	BPMC8 Top management frequently communicates with project team and users.
	BPMC9 Organization has empowered

	process owners, who are responsible.
	BPMC10 Co-workers have confidence and trust in each other.
	BPMC11 There is performance recognition among coworkers.
	BPMC12 Organization uses external consultants when needed.
	BPMC14 Management evaluates customer expectations when establishing the organization's vision.
TOTAL MEDIUM IMPORTANCE: 4	TOTAL HIGH IMPORTANCE: 11

R (Pearson) Correlations For People Importance

Below are correlations found between BPMC People importance in this survey:

People Importance: BPMC14   P-value: 0

People Importance: BPMC5   Correlation: 0.58

This indicates that respondents who think that BPMC14 is important may also think that BPMC5 is important. In Organization Gamma importance mean of BPMC14 was 2.3 and importance of BPMC5 is 2.2. Based on that respondents see those two factors as medium importance. This however does not mean that importance of one factor causes the importance of other.

R (Pearson) Correlations Between People Value And Importance

In this report, correlation values 0.50 or above are considered as correlating for BPMC People value and importance. Correlations below 0.50 are regarded as uncorrelated. Please, see the table below for correlated values:

People Value: BPMC2   P-value: 0.0

People Importance: BPMC2   Correlation: 0.53

This indicates that the more important respondents think BPMC2 is, the higher value it may receive. The importance's mean was 2.6 and value mean 4.0, so respondents agree that Organization Gamma's managers constructively use their subordinates' ideas and it is important.

7.6.4.3 Open ended comments on People Factors

What do you think Organization Gamma should do to improve those People BPMC Factors that you answered either strongly disagree or disagree?

Communicate more with the subordinates.

Use consultants or Organization Gamma's people more often to improve processes.

We should be more customer focused.

Not use HRM system or Resource Planner software for example.

Managers should listen to their subordinates and people who have long working experience. They also know the needs of the customers.

Decisions should be communicated in a manner that respects employees. Grounds of decisions should be brought onward.

Management does not understand process changes that improve software development. Because they do not understand these improvements they are not interested in them.

Basic knowledge of processes should be improved among consultants (and all other employees too) to everybody to play this game with same rules-> improves quality, standards are used. For each process there should be a dedicated process owner who spreads information about his/her process over the whole organization (where applied).

External consultants are not used (according to what I know) and we have some of the best competencies in house. We should use the same people for improving our internal processes that we use to do the same for our customer. We should be a marked leader in many areas, but we internally we still function poorly.

Management should be self-enthusiastic about their vision and strategy and implement those ideas widely in the organization. Continuous communication is the key to empower employees to work towards the vision in everyday work. It is unclear how customer expectations are considered.

Clear process owners should be set. Or if those are set then more clearly communicate how it goes in Organization Gamma.

Top management frequently communicates with project team and users.

- As far as I know TOP management communicates in Q- infos. Not heard them communicating with project teams and users.

Organization has empowered process owners, who are responsible.

- If there are process owners at least those are not well communicated since I've not heard them.

As usually, Managers should think how to communicate inside Organization Gamma. Not one roadshow save the situation, if employee is not in that city's info, it doesn't do from somewhere else.

What other comments do you have related to these People BPMC Factors in Organization Gamma?

CPP training should be arranged annually.

Olen hämmästynyt, että annoin näin hyvät arvosanat. Organisaatio Gamman TOP-management on tehnyt hyvää työtä strategian jalkauttamisessa middle managementille.

Our internal processes ought to work smoothly and without needing to save the same data to 3-4 different systems. We are here to do the work that our customers' have bought, not to type same data again and again to different, non-working, slowly answering systems.

We still have concrete technological silos preventing efficient process improvements.

Organization Gamma is Professional providing IT-Solutions for customers to help them to "save money" by enhancing Business Processes but seems that "Suutarinlapsella ei ole Kenkiä" - is very valid in this company.

These were quite much about Mangers and Top Management. Do we have anything else than Manager - Employee structures?

7.6.4.4 Summary of BPMC People Factors

Prioritization for these factors can be calculated in following way: mean of reversed importance multiplied by value. Priorities are reversed to get a list of factors where smallest value is the most important (in original data highest priority had number 3 and lowest 1, so those are reversed). Using previously described calculation we get following prioritized list of BPMC People factors for Organization Gamma:

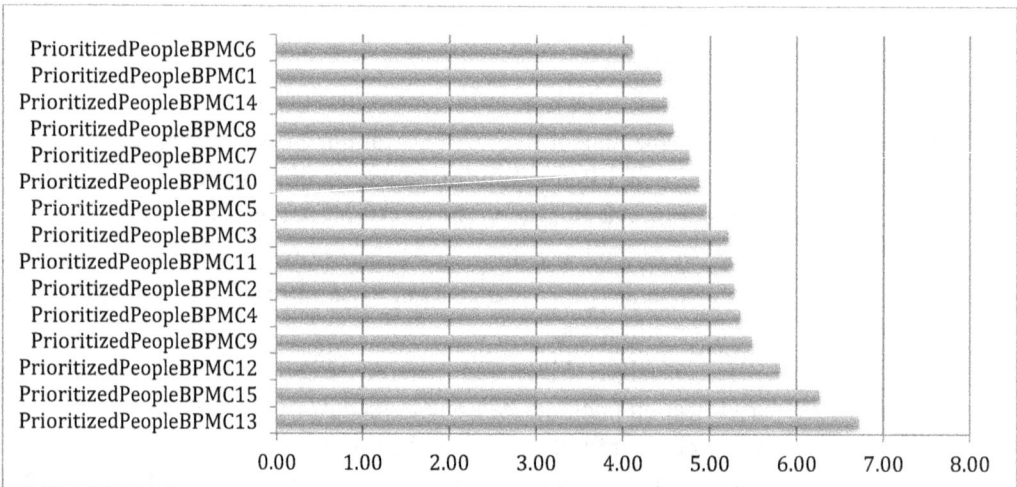

BPMC6 indicates that there is a need for having more trust between supervisors and their subordinates. Organization Gamma should evaluate further how this trust could be build (for example using trust based management).

BPMC6 is correlated with BPMC1, BPMC2, BPMC4 and BPMC8. These factors are also quite high on prioritization list, so Organization Gamma should look into ways to improve especially on factors BPMC1, BPMC4 and BPMC8. Since BPMC2 factor is already on quite high level in Organization Gamma, it does not have that high priority.

BPMC1 (Managers share vision and information with their subordinates) may be improved by having discussions between managers and subordinates about the ways in which they would like to receive information, how often and in what format.

BPMC4 (Top management generally supports changes in processes) could be improved by clearer support from top management towards process changes. Top management should evaluate their views on process management and tell subordinates what are the ways they are willing to show support for changes in processes.

BPMC8 (Top management frequently communicates with project team and users) could be improved by having more good quality communication between top management and project teams. Respondents would like to get more frequently communication from top management.

Since BPMC4 seems to be correlated to BPMC14, it may mean that when one is increased also the other increases. Organization Gamma should look into ways to improve BPMC14 also. Currently respondents would like to management to evaluate customer expectations when establishing the organization's vision. Top management should look for methods that help them to identify and measure customer expectations when forming vision for Organization Gamma.

BPMC7 also needs attending from organization to improve. Respondents have indicated that top management generally should have more realistic expectations of the process improvement projects. Top management could re-evaluate the ways they set and measure expectations towards process improvement projects.

Rest of the People BPMC factors in Organization Gamma are on a higher level. Measuring them again later could give information on trend where they are moving.

7.6.5   BPMC – Process

BPMC Survey process factors contain BPMC factors from BPMC16 until BPMC30:
BPMC16 The performance measurements adequately correspond to the processes and changes into them.
BPMC17 Everyone knows the cost of customer acquisition, the annual value of a customer and the cost of a   customer complaint.

BPMC18 The reward system adjusts to serve the employees after the changes.
BPMC19 There are training programs to update employees' skills.
BPMC20 BPM concepts and methodologies are known and understood.
BPMC21 The project plan for process improvement is adequate.
BPMC22 People are eager to improve the existing state of processes.
BPMC23 Business process improvement efforts are important for the organization.
BPMC24 Organizational structure can be easily changed when needed.
BPMC25 No one has to worry about losing his or her job because of process changes.
BPMC26 Employees feel comfortable with the new working environment.
BPMC27 Organization has standard methodology for improving processes.
BPMC28 Organization is able to respond to changes in markets quickly.
BPMC29 Initiatives in organization respect each other and are heading in the same direction.
BPMC30 People know the whole system they are part of.

These factors were measured from two perspectives: how do respondents feel these statements apply to Organization Gamma (value) and how important they think each statement is (importance).

7.6.5.1 BPMC Process Value

Process value describes how respondents valued Organization Gamma in BPMC factors 16-30. This was measured by asking them how much do they agree or disagree with statements regarding this organization.

Value questions were measured with Likert scale: 1 = Strongly disagree, 2 = Disagree, 3 = Undecided, 4 = Agree, 5 = Strongly agree

Means table and graph

Variables	count	average	unique (number of values)	median	standard_deviation
Process Value: BPMC16	27	2.8	5	3.0	
Process Value: BPMC17	31	1.9	5	2.0	0.7718152
Process Value: BPMC18	29	2.4	5	2.0	1.052794

Process Value: BPMC19	32	3.3	5	4.0	1.124776
Process Value: BPMC20	25	2.0	5	2.0	0.7071068
Process Value: BPMC21	22	2.6	5	2.5	0.6661254
Process Value: BPMC22	29	3.1	5	3.0	1.066738
Process Value: BPMC23	30	4.0	5	4.0	1.050452
Process Value: BPMC24	29	3.0	5	3.0	1.148998
Process Value: BPMC25	26	3.4	5	4.0	1.238485
Process Value: BPMC26	28	3.0	5	3.0	0.8380816
Process Value: BPMC27	22	2.2	5	2.0	0.6644986
Process Value: BPMC28	28	3.2	5	3.0	0.9172076
Process Value: BPMC29	25	3.6	5	4.0	0.6377042
Process Value: BPMC30	30	2.5	5	2.0	

Process Value

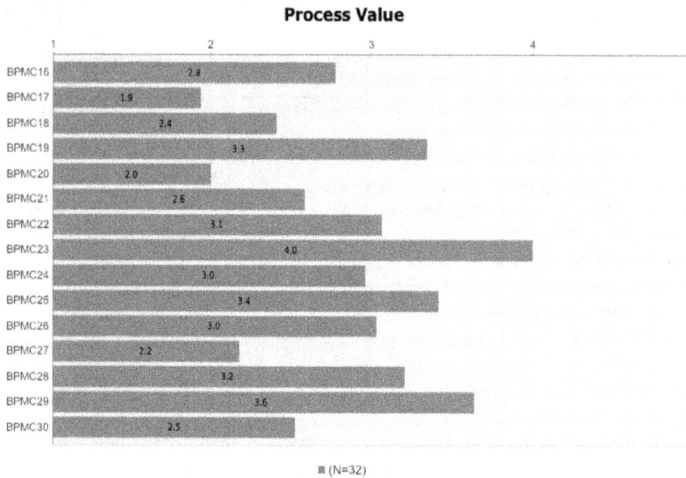

■ (N=32)

These mean values show that we can divide the responses into three categories: Negative (<2.9), Undecided (2.9 <= x =< 3.1) and Positive (>3.1). Using the means values from above factors go into these categories in the following way:

Negative	Undecided	Positive
BPMC16 The performance measurements adequately correspond to the processes and changes into them	BPMC22 People are eager to improve the existing state of processes	BPMC19 There are training programs to update employees' skills
BPMC17 Everyone knows the cost of customer acquisition, the annual value of a customer and the cost of a customer complaint	BPMC24 Organizational structure can be easily changed when needed	BPMC23 Business process improvement efforts are important for the organization
BPMC18 The reward system adjusts to serve the employees after the changes	BPMC26 Employees feel comfortable with the new working environment	BPMC25 No one has to worry about losing his or her job because of process changes
BPMC20 BPM concepts and methodologies are known and understood		BPMC28 Organization is able to respond to changes in markets quickly.
BPMC21 The project plan for process improvement is adequate		BPMC29 Initiatives in organization respect each other and are heading in the same direction
BPMC27 Organization has standard methodology for improving processes		
BPMC30 People know the whole system they are part of		
TOTAL NEGATIVE: 7 (47%)	TOTAL	TOTAL POSITIVE: 5

			UNDECIDED: 3 (20%)	(33%)

As table above shows, only 33% of process value factors are positive in Organization Gamma. There are 7 factors that need improvement (47%). Respondents have not decided whether they feel positive or negative regarding three factors.

R (Pearson) Correlation for Process value

In this report, correlation values 0.50 or above are considered as correlating for BPMC PRocess value factors. Correlations below 0.50 are regarded as uncorrelated. Please, see the table below for correlated values:

Process Value: BPMC23   P-value: 0.0

Process Value: BPMC28   Correlation: 0.59

This information may be used to evaluate how change in certain process value may affect other process values also. In Organization Gamma mean value for BPMC23 was 4.0 and for BPMC28 it was 3.2. This indicates that respondents agree to these statements.

7.6.5.2 BPMC Process Factors' Importance

Process factors' importance describes how important respondents think BPMC factors 16-30 are. This was measured by asking them how important they think each statement is.

Importance of these process factors was measured with scale: 1 = Low, 2 = Medium, 3 = High

Means for BPMC process factors' importance

Variables	count	average	unique (number of values)	median	standard_deviation	
Process Imp.: BPMC16	30	2.1	3		2.0	
Process Imp.: BPMC17	31	2.1	3		2.0	0.7184212
Process Imp.: BPMC18	31	2.2	3		2.0	0.5226073
Process Imp.: BPMC19	31	2.6	3		3.0	0.5641627

Process Imp.: BPMC20	30	2.0	3		2.0	0.6149479
Process Imp.: BPMC21	29	2.1	3		2.0	0.5570861
Process Imp.: BPMC22	30	2.4	3		2.0	0.6214554
Process Imp.: BPMC23	30	2.4	3		3.0	0.7701321
Process Imp.: BPMC24	30	2.1	3		2.0	0.6617636
Process Imp.: BPMC25	30	2.3	3		3.0	0.5632418
Process Imp.: BPMC26	30	2.3	3		2.0	0.6512588
Process Imp.: BPMC27	29	2.0	3		2.0	0.5658596
Process Imp.: BPMC28	30	2.7	3		3.0	0.5208305
Process Imp.: BPMC29	31	2.2	3		2.0	0.4973046
Process Imp.: BPMC30	31	2.3	3		2.0	

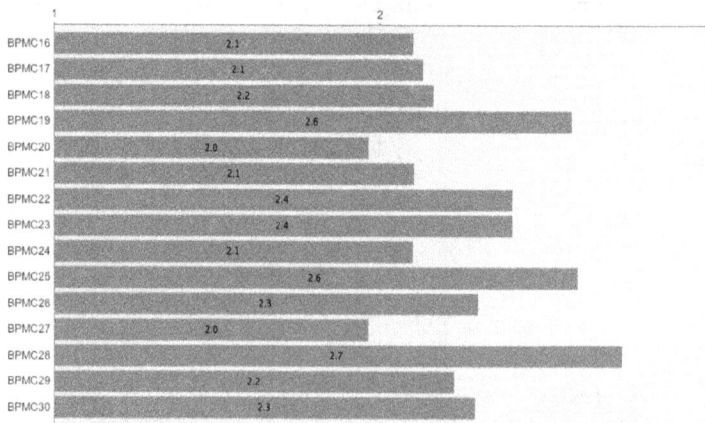

Process Importance

BPMC16 2.1
BPMC17 2.1
BPMC18 2.2
BPMC19 2.6
BPMC20 2.0
BPMC21 2.1
BPMC22 2.4
BPMC23 2.4
BPMC24 2.1
BPMC25 2.6
BPMC26 2.3
BPMC27 2.0
BPMC28 2.7
BPMC29 2.2
BPMC30 2.3

▦ (N=31)

Based on value in above table and graph we can conclude that respondents indicate that these process BPMC factors are important for organization. None of the factors were regarded as low importance. Following Process BPMC factors are regarded as medium or high importance:

Medium importance (1.8 <= x =< 2.2)	High importance (>2.2)
BPMC16 The performance measurements adequately correspond to the processes and changes into them	BPMC19 There are training programs to update employees' skills
BPMC17 Everyone knows the cost of customer acquisition, the annual value of a customer and the cost of a customer complaint	BPMC22 People are eager to improve the existing state of processes
BPMC18 The reward system adjusts to serve the employees after the changes	BPMC23 Business process improvement efforts are important for the organization
BPMC20 BPM concepts and methodologies are known and understood	BPMC25 No one has to worry about losing his or her job because of process changes
BPMC21 The project plan for process improvement is adequate	BPMC26 Employees feel comfortable with the new working environment
BPMC24 Organizational structure can be easily changed when needed	BPMC28 Organization is able to respond to changes in
BPMC27 Organization has standard methodology for improving processes	BPMC30 People know the whole system they are part of
BPMC29 Initiatives in organization respect each other and are heading in the same direction	
TOTAL MEDIUM IMPORTANCE: 8	TOTAL HIGH IMPORTANCE: 7

R (Pearson) Correlation for Process Importance

In this report, correlation values 0.50 or above are considered as correlating for BPMC Process importance factors. Correlations below 0.50 are regarded as uncorrelated. Please, see the table below for correlated values:

Process Importance: BPMC17	P-value: 0.0	
Process Importance: BPMC24	Correlation: 0.63	
Process Importance: BPMC20	P-value: 0.0	
Process Importance: BPMC21	Correlation: 0.63	
Process Importance: BPMC20	P-value: 0.0	
Process Importance: BPMC23	Correlation: 0.54	
Process Importance: BPMC23	P-value: 0.0	
Process Importance:	Correlation: 0.60	

BPMC24		
Process Importance: BPMC25	P-value: 0.0	
Process Importance: BPMC26	Correlation: 0.64	
Process Importance: BPMC28	P-value: 0.0	
Process Importance: BPMC29	Correlation: 0.51	

Quite many of process factors are related to each other through their importance. This however does not mean that importance of one factor causes the other.

7.6.5.3 Open ended comments on Process Factors

What do you think Gamma should do to improve those Process BPMC Factors that you answered either strongly disagree or disagree?

The general knowledge of the BPMC factors could greatly be improved by informing the staff.

More training of people on general level i.e. the finances of Organization Gamma / business units. Involve people more to the organization changes; open discussion is better than sudden surprises.

Hyvät asiat eivät näy tarpeeksi hyvin asiantuntijoille. ylin johto ja keskijohto ovat sitoutuneita, mutta asiantuntijat eivät.

Reward system is not anyhow dependent on processes.

At least in BSS unit there are no training programs. EIM/BI has Organization Gamma University etc. but they are first class employees and BSS is just something from history.

Everyone ought to know customer situations.

Reward system ought to give everyone equal share + special bonus to those who have achieved something major.

Reward system should apply to all consultants, no matter junior or senior. And to administrative staff, too.

The questionnaire seems to assume that the organization is undergoing some planned changes. I do not think that is the case with Organization Gamma. Our top management is trying to make us more efficient by not changing anything.

Lack of management support is the key issue here. The current organizational structure efficiently prevents any true process improvement across the whole organization. We can only improve inside our own "silo".

We measure utilization on the ground level. We don't measure customer satisfaction, communication, training, use of intranet more clearly to communicate internal structures

Everyone knows the cost of customer acquisition, the annual value of a customer and the cost of a customer complaint.

- I've not heard this would have been communicated. Neither saw this being important issue for the Mgmt.

The reward system adjusts to serve the employees after the changes.

- Not seen this happening.

Organizational structure can be easily changed when needed.

- Organization structure is not easy to change but needs tough decision even from TOP Management. Correcting actions hard to make if noticed something went wrong in the change because those would need decision from TOP Mgmt as well.

Business process improvement efforts are important for the organization.

- BPM process improvements are very important to be able make company more effective.

What are the Organization Gamma's business process improvements? Please answer something else than strategy.

Training program for every employee.

What other comments do you have related to these Process BPMC Factors in Gamma?

Organization Gamma is very flexible in changing the organization, but the changes are driven by only a hand full of people.

The processes for support functions like HR and IT are carved to stone. They are not supporting the business anymore, they are the only something that prevent the business from working efficiently. They should step down from the ivory towers and start serving their customers.

7.6.5.4 3.4 Summary of BPMC Process Factors

Prioritization for these factors can be calculated in following way: mean of reversed importance multiplied by value. Priorities are reversed to get a list of factors where smallest value is the most important (in original data highest priority had number 3 and lowest 1, so those are reversed). Using previously described calculation we get following prioritized list of BPMC Process factors for Organization Gamma:

238

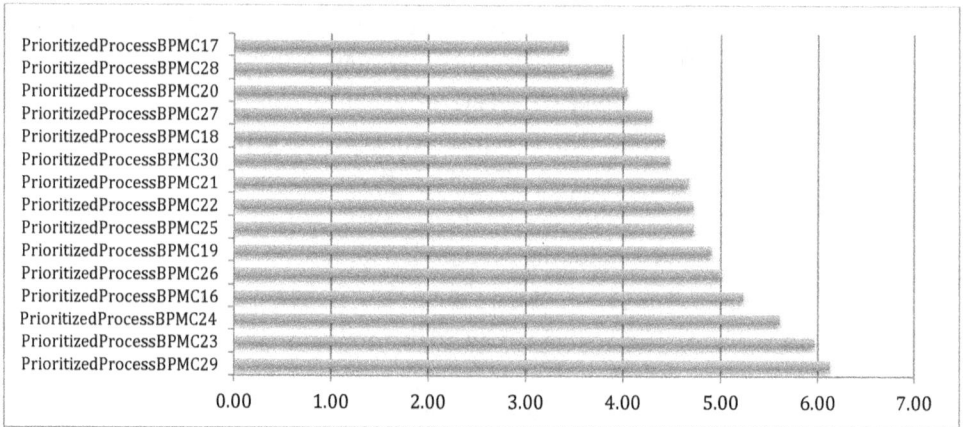

Organization Gamma has more capabilities to develop on process side than on people side. As the table shows (and if compared to equivalent table for people factors), there are several factors that are thought to be important by respondents but at the same time their value is average or below.

BPMC17 (Everyone knows the cost of customer acquisition, the annual value of a customer and the cost of a customer complaint) is perceived to be medium important, but it has very low value. This is a clear indication that employees do not know these measurements, but they think it would be important to know them. Organization should develop a way to let everyone know what are the values of these measurements.

BPMC28 (Organization is able to respond to changes in markets quickly) has been seen little bit on the positive side by respondents, but still it is very close to undecided. However, this factor is perceived to be of high importance, so management should work on being able to respond market changes quicker. Since respondents have evaluated correlating factor BPMC23 (Business process improvement efforts are important for the organization) high value and importance, it may explain that organization is working on process improvement, but slowly. Management should look into ways to make this process faster.

BPMC20 (BPM concepts and methodologies are known and understood) has very low value with medium importance. Like background information showed earlier, only 29% of employees have received formal training for business process development. This indicates that management should consider training people on BPM more.

Respondents also disagree on medium importance statement BPMC27 (Organization has standard methodology for improving processes). It is logical that since BPM concepts and methodologies are not known well, they are not used in standardized way either. Management should consider adopting some standard method for process development in organization and teaching it to employees.

Based on this survey the respondents disagree that reward system adjusts to serve the employees after the changes (BPMC18). This indicates that the way reward system is adjusted is not as flexible as process changes would require.

BPMC30 (People know the whole system they are part of) is disagreed by respondents also. They think it is important for them to know their role in organization. Management should find ways to bring more visibility to people's work in relation to whole system they are part of. Possibly this could be achieved through standardized process management, which people have access to.

Respondents disagree on BPMC21 (The project plan for process improvement is adequate). This may tell that process improvement should be planned better and it may also mean that employees are not aware of project plans for process improvements.

BPMC22 (People are eager to improve the existing state of processes) is undecided by respondents, even though it is slightly on positive side. Lack of standard methods and skills in process improvement may affect this, so management should get people more involved with process improvement projects.

Process factor BPMC16 (The performance measurements adequately correspond to the processes and changes into them) is disagreed by respondents slightly and they think it is medium importance. Organization Gamma should look into their performance measurements to see which parts of them are not adequately corresponding to processes.

Also rest of the factors BPMC24, BPMC26 should be evaluated by the Organization Gamma, how to improve them.

7.6.6   BPMC – Technology

BPMC Survey technology factors contain BPMC factors from BPMC31 until BPMC35:

BPMC31 Information technology is integrated in business plan of the organization.

BPMC32 The organization extensively uses the information systems.

BPMC33 There are efficient communication channels in transferring information.

BPMC34 Legacy information systems are reengineered if necessary.

BPMC35 IT is aligned with business process management strategy.

These factors were measured from two perspectives: how do respondents feel these statements apply to Organization Gamma (value) and how important they think each statement is (importance).

7.6.6.1 BPMC Technology Value

Technology value describes how respondents valued Organization Gamma in BPMC factors 31-35. This was measured by asking them how much do they agree or disagree with statements regarding this organization.

Value questions were measured with Likert scale: 1 = Strongly disagree, 2 = Disagree, 3 = Undecided, 4 = Agree, 5 = Strongly agree

Means table and graph

Variables	count	average	unique (number of values)	median	standard_ deviation	
Tech.Value: BPMC31	31	3.3	5		4.0	
Tech.Value: BPMC32	32	3.2	5		4.0	1.077632
Tech.Value: BPMC33	33	3.3	5		4.0	1.131505
Tech.Value: BPMC34	24	2.9	5		3.0	1.248187
Tech.Value: BPMC35	24	3.0	5		3.0	

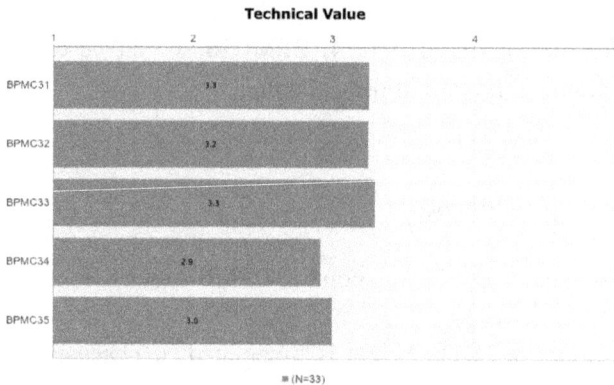

Technical Value

These mean values show that we can divide the responses into three categories: Negative (<2.9), Undecided (2.9 <= x =< 3.1) and Positive (>3.1). Using the means values from above factors go into these categories in the following way:

Undecided	Positive
BPMC34 Legacy information systems are reengineered if necessary	BPMC31 Information technology is integrated in business plan of the organization
BPMC35 IT is aligned with business process management strategy.	BPMC32 The organization extensively uses the information systems

	BPMC33 There are efficient communication channels in transferring information
TOTAL UNDECIDED: 2 (40%)	TOTAL POSITIVE: 3 (60%)

As table above shows, 60% of technology value factors are positive in Organization Gamma. There are only two technology factors that are undecided. From those two factors BPMC34 is slightly negative (disagree) and BPMC35 is slightly positive (agree). It is also notable that none of the technology factors are highly agreed either. This may show uncertainty amongst employees whether they agree or disagree to these statements in Organization Gamma.

7.6.6.2 BPMC Technology Factors' Importance

Technology factors' importance describes, how important respondents think BPMC factors 31-35 are. This was measured by asking them how important they think each statement is.

Importance of these people factors was measured with scale: 1 = Low, 2 = Medium, 3 = High

Means for BPMC technology factors' importance

Variables	count	average	unique (number of values)	median	standard_deviation	
Technical Imp.: BPMC31	31	2.4	3		2.0	
Technical Imp.: BPMC32	30	2.5	3		2.5	0.5713465
Technical Imp.: BPMC33	31	2.5	3		2.0	0.5679619
Technical Imp.: BPMC34	29	2.1	3		2.0	0.6732027
Technical Imp.: BPMC35	30	2.4	3		2.0	

Technical Importance

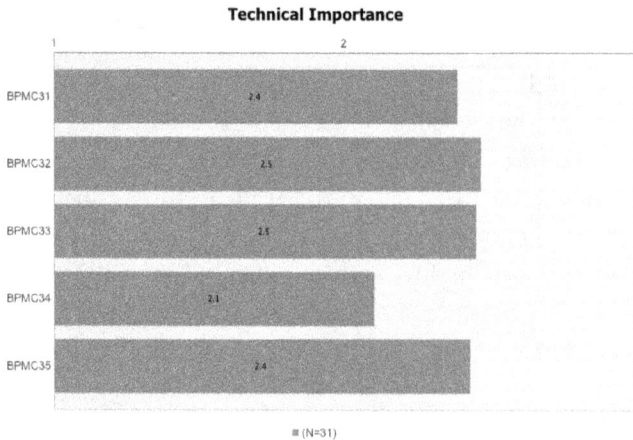

(N=31)

Based on value in above table and graph we can conclude that respondents indicate that these technology BPMC factors are medium or slightly highly important for organization. None of the factors were regarded as low importance. Following Technology BPMC factors are regarded as medium or high importance:

Medium importance (1.8 <= x =< 2.2)	High importance (>2.2)
BPMC34 Legacy information systems are reengineered if necessary	BPMC31 Information technology is integrated in business plan of the organization
	BPMC32 The organization extensively uses the information systems.
	BPMC33 There are efficient communication channels in transferring information
	BPMC35 IT is aligned with business process management strategy
TOTAL MEDIUM IMPORTANCE: 1	TOTAL HIGH IMPORTANCE: 4

R (Pearson) Correlation for Technical importance:

In this report, correlation values 0.50 or above are considered as correlating for BPMC Technology importance factors. Correlations below 0.50 are regarded as uncorrelated. Please, see the table below for correlated values:

Technical Importance: BPMC32   P-value: 0

Technical Importance: BPMC33   Correlation: 0.68

This indicates that respondents who think that BPMC32 is important may also think that BPMC33 is important. In Organization Gamma importance mean of BPMC32 was 2.5 and importance of BPMC33 is 2.5. Based on that respondents see those two factors as high importance. This however does not mean that importance of BPMC32 causes the also the importance of BPMC33.

7.6.6.3 Open ended comments on Technology Factors

What do you think Gamma should do to improve those Technical BPMC Factors that you answered either strongly disagree or disagree?

Our IT is just to serve a IT support, not to be aligned with business processes. The business units have to take care the IT. IT seems not having a clue what our company does. The current systems are under used for supporting business.

Our internal it systems are not so good. Organization Gamma People is disaster and work hour logging system is very old. It's ironic that we sell top of the line BI solutions and then our controllers and managers has to make reports by hand with Excel and use lots of time to generate those reports.

Also we sell Document Management systems, but we internally use network drive to save documents and other files.

We sell fine MOSS intranet solutions and our own intranet is made with minimal budget.

When we sell document management systems to customers we ourselves should use one BUT we DO NOT.

Organization Gamma should improve its strategy on social media networks (as it has recenly) and to organize a channel to improve communication between different units (EIM - hr - asiakastuki). And travel invoices in electronic form, thanks!

More and more, we are just circumventing the official IT systems, because they just aren't very good. Technical decisions from the Organization Gamma level and up are usually bad - they do not listen to us, even though we are the professionals.

Just wait until the new ERP is forced down our throats.

Our internal functions do not use the same cutting edge techniques we sell to our customers (for example reporting solutions etc.).

The administrative persons have a high daily workload. However, my assumption is that we could easily remove half of the tasks with simple process improvement exercise and implementing some simple IT solutions to support them...

IT does not see the customer (=us), or even most importantly their customer's customer does not affect their way of working in any way.

The current IT improvement project(s) are only internal tinkering of the ""IT-nerds"". They should take the external customers into consideration when planning the future."

We send travel expense receipts around Country at the moment. We collect CV:s every other week in emails. We have multiple communication channels but none of them are really effective in covering most of the employees. Plans are not integrated with the actuals from work hour logging system. Analysis based on work hour logging system mainly (I assume) done in Excel.

"Information technology is integrated in business plan of the organization.

- At least this is not visible for workers... well we have work hour logging system :)

Legacy information systems are reengineered if necessary.

- We have legacy systems, which are not re-engineered, but those are being planned to be bought from other companies.

IT is aligned with business process management strategy.

- IF IT is aligned with BPM Strategy it has not been communicated."

What other comments do you have related to these Technical BPMC Factors in Gamma?

We should be the professionals in this field, still our systems are either old or the data is not utilized in open and modern way. We build more modern systems for our client than we have.

Top management and Sales personnel: Ask yourself this:

If you were buying a document management system would you buy it from a company that itself uses one OR from a company that do not use document management system in their own business?

IT support is heavily resourced, but I really do not know what they really do all day.

We have a really high percentage of people allocated in administrative tasks doing manual paper pushing with excel and other "obsolete" tools.

The People in Organization Gamma knows best what kind of tools they would need in their work. Making BPM- analysis for different people in different roles would give understanding what should be done for the systems. Also Organization Gamma has lot of BPM knowledge, which should be used. Also it would be beneficial to think carefully whether implementing solutions for own usage benefit the company -> It is very expensive to build the system -> but if you can sell the system to other companies then it would be very profitable compared to system which would be bought from external vendor which is also expensive but not very usable at the same time.

I do not know our business plan, so how I could compare that to our IT?

7.6.6.4 Summary of BPMC Process Factors

Prioritization for these factors can be calculated in following way: mean of reversed importance multiplied by value. Priorities are reversed to get a list of factors where smallest value is the most important (in original data highest priority had number 3 and lowest 1, so those are reversed). Using previously described calculation we get following prioritized list of BPMC Technology factors for Organization Gamma:

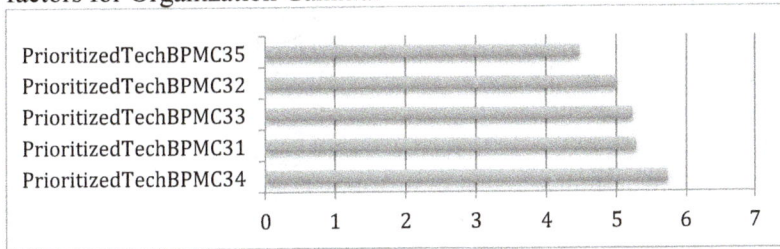

Technological capabilities to promote BPM success are on average level in Organization Gamma. The statistics show that respondents do not feel that there are big hurdles in technological support, but they do not seem to strongly agree either. Respondents are quite undecided in this matter.

BPMC35 (IT is aligned with business process management strategy.) Organization could make it more clear that how IT systems support business processes. This matter might also be linked to lack of standardized process management system, which would make the links more visible. Organization should look into possibilities how to evaluate whether IT systems are aligned with BPM.

BPMC32 (The organization extensively uses the information systems.) Respondents slightly agree on this statement and they think it is important to use information systems. Organization should evaluate where in processes there are places to use information systems more efficiently.

BPMC34 (Legacy information systems are reengineered if necessary.) Respondents slightly disagree with this statement. Organization should evaluate which legacy information systems may be in a need of reengineering.

7.6.7 Cronbach's Alpha for all BPMC factors

This Cronbach's Alpha shows internal consistency of this survey. The consistency is higher when there are more variables in a survey. Below is a table of variables and their Alpha values, if item is deleted from survey.

Variables	Alpha if item deleted
Process Value: BPMC19	0.8713162
People Value: BPMC15	0.8660175
Process Value: BPMC26	0.8652421
Process Value: BPMC21	0.865153
People Value: BPMC10	0.8641223
Process Value: BPMC29	0.8641014
People Value: BPMC9	0.8632292
Technical Value: BPMC33	0.8630801
People Value: BPMC8	0.8627247

246

Process Value: BPMC27	0.8614933
People Value: BPMC12	0.860736
Process Value: BPMC17	0.859795
People Value: BPMC14	0.8594372
People Value: BPMC11	0.859417
Process Value: BPMC20	0.8593226
People Value: BPMC3	0.8589957
Process Value: BPMC30	0.8583381
People Value: BPMC1	0.8580912
Technical Value: BPMC32	0.8571672
Technical Value: BPMC35	0.8569844
People Value: BPMC5	0.856775
Process Value: BPMC24	0.8565609
People Value: BPMC2	0.8563052
People Value: BPMC13	0.8553035
Process Value: BPMC25	0.8550047
People Value: BPMC7	0.8549735
Process Value: BPMC18	0.8546189
People Value: BPMC6	0.8544915
People Value: BPMC4	0.853583
Technical Value: BPMC31	0.8511426
Process Value: BPMC28	0.8510121
Process Value: BPMC23	0.8507966
Process Value: BPMC22	0.8494647
Process Value: BPMC16	0.8476194
Technical Value: BPMC34	0.8431227

Internal consistency level of this survey based on Cronbach's Alpha value is: 0.8616 (good). Since this survey measures Business Process Management Capabilities (BPMC) of Organization Gamma, Cronbach's Alpha shows how well this survey is able to measure that from overall perspective.

7.6.8 Open ended comments on overall process development in Organization Gamma

What do you think Gamma should do to improve its business processes?

Improve how information is shared within the organization.

Open and transparent processes and measurement. Modern it solutions should be implemented and the data analyzed in 2010 way, not 90s way.

Improve our IT systems.

Key account managers should talk more with customers instead of polling Hilma.

Why don't we concentrate on high-level consultation on such substance matters where we have decades of experience?

"The shoemaker's children go barefoot"! We should utilize the internal expertise in BPM and providing IT solutions inside the company. We really cannot say we are number one, when our internal processes and tools are inefficient and obsolete.

What are the coce competences of a consultant - what should they be doing.

improve communication. New people are a bit lost how things work or who should they contact if they have "great ideas"

Focus on those business processes that affect the everyday life of regular consultants the most (for example HR processes, competence management processes etc.)

We should need to re-engineer "work hour logging system" :)

Draw them, and show to employees.

7.6.9 Summary of BPMC survey results

Following table shows number of negative, undecided and positive value factors in whole BPMC survey:

Factors	Negative	Undecided	Positive
People	1	5	9
Process	7	3	5
Technology	0	2	3
	TOTAL NEGATIVE: 8 (23%)	TOTAL UNDECIDED: 10 (28%)	TOTAL POSITIVE: 17 (49%)

As table above shows, Organization Gamma is mainly on positive side regarding BPM capabilities measured in this survey. There are some areas to be developed especially on process capabilities, but people capabilities seem to be on a good level. Technological capabilities in Organization Gamma are not very clear, since respondents indicated that they are something between undecided and positive. Organization should take measures to strengthen negative capabilities and to increase undecided capabilities to positive side.

Following table shows number of low, medium and high importance factors in whole

BPMC survey:

Factors	Low importance	Medium	High importance
People	0	4	11
Process	0	8	7
Technology	0	1	4
	TOTAL LOW: 0 (0%)	TOTAL MEDIUM: 13 (37%)	TOTAL HIGH: 22 (63%)

248

Table above shows, that capabilities measured in this survey have all been either medium or high importance. Over 60% of respondents indicated that these issues are important for the organization.

Using the importance together with value given to organization (value means multiplied by importance means), we can get graph below showing the capabilities the Organization Gamma should focus on improving in order of importance (high to low):

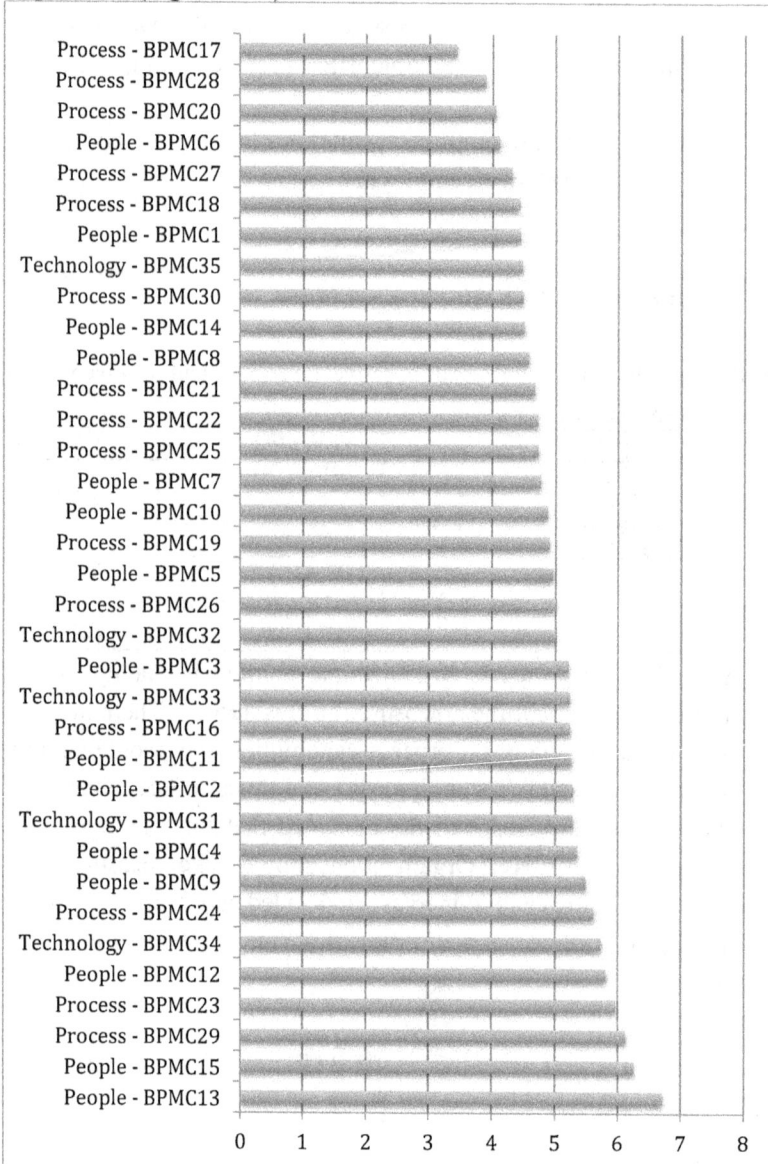

Since the importance is reversed (the higher importance has smaller number), the most important factors are at the beginning of the list and least important factors are at the end of the list.

7.6.10 Open ended comments on this BPMC survey

Please, share your thoughts and feedback on this BPMC survey?

Due to my lack of knowledge in this field, the questions were somewhat unclear at times.

Excellent idea!

Doesn't really understand what BPMC is all about, but hope that this survey improves way of working in Organization Gamma.

Felt like Great place to work enquiry ;) but shorter. Good luck for your work!

There is much I don't know of our company, but answered by gut feeling.

Managers place confidence between supervisors and their subordinates. What does that even mean? You just don't use between with confidence. http://www.learnersdictionary.com/search/confidence

Thank you for providing a good channel for my five-minute rampage on the inefficient process management inside the company :)

I felt that some of the questions were on a bit too abstract level, which made answering them a bit difficult.

Questions were little bit confusing and hard to understand at first read.

It is not described whether Organization Gamma uses the results for own good.

I did not get the idea behind this survey. I hope that my questions will help you to succeed your dissertation.

These open-ended comments on this survey indicate that the researcher needs to improve the wording in BPMC questions, so that they are more understandable for employees. If other respondents were feeling also that these questions were hard for them to understand, that may also explain low response rate.

7.7   Appendix III - Organization Alpha Case Report

7.7.1   *Executive summary*

Based on background information of 25 respondents, we can state that the survey has been able to receive responses from different organizational levels, with 22% respond rate. Respondents have wide background in their experience in process development. All respondents had adequate command of English to be able to understand the questions in this survey. Background information numbers also indicate, that offering training in developing processes may raise people's own perception on their skills and knowledge in developing processes.

In People BPMC factors, Organization Alpha should turn close attention especially to BPMC5 (Managers have sufficient knowledge about process changes) and BPMC8 (The organization has appointed responsible people for processes). Rest of the People factors are on a higher level. This document gives ideas on how to improve those capabilities. The suggestion is to state the processes and process responsibilities clearly. Also communicate road map for process development for every process is seen as important. People seem to have desire for BPM and CEM trainings to get more customer centric methods.

Overall score in Process BPMC factors is lower than in People factors. There are several factors that respondents disagree with, even though they are perceived to be medium or high importance. Organization should evaluate how to improve at least following process capabilities: BPMC18 (The bonus scheme adjusts to process changes), BPMC27 (The organization has a standard methodology for improving processes), BPMC16 (The performance measurements adequately correspond to the process changes), BPMC17 (I know the cost of customer acquisition, the annual value of a customer and the cost of a customer complaint), BPMC19 (There are training programs available to update my skills), BPMC21 (The plans for process improvement projects are adequate), BPMC24 (Organizational structure can be easily changed when needed), BPMC28 (The organization is able to respond to changes in markets quickly) and BPMC29 (Initiatives in the organization are heading in the same direction).

Technological capabilities to promote BPM success are on average level in Organization Alpha. The statistics show that respondents do not feel that there are big hurdles in technological support, but they do not seem to strongly agree either. Respondents are quite undecided in this matter. However, information systems should be in development focus because Alpha should automate more processes to be efficient (many internal systems and data synchronizations are based on MS Excel).

Open-ended questions for each BPMC category contain relevant and interesting information from individual respondents. People responsible for developing business processes should take a look at those comments and make their own conclusions from them. Real name of organization and IT systems have been replaced with general terms to protect the anonymity of Organization Alpha and its employees.

As a summary, Organization Alpha is mainly on positive side regarding BPM capabilities measured in this survey. There are some areas to be developed especially on process capabilities, but people capabilities seem to be on a good level. Technological capabilities in Organization Alpha are not very clear, since respondents indicated that they are something between undecided and positive. Organization should take measures to strengthen negative (respondents disagree) capabilities and to increase undecided capabilities to positive (respondents agree) side.

7.7.2 Suggestions for actions to improve BPM Capabilities in Organization Alpha

BPMC5 (Managers have sufficient knowledge about process changes.) can be improved by improving the communication between management and those parties that are involved with process changes. The managers should proactively follow, how processes could be and are changed in the organization. Standardized way with communication plan will also help managers to have sufficient knowledge about process changes.

BPMC8 (Top management frequently communicates with project team and users) could be improved by having more good quality communication between top management and project teams. Respondents would like to get more frequently communication from top management. Management should not alienate itself from the production and people doing daily work.

Process factor BPMC16 (The performance measurements adequately correspond to the processes and changes into them) is disagreed by respondents slightly and they think it is medium importance. Organization Alpha should look into their performance measurements to see which parts of them are not adequately corresponding to processes.

BPMC17 (Everyone knows the cost of customer acquisition, the annual value of a customer and the cost of a customer complaint) is perceived to be medium important, but it has very low value. This is a clear indication that employees do not know these measurements, but they think it would be important to know them. Organization should develop a way to let everyone know what are the values of these measurements.

BPMC19 (There are training programs available to update my skills). The organization should have clear training plan, which is based on the strategy and customer needs. These programs should be available for employees to improve their skills. Training can be used as strategic method to take the organization forward to desired direction. HR department is recommended to evaluate current skills and future needs and to make a training plan to fill in the gap.

Respondents disagree on BPMC21 (The project plan for process improvement is adequate). This may tell that process improvement should be planned better and it may also mean that employees are not aware of project plans for process improvements.

BPMC24 (Organizational structure can be easily changed when needed). The organizational structure should be a way to organize people into functional units that fill in different strategic purposes in an organization. These should be designed in such a way that they can be changed when needed.

Respondents disagree on statement BPMC27 (Organization has standard methodology for improving processes). It is logical that since BPM concepts and methodologies are not known well, they are not used in standardized way either. Management should consider adopting some standard method for process development in organization and teaching it to employees (such as the CEI Method).

BPMC28 (Organization is able to respond to changes in markets quickly) has been seen little bit on the positive side by respondents, but still it is very close to undecided. However, this factor is perceived to be of high importance, so management should work on being able to respond market changes quicker. Since respondents have evaluated correlating factor BPMC23 (Business process improvement efforts are important for the organization) high value and importance, it may explain that organization is working on process improvement, but slowly. Management should look into ways to make this process faster.

BPMC29 (Initiatives in the organization are heading in the same direction). The organization should have a clear strategy, which dictates what initiatives are needed. Strategy can also help managers to make sure that all of them are taking the organization in the same direction.

BPMC32 (The organization extensively uses information systems.) Respondents slightly agree on this statement and they think it is important to use information systems. Organization should evaluate where in processes there are places to use information systems more efficiently.

BPMC34 (Existing information systems are reengineered if necessary.) Respondents slightly disagree with this statement. Organization should evaluate which legacy information systems may be in a need of reengineering.

BPMC35 (The information systems are aligned with the organization's strategy.) Organization could make it more clear that how IT systems support business processes. This matter might also be linked to lack of standardized process management system, which would make the links more visible. Organization should look into possibilities how to evaluate whether IT systems are aligned with BPM.

7.7.3   Background information

Background information shows what kind of respondents this survey had. All 25 respondents gave an answer to these background questions, so there were no missing values to handle.

7.7.3.1 General description

BPMC survey in Organization Alpha was able to receive 25 responses. Target audience was 115 people, so it gives 22% response rate. The group of respondents contains a lot of managers (84%). The survey was done during December 2012 - January 2013. The survey link was emailed to employees three times. Board of Directors promoted answering to survey.

Anonymity of respondents was assured through general invitation that was sent in email to all employees in Organization Alpha. So, no respondents can be traced back and this was mentioned in invitation letter.

The graphs below show the basic information about the respondents:

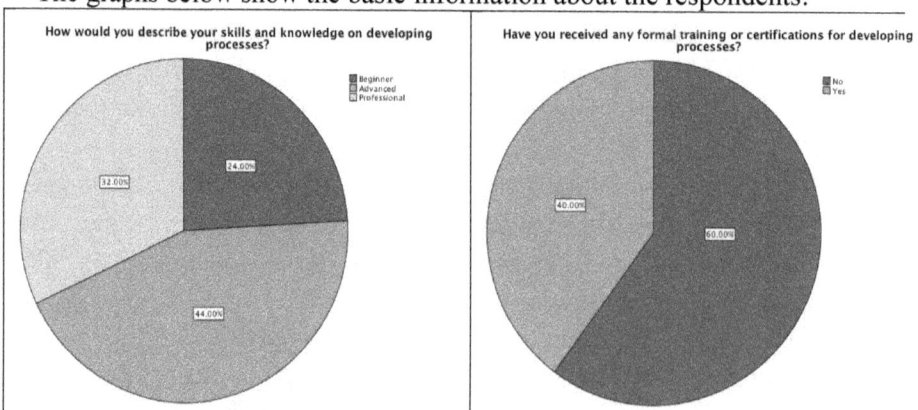

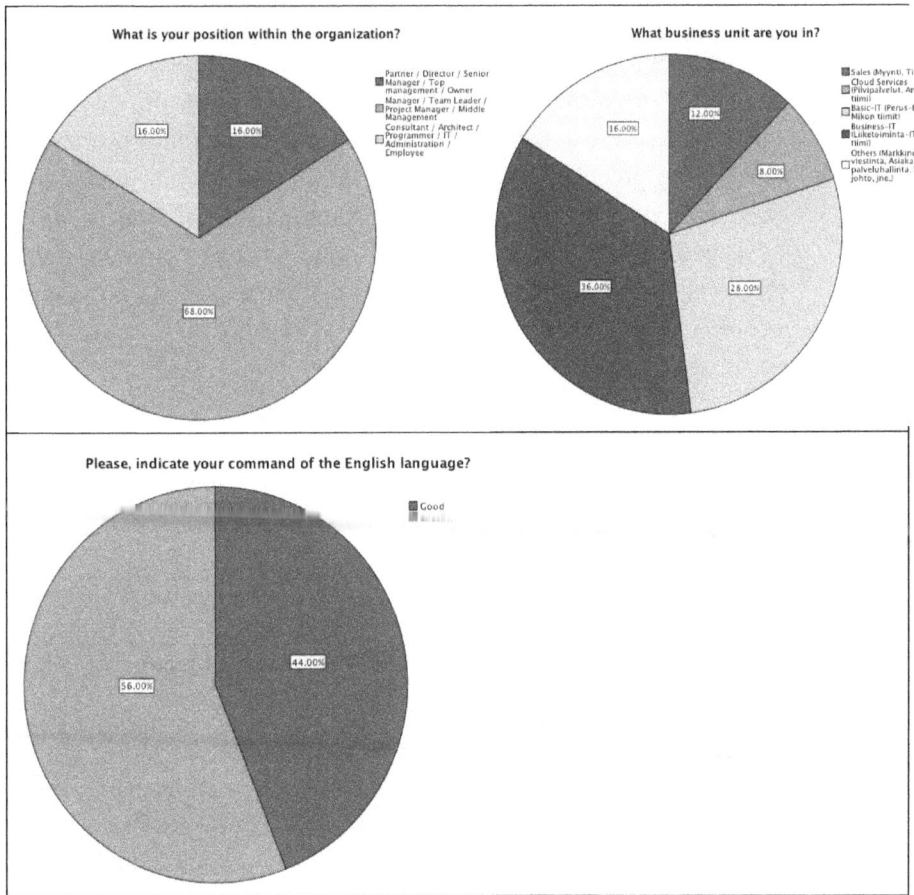

What is your position within the organization?

What business unit are you in?

Please, indicate your command of the English language?

7.7.3.2 Relationship between process skills and formal training

How would you describe your skills and knowledge on developing processes?		Have you received any formal training or certifications for developing processes?		Total
		No	Yes	
Beginner	Count	6	0	6
	%	100.0%	0.0%	100.0%
Advanced	Count	8	3	11
	%	72.7%	27.3%	100.0%
Professional	Count	1	7	8
	%	12.5%	87.5%	100.0%
Total	Count	15	10	25

256

| | % | 60.0% | 40.0% | 100.0% |

Background information shows 76% of respondents feel that they are either advanced or professionals in process development, but only 40% of respondents have received some kind of formal training or certifications in developing processes. Table above shows that people who are on beginner level have not received any process training. On the other hand only 40% of advanced or professional people have received process training. These numbers indicate, that offering training in developing processes may raise people's own perception on their skills and knowledge on developing processes.

7.7.3.3 Relationship between process skills and position

			What is your position within the organization?		
How would you describe your skills and knowledge on developing processes?			Partner / Director / Senior Manager / Top management / Owner	Manager / Team Leader / Project Manager / Middle Management	Consultant / Architect / Programmer / IT / Administration / Employee
	Beginner	Count	0	6	0
		%	0.0%	100.0%	0.0%
	Advanced	Count	2	8	1
		%	18.2%	72.7%	9.1%
	Professional	Count	2	3	3
		%	25.0%	37.5%	37.5%
Total		Count	4	17	4
		%	16.0%	68.0%	16.0%

Table above shows that different positions have quite equal skills in process development even though there has not been official training to 60% of them. This indicates that management level employees have acquired their skills in process development through practical work rather than through official training.

7.7.3.4 Summary of background information

Based on background information of 25 respondents, we can state that the survey has been able to receive responses from different organizational levels, even though focusing more on the managerial positions. Respondents have wide background in their experience in process development. All respondents had adequate command of English to be able to understand the questions in this survey. Background information numbers also indicate, that offering training in developing processes may raise people's own perception on their skills and knowledge in developing processes. Since level of trained people in Organization Alpha is quite low (40%), it is suggested to train more people for process development.

7.7.4   BPMC – People factors

BPMC Survey people factors contain BPMC factors from BPMC1 until BPMC15:

BPMC1 Managers share vision and information with you.

BPMC2 Senior management has confidence and trust in you and your managers.

BPMC3 Managers constructively use your ideas.

BPMC4 Managers have realistic expectations of process changes.

BPMC5 Managers have sufficient knowledge about process changes.

BPMC6 Managers frequently communicate with you.

BPMC7 Managers support changes in processes.

BPMC8 The organization has appointed responsible people for processes.

BPMC9 You are empowered to make decisions.

BPMC10 There is open communication between you and your managers.

BPMC11 Co-workers have confidence and trust in each other.

BPMC12 Teamwork between co-workers is the standard way to solve problems within this organization.

BPMC13 There is performance recognition among co- workers.

BPMC14 Managers evaluate customer expectations when establishing the organization's vision.

BPMC15 The organization uses external consultants when needed.

These factors were measured from two perspectives: how do respondents feel these statements apply to Organization Alpha (value) and how important they think each statement is (importance).

7.7.4.1 BPMC People Value

People value describes how respondents valued Organization Alpha in BPMC factors 1-15. This was measured by asking them how much do they agree or

258

disagree with statements regarding this organization. Value questions were measured with Likert scale: 1 = Strongly disagree, 2 = Disagree, 3 = Undecided, 4 = Agree, 5 = Strongly agree

Means for People BPMC Factors

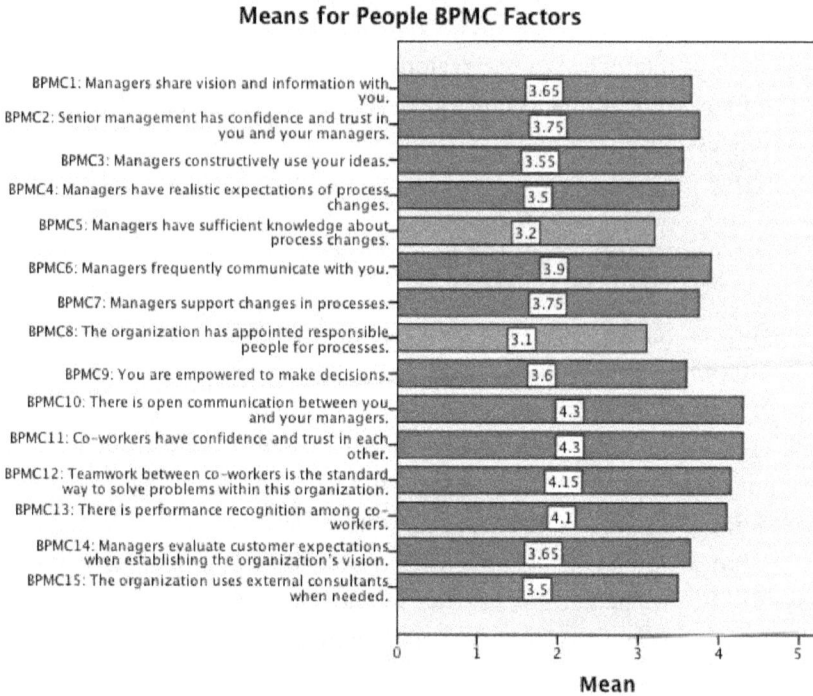

Factor	Mean
BPMC1: Managers share vision and information with you.	3.65
BPMC2: Senior management has confidence and trust in you and your managers.	3.75
BPMC3: Managers constructively use your ideas.	3.55
BPMC4: Managers have realistic expectations of process changes.	3.5
BPMC5: Managers have sufficient knowledge about process changes.	3.2
BPMC6: Managers frequently communicate with you.	3.9
BPMC7: Managers support changes in processes.	3.75
BPMC8: The organization has appointed responsible people for processes.	3.1
BPMC9: You are empowered to make decisions.	3.6
BPMC10: There is open communication between you and your managers.	4.3
BPMC11: Co-workers have confidence and trust in each other.	4.3
BPMC12: Teamwork between co-workers is the standard way to solve problems within this organization.	4.15
BPMC13: There is performance recognition among co-workers.	4.1
BPMC14: Managers evaluate customer expectations when establishing the organization's vision.	3.65
BPMC15: The organization uses external consultants when needed.	3.5

Mean

These mean values show that we can divide the responses into three categories: Negative (<2.8), Undecided (2.8 <= x =< 3.2) and Positive (>3.2). The researcher decided these thresholds for different categories. The thought pattern behind is that values close to 3 mean that respondents are undecided whether to have positive or negative standing. So, this undecided mean value is given +/- 0.2 units to sway on both negative and positive side. Any mean value differentiating more than 0.1 units from 3 are regarded either as negative (respondents disagree with statement) or positive (respondents agree with statement). This same logic is used also later on Process and Technology categories. Using the means values from above factors go into these categories in the following way: Undecided: 13% and positive 87%. In organization Alpha there were no negative capabilities.

Organization Alpha should take actions to improve appointing responsible people for processes. Also Alpha's managers should get more familiar with process changes in the organization.

7.7.4.2   BPMC People Factors' Importance

People factors' importance describes, how important respondents think BPMC factors 1-15 are. This was measured by asking them how important they think each statement is. Importance of these people factors was measured with scale: 1 = Low, 2 = Medium, 3 = High

Mean values for People BPMC Factors' Importance

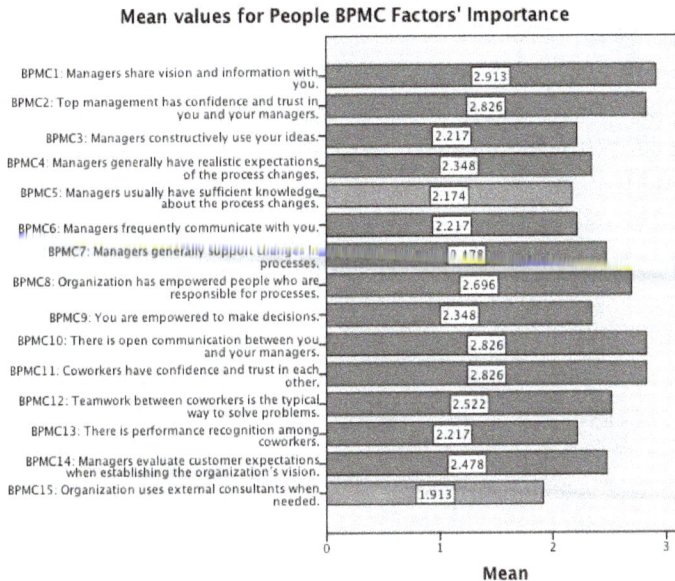

	Mean
BPMC1: Managers share vision and information with you.	2.913
BPMC2: Top management has confidence and trust in you and your managers.	2.826
BPMC3: Managers constructively use your ideas.	2.217
BPMC4: Managers generally have realistic expectations of the process changes.	2.348
BPMC5: Managers usually have sufficient knowledge about the process changes.	2.174
BPMC6: Managers frequently communicate with you.	2.217
BPMC7: Managers generally support changes in processes.	2.478
BPMC8: Organization has empowered people who are responsible for processes.	2.696
BPMC9: You are empowered to make decisions.	2.348
BPMC10: There is open communication between you and your managers.	2.826
BPMC11: Coworkers have confidence and trust in each other.	2.826
BPMC12: Teamwork between coworkers is the typical way to solve problems.	2.522
BPMC13: There is performance recognition among coworkers.	2.217
BPMC14: Managers evaluate customer expectations when establishing the organization's vision.	2.478
BPMC15: Organization uses external consultants when needed.	1.913

These mean values show that we can divide the responses into three categories: Low (<1.8), Medium (1.8 <= x =< 2.2) and High (>2.2). The researcher decided these thresholds for different categories. The thought pattern behind is that values close to 2 mean that respondents think the statement is of medium importance. So, this medium mean value is given +/- 0.2 units to sway on both low and high side. Any mean value differentiating more than 0.2 units from 2 are regarded either as low or high. This same categorization is used later also on Process and Technology importance.

Based on mean values of importance in above table and graph we can conclude that respondents indicate that these people BPMC factors are important for organization. None of the factors were regarded as low importance (mean value below 1.8). Following People BPMC factors are regarded as medium or high importance: Medium importance 13% and high importance 87%.

260

7.7.4.3 Open ended comments on People Factors

What do you think Organization Alpha should do to improve those People BPMC Factors that you answered either strongly disagree or disagree?

State the processes and process responsibilities clearly. Communicate road map for process development for every process.

Managers should communicate more, da? ;P

Prosessin kehitykseen pitäisi sitoutua pitkäjänteisesti. Prosessin kehitys pitäisi organisoida siten, että johto voisi ohjata sitä järkevällä tavalla siten, ettei ajankäytöllisesti ohjaustyö olisi mahdollista. Prosessin kehitysryhmät eivät saisi olla liian isoja. Resursointi pitäisi sovittaa paremmin liiketoiminnan kanssa. Prosessin kuvauksen ja jalkautuksen tekemisen tavat pitäisi olla selvillä ja yhteisesti hyväksytty ennen kuin niihin ryhdytään. Tavat eivät voi olla kymmenien ihmisten workshoppeja vaan työstäminen pitäisi tapahtua pienellä ryhmällä. Ohjausmalli selkeä ja tehokas. Jalkaituksen suunnittelu tärkeää. Käytetään ulkoista apua, mutta silti sovitetaan se Alphaan- ei edelleenkään kymmenien ihmisten workshoppeja.

More open internal communication and more systematic interaction with customers and potential customers. Clear responsibilities and processes.

Process training (and possibly certificates) regarding best practices and standards (e.g. ITIL, Prince2, Cobit etc.). - Management commitment -> adequate allocation of resources, be present in meetings etc. - Appoint responsible people for processes

Build discipline in growth oriented process development, nurture strategic competences and differentiate them from operational ones, avoid halo-effect in business management.

Treat teams and employees equally important, regardless of the importance of current project/customer challenge. There should be time and practices to lead in a wider perspective as are currently done.

Kannustetaan selkeäämmin kaikkia enemmän asiakaslähtöisyyteen ja jaetaan tietoa enemmän. Valutetaan aktiivisesti kaikille tietoa siitä mikä johdossa milläkin hetkellä mietityttää. Annetaan tämän avulla fiksulle porukalle enemmän mahdollisuuksia korjata asioita suoraan.

More communication and realistic resource planning cross-over units. We have insufficient human resources for long-term internal development or process owners are not motivated as it does not bring up short-term turnover. We don't need to do everything by ourselves. KPIs are more or less focused on short-term sales or planning is so high-level that it will not support daily operations.

Managers should realize that the change needs time, resources and change management to apply. When you need to start to do things that you have not done before and if your team members are already running the 40+ saldo hours, no progress...

Management to align strategy both with Mother Company and Alpha functions. Increase cross function awareness within Alpha.

7.7.4.4 *Summary of BPMC People Factors*

Prioritization for these factors can be calculated in following way: mean of reversed importance multiplied by value. Priorities are reversed to get a list of factors where smallest value is the most important (in original data highest priority had number 3 and lowest 1, so those are reversed). Using previously described calculation we get following prioritized list of BPMC People factors for Organization Alpha:

BPMC5 (Managers have sufficient knowledge about process changes.) can be improved b y improving the communication. The managers should proactively follow how processes could be and are changed in the organization.

BPMC8 (Top management frequently communicates with project team and users) could be improved by having more good quality communication between top management and project teams. Respondents would like to get more frequently communication from top management.

Rest of the People BPMC factors in Organization Alpha are on a higher level. Measuring them again later could give information on trend where they are moving.

7.7.5   *BPMC – Process*

BPMC Survey process factors contain BPMC factors from BPMC16 until BPMC30:

BPMC16 The performance measurements adequately correspond to the process changes.

BPMC17 I know the cost of customer acquisition, the annual value of a customer and the cost of a customer complaint.

BPMC18 The bonus scheme adjusts to process changes.

BPMC19 There are training programs available to update my skills.

BPMC20 I know and understand Business Process Management (BPM) concepts and methodologies.

BPMC21 The plans for process improvement projects are adequate.

BPMC22 I am eager to improve the existing state of our processes.

BPMC23 Process improvement efforts are important for the organization.

BPMC24 Organizational structure can be easily changed when needed.

BPMC25 No one has to worry about losing his or her job because of process changes.

BPMC26 I feel comfortable with the new working environment after process changes.

BPMC27 The organization has a standard methodology for improving processes.

BPMC28 The organization is able to respond to changes in markets quickly.

BPMC29 Initiatives in the organization are heading in the same direction.

BPMC30 I know what I do within my organization and how it affects the result

These factors were measured from two perspectives: how do respondents feel these statements apply to Organization Alpha (value) and how important they think each statement is (importance).

7.7.5.1 BPMC Process Value

Process value describes how respondents valued Organization Alpha in BPMC factors 16-30. This was measured by asking them how much do they agree or disagree with statements regarding this organization. Value questions were measured with Likert scale: 1 = Strongly disagree, 2 = Disagree, 3 = Undecided, 4 = Agree, 5 = Strongly agree

Means for Process BPMC Factors

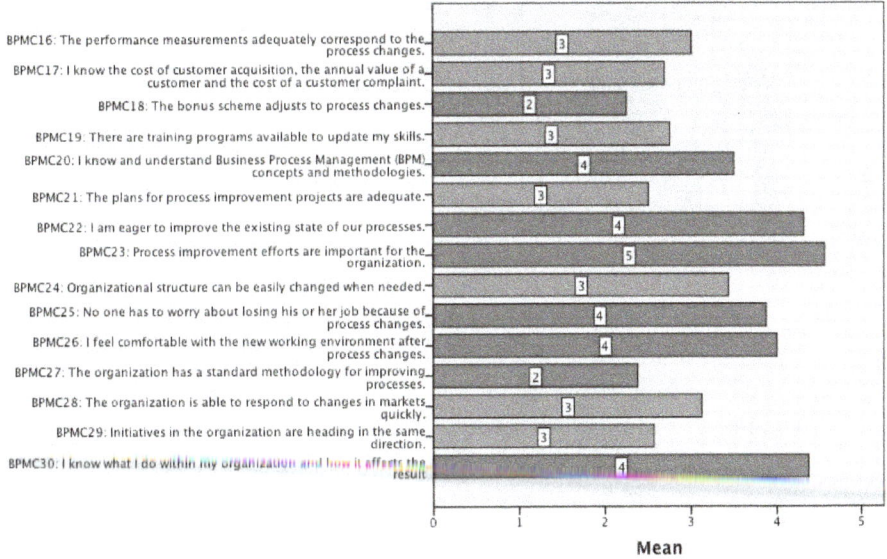

These mean values show that we can divide the responses into three categories: Negative (<2.8), Undecided (2.8 <= x =< 3.2) and Positive (>3.2). Using the means values from above factors go into these categories in the following way:

Negative	Undecided	Positive
BPMC18 The bonus scheme adjusts to process changes	BPMC16 The performance measurements adequately correspond to the process changes	BPMC20 I know and understand Business Process Management (BPM) concepts and methodologies
BPMC27 The organization has a standard methodology for improving processes	BPMC17 I know the cost of customer acquisition, the annual value of a customer and the cost of a customer complaint	BPMC22 I am eager to improve the existing state of our processes
	BPMC19 There are training programs available to update my skills	BPMC23 Process improvement efforts are important for the organization
	BPMC21 The plans for process improvement projects are adequate	BPMC25 No one has to worry about losing his or her job because of process changes
	BPMC24 Organizational structure can be easily changed when needed	BPMC26 I feel comfortable with the new working environment after process changes
	BPMC28 The organization is able to respond to changes in markets quickly.	BPMC30 I know what I do within my organization and how it affects the

		result
	BPMC29 Initiatives in the organization are heading in the same direction	
TOTAL NEGATIVE: 2 (13%)	TOTAL UNDECIDED: 7 (47%)	TOTAL POSITIVE: 6 (40%)

As table above shows, 40% of process value factors are positive in Organization Alpha. There are 9 factors that need improvement (60%).

7.7.5.2 BPMC Process Factors' Importance

Process factors' importance describes how important respondents think BPMC factors 16-30 are. This was measured by asking them how important they think each statement is. Importance of these process factors was measured with scale: 1 = Low, 2 = Medium, 3 = High.

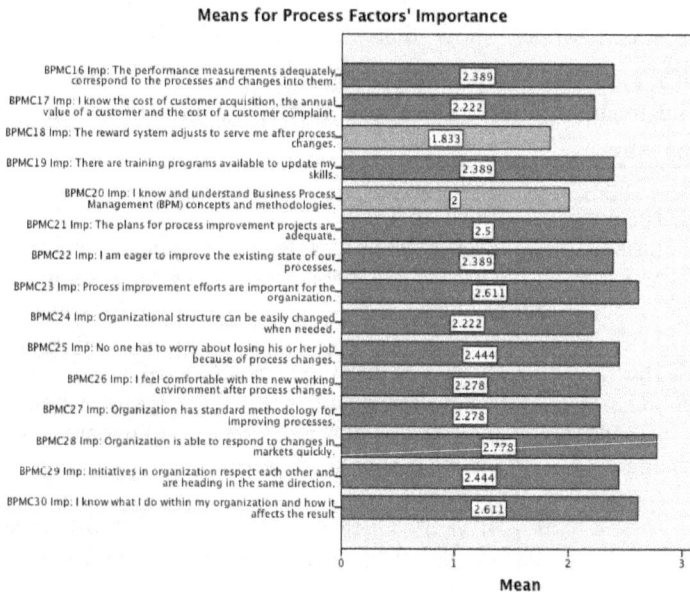

Means for Process Factors' Importance

Factor	Mean
BPMC16 Imp: The performance measurements adequately correspond to the processes and changes into them.	2.389
BPMC17 Imp: I know the cost of customer acquisition, the annual value of a customer and the cost of a customer complaint.	2.222
BPMC18 Imp: The reward system adjusts to serve me after process changes.	1.833
BPMC19 Imp: There are training programs available to update my skills.	2.389
BPMC20 Imp: I know and understand Business Process Management (BPM) concepts and methodologies.	2
BPMC21 Imp: The plans for process improvement projects are adequate.	2.5
BPMC22 Imp: I am eager to improve the existing state of our processes.	2.389
BPMC23 Imp: Process improvement efforts are important for the organization.	2.611
BPMC24 Imp: Organizational structure can be easily changed when needed.	2.222
BPMC25 Imp: No one has to worry about losing his or her job because of process changes.	2.444
BPMC26 Imp: I feel comfortable with the new working environment after process changes.	2.278
BPMC27 Imp: Organization has standard methodology for improving processes.	2.278
BPMC28 Imp: Organization is able to respond to changes in markets quickly.	2.778
BPMC29 Imp: Initiatives in organization respect each other and are heading in the same direction.	2.444
BPMC30 Imp: I know what I do within my organization and how it affects the result	2.611

Based on value in above table and graph we can conclude that respondents indicate that these process BPMC factors are important for organization. None of the factors were regarded as low importance. Only two factors were regarded as medium importance and rest as high.

7.7.5.3 Open ended comments on Process Factors

What do you think Alpha should do to improve those Process BPMC Factors that you answered either strongly disagree or disagree?

Build framework for process development

BPM-courses!

Business process management training, if it is necessary to understand these concepts.

Miksi organisaatiomuutoksen pitäisi tapahtua nopeasti? Vastasin jo ed. sivulla prosessin kehitystä koskeviin kysymyksiin. Prosessin kehityksen pitää olla pitkäjänteistä, kehittämisen mallin pitää olla selkeä, ei liikaa työllistävä, ohjausmallin pitäisi olla tehokas, kymmenien ihmisten workshopit ei toimi, mittareita ei pidä olla liikaa ja niiden pitäisi olla mahd. konkreettisia, prosessin kehitys ei saa työllistää yli liiketoiminnan liikaa, prossin muutosten iteraatioiden pitäisi olla lyhyitä, kaikkea ei kannata muuttaa parhaaksi kerralla. Prosessin kehitystä ei saisi nostaa liian korkealle prioriteetille, jotta siitä ei tule itse tarkoitus.

There should be a real process plan and we should accept processes as a natural part of our business.

- Agree performance measurements for processes - nominate process roles & agree on responsibilities - organize / faciliate more than "just technical" trainings and courses.

- Management commitment needed: resources etc.

Accept more uncertainty and challenges in business management to secure the focus in customer satisfaction and service quality

Asiakkaat haluavat osaamista, eivät aina niputtamista. Parhaiden asioiden ei pidäkkään olla aina selkeitä paketteja ja laatikkoja. Parhaat jutut ovat vaikeita. Siksi juuri kaikki eivät niitä osaa tehdä.

When planning the next merger, please do some kind of process development and thinking forehand.

More information about the costs and values of customers

7.7.5.4 Summary of BPMC Process Factors

Organization Alpha has more capabilities to develop on process side than on people side. As the table shows (and if compared to equivalent table for people factors), there are several factors that are thought to be important by respondents but at the same time their value is average or below.

Based on this survey the respondents disagree that reward system adjusts to serve the employees after the changes (BPMC18). This indicates that the way reward system is adjusted is not as flexible as process changes would require.

BPMC17 (Everyone knows the cost of customer acquisition, the annual value of a customer and the cost of a customer complaint) is perceived to be medium important, but it has very low value. This is a clear indication that employees do not know these measurements, but they think it would be important to know them. Organization should develop a way to let everyone know what are the values of these measurements.

Respondents disagree on statement BPMC27 (Organization has standard methodology for improving processes). It is logical that since BPM concepts and methodologies are not known well, they are not used in standardized way either. Management should consider adopting some standard method for process development in organization and teaching it to employees (such as the CEI Method).

BPMC28 (Organization is able to respond to changes in markets quickly) has been seen little bit on the positive side by respondents, but still it is very close to undecided. However, this factor is perceived to be of high importance, so management should work on being able to respond market changes quicker. Since respondents have evaluated correlating factor BPMC23 (Business process improvement efforts are important for the organization) high value and importance, it may explain that organization is working on process improvement, but slowly. Management should look into ways to make this process faster.

Respondents also disagree on medium importance statement BPMC27 (Organization has standard methodology for improving processes). It is logical that since BPM concepts and methodologies are not known well, they are not used in standardized way either. Management should consider adopting some standard method for process development in organization and teaching it to employees.

Respondents disagree on BPMC21 (The project plan for process improvement is adequate). This may tell that process improvement should be planned better and it may also mean that employees are not aware of project plans for process improvements.

Process factor BPMC16 (The performance measurements adequately correspond to the processes and changes into them) is disagreed by respondents slightly and they think it is medium importance. Organization Alpha should look into their performance measurements to see which parts of them are not adequately corresponding to processes.

BPMC19 (There are training programs available to update my skills). The organization should have clear training plan, which is based on the strategy and customer needs. These programs should be available for employees to improve their skills. Training can be used as strategic method to take the organization forward to desired direction. HR department is recommended to evaluate current skills and future needs and to make a training plan to fill in the gap.

BPMC24 (Organizational structure can be easily changed when needed). The organizational structure should be a way to organize people into functional units that fill in different strategic purposes in an organization. These should be designed in such a way that they can be changed when needed.

BPMC29 (Initiatives in the organization are heading in the same direction). The organization should have a clear strategy, which dictates what initiatives are needed. Strategy can also help managers to make sure that all of them are taking the organization in the same direction.

7.7.6 BPMC – Technology

BPMC Survey technology factors contain BPMC factors from BPMC31 until BPMC35:

BPMC31 The business plan of the organization also takes the information systems into consideration.

BPMC32 The organization extensively uses information systems.

BPMC33 There are efficient communication channels for transferring information.

BPMC34 Existing information systems are reengineered if necessary.

BPMC35 The information systems are aligned with the organization's strategy.

These factors were measured from two perspectives: how do respondents feel these statements apply to Organization Alpha (value) and how important they think each statement is (importance).

7.7.6.1 BPMC Technology Value

Technology value describes how respondents valued Organization Alpha in BPMC factors 31-35. This was measured by asking them how much do they agree or disagree with statements regarding this organization. Value questions were measured with Likert scale: 1 = Strongly disagree, 2 = Disagree, 3 = Undecided, 4 = Agree, 5 = Strongly agree.

Means for BPMC Technology Factors

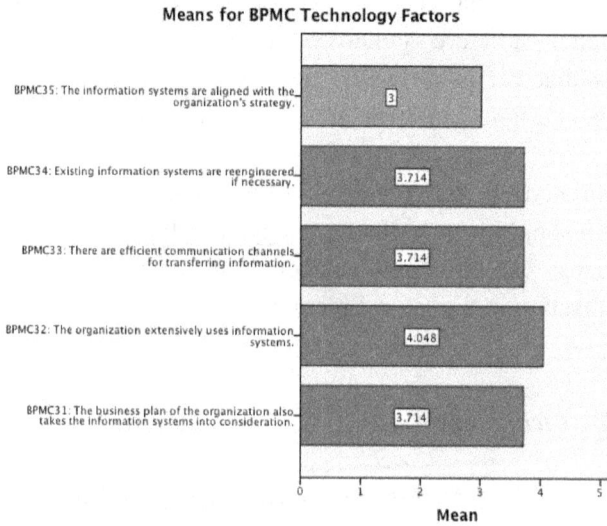

These mean values show that we can divide the responses into three categories: Negative (<2.8), Undecided (2.8 <= x =< 3.2) and Positive (>3.2). Using the means values from above factors go into these categories in the following way:

Undecided	Positive
BPMC35 IT is aligned with business process management strategy.	BPMC31 Information technology is integrated in business plan of the organization
	BPMC32 The organization extensively uses the information systems
	BPMC33 There are efficient communication channels in transferring information
	BPMC34 Legacy information systems are reengineered if necessary
TOTAL UNDECIDED: 1 (20%)	TOTAL POSITIVE: 4 (80%)

As table above shows, 80% of technology value factors are positive in Organization Alpha. There is only one technology factor that is undecided. It is also notable that none of the technology factors are highly agreed either. This may show uncertainty amongst employees whether they agree or disagree to these statements in Organization Alpha.

7.7.6.2 BPMC Technology Factors' Importance

Technology factors' importance describes, how important respondents think BPMC factors 31-35 are. This was measured by asking them how important they think each statement is. Importance of these people factors was measured with scale: 1 = Low, 2 = Medium, 3 = High.

Means for Technology Importance Factors

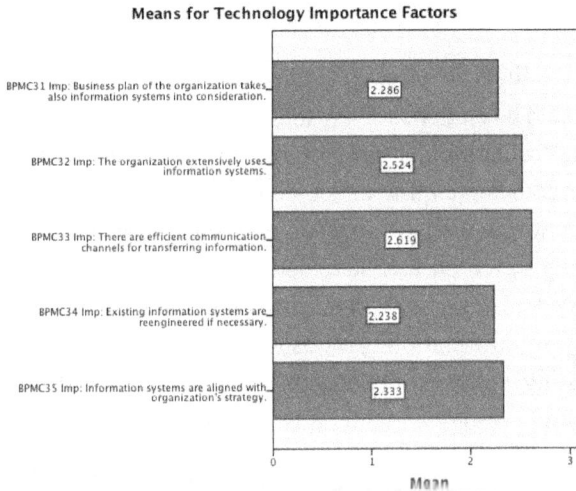

Based on value in above table and graph we can conclude that respondents indicate that these technology BPMC factors are medium or slightly highly important for organization. None of the factors were regarded as low importance.

7.7.6.3 Open ended comments on Technology Factors

What do you think Alpha should do to improve those Technical BPMC Factors that you answered either strongly disagree or disagree?

Plan strategy in a deeper way it has been done before

Vaihtelee. Työkalut laahaavat joiltain osin jäljessä. Joiltain osin tilanne ok ja kehitetään voimakkaasti. Zapista Dynamoon (Service Nowiin) nopeammin kiitos.

Information systems should be in our focus because we should automate our processes and work as much as possible. Unit prices are going down all the time and we should be more efficient in the future.

Do a current state analysis vs. target state, and make a development project to improve the situation (regarding information channels and systems).

Käytetään aika paljon aikaa omien asioiden tunkkaamiseen. tämä toisaalta hyvä, koska silloin tiedetään mistä puhutaan.

Too many information systems addressing the same issues.

Simple is good. Too many internal systems and data synchronization based on excel. Personally I spend mainly my time with email and excel (linked to several resources). Forecasting is manual process.

7.7.6.4 Summary of BPMC Process Factors

Technological capabilities to promote BPM success are on average level in Organization Alpha. The statistics show that respondents do not feel that there are big hurdles in technological support, but they do not seem to strongly agree either. Respondents are quite undecided in this matter.

BPMC32 (The organization extensively uses information systems.) Respondents slightly agree on this statement and they think it is important to use information systems. Organization should evaluate where in processes there are places to use information systems more efficiently.

BPMC34 (Existing information systems are reengineered if necessary.) Respondents slightly disagree with this statement. Organization should evaluate which legacy information systems may be in a need of reengineering.

BPMC35 (The information systems are aligned with the organization's strategy.) Organization could make it more clear that how IT systems support business processes. This matter might also be linked to lack of standardized process management system, which would make the links more visible. Organization should look into possibilities how to evaluate whether IT systems are aligned with BPM.

7.7.7   Open ended comments on overall process development in Organization Alpha

What do you think Alpha should do to improve its business processes?

Build framework and give resources for development

Määritellä ja jalkauttaa ne henkilökunnalle, sekä luoda selkeä malli prosessien jatkuvalle kehittämiselle. Prosesseille pitäisi myös sopia selkeät omistajat.

Asiakkaan liiketoimintatarpeen huomioiminen tärkeintä. Ei ainakaan tehdä tästä tekemisestä liian jäykkää.

1. Public statement from CEO and the management team that business processes are important and strategic. 2. Clear responsibilities, who is in charge for process planing, processes, functions and so on. 3. Simple and realistic plan how to improve our business processes 2013-2015.

See comments I wrote in this survey earlier.

Self-evaluate the most critical process chains and objectively seek alternative ways to do things better - even radical ones.

keep it simple for the customer in finnish in Finland

Lopetetaan pelkästään roolivaraiset yhteenniputtamiset ja ihmisiä ärsyttävä"selkeyttävä" laatikkoleikki. Ei kannata muuttaa sioista jos ei

271

varmasti ymmärrä seurauksia. Lattikkoleikkiä ei kannata ottaa kivana leikkinä jossa pääsee kokeilemaan. Sellainen ajattelu on tyhmää. Keskitytään myynnissä erityisesti sisältöosaamiseen. Myönnetään että kaikilla on omat vahvuuusalueet ja että kukaan ei uskottavasti hanskaa "kaikkea". Panostetaan enemmän pienempään dedikoituun osaamiseen kaupan cloussausvaiheessa ja yhdistetään tähän konsernin tukema liidien genrointi. Vältetään viimeiseen asti ihmisten "kastittamista" eri organisaatioiden osissa.

Screening current setups, revalue, setup targets, calculate resources needed and setup owners / targets /performance measures

Systematic and long-term way of developing, listen people and understand every day work, ensure resources, implementation and training

7.7.8 Summary of BPMC survey results

Following table shows number of negative, undecided and positive value factors in whole BPMC survey:

Factors	Negative	Undecided	Positive
People	0	2	13
Process	2	7	6
Technology	0	1	4
	TOTAL NEGATIVE: 2 (7%)	TOTAL UNDECIDED: 10 (28%)	TOTAL POSITIVE: 23 (65%)

As table above shows, Organization Alpha is mainly on positive side regarding BPM capabilities measured in this survey. There are some areas to be developed especially on process capabilities, but people capabilities seem to be on a good level. Technological capabilities in Organization Alpha are not very clear, since respondents indicated that they are something between undecided and positive. Organization should take measures to strengthen negative capabilities and to increase undecided capabilities to positive side.

Following table shows number of low, medium and high importance factors in whole BPMC survey:

Factors	Low importance	Medium	High importance
People	0	2	13
Process	0	2	13
Technology	0	0	5
	TOTAL LOW: 0 (0%)	TOTAL MEDIUM: 4 (11%)	TOTAL HIGH: 31 (89%)

Table above shows, that capabilities measured in this survey have all been either medium or high importance. 89% of respondents indicated that these issues are important for the organization.

7.7.9 Open ended comments on this BPMC survey

Please, share your thoughts and feedback on this BPMC survey?

Interesting. Maybe something will happen?

The questions were presented on such a general level that specific answers concerning our organization were a bit difficult to figure out.

Ihan kiva

Onpa prosessipainotteinen kysely. Sen pitäisi olla lähtökohta myös esim. Jatkuvuuspalveluiden kehityksessä. Hienoa, kun tällaista tehdään. Olisi ollut ehkä hyvä nimetä Business Processit tämän kyselyn alkuun.

Great! It is important to ask this kind of questions.

Excellent to study and promote the value of business processses and it's value regarding Alpha's ability to reach it's goals (and ultimately for Alpha's Customers to reach their objectives).

Crucially important topics, survey as a method questionable, overall length of the survey close to max to maintain focus

On hienoa että asioita mietitään. Meillä on paljon asioita joita voi vielä parantaa

Do not think that I have insight in evaluating this topic.

OK, but why practical English in practice in Finnish company?

Interesting survey and question layout

The definition of "Your organization" can be interpreted both as Alpha or my workgrop/team/unit/...

How easy did you find the questions in this survey to understand?

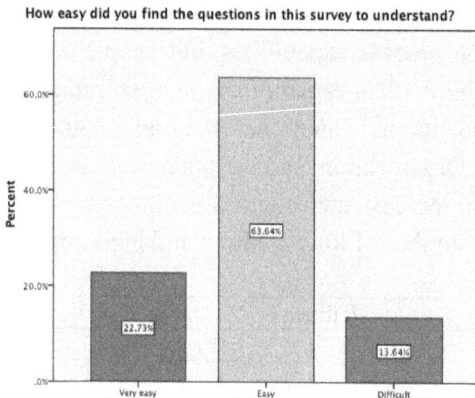

How easy did you find the questions in this survey to understand?

7.8   Appendix IV - Organization Epsilon Case Report

7.8.1   *Executive summary*

Based on background information of 51 respondents, it is possible to state that the survey has been able to receive responses from different organizational levels, with 43% respond rate. Respondents have wide background in their experience in process development. All respondents had adequate command of English to be able to understand the questions in this survey. Background information numbers also indicate, that offering training in developing processes may raise people's own perception on their skills and knowledge in developing processes.

In People BPMC factors, Organization Epsilon should turn close attention especially to BPMC1 (Managers share vision and information with you), BPMC4 (Managers have realistic expectations of process changes) and BPMC13 (There is performance recognition among co-workers). Rest of the People factors are on a higher level, but even though these ones were on positive side company should improve them higher.

Process BPMC factors are quite high for Epsilon. Organization should evaluate how to improve at least the following process capabilities: BPMC16 (The performance measurements adequately correspond to the process changes) and BPMC28 (The organization is able to respond to changes in markets quickly). These BPMC Process factors are barely on the positive side: BPMC17 (I know the cost of customer acquisition, the annual value of a customer and the cost of a customer complaint), BPMC27 (The organization has a standard methodology for improving processes) and BPMC29 (Initiatives in the organization are heading in the same direction).

Technological capabilities to promote BPM success are on average level in Organization Epsilon. The statistics show that respondents do not feel that there are big hurdles in technological support, but they do not seem to strongly agree either. Respondents are quite undecided in this matter. However, information systems should be in development focus because Epsilon had below the average value for the information systems being aligned with the organization's strategy.

Open-ended questions for each BPMC category contain relevant and interesting information from individual respondents. People responsible for developing business processes should take a look at those comments and make their own conclusions from them. Real name of organization and IT systems have been replaced with general terms to protect the anonymity of Organization Epsilon and its employees.

As a summary, Organization Epsilon is clearly on the positive side regarding BPM capabilities measured in this survey. There are some areas to be developed especially on process and IT capabilities, but people capabilities seem to be on a good level even though open-ended comments are giving clear indications for need to train the managers. Technological capabilities in Organization Epsilon are not very clear, since respondents indicated that they are something between undecided and positive.

7.8.2 Suggestions for actions to improve BPM Capabilities in Organization Epsilon

BPMC1 (Managers share vision and information with their subordinates) may be improved by having discussions between managers and subordinates about the ways in which they would like to receive information, how often and in what format. After that appropriate ideas from those discussions may be taken in use.

BPMC4 (Top management generally supports changes in processes) could be improved by clearer support from top management towards process changes. Top management should evaluate their views on process management and tell subordinates what are the ways they are willing to show support for changes in processes.

BPMC13 (There is performance recognition among co- workers) can be enhanced by promoting positive ways for employees to give each other appraisals. This should be on-going behavior and the appraisal should come from one employee to another as soon as there has happened something positive performance wise. The feedback should be genuine and timely.

Epsilon should consider regular team meetings whereby workers can express their concerns and grievances. Gathering and using the ideas presented by the team in those meetings make each person feel like they are meant to be here.

Epsilon should give leadership training to its managers, to enable them to communicate and deal with employees better.

Process factor BPMC16 (The performance measurements adequately correspond to the processes and changes into them) is disagreed by respondents slightly and they think it is medium importance. Organization Alpha should look into their performance measurements to see which parts of them are not adequately corresponding to processes.

BPMC28 (Organization is able to respond to changes in markets quickly) has been seen little bit on the positive side by respondents, but still it is very close to undecided. However, this factor is perceived to be of high importance, so management should work on being able to respond market changes quicker.

Since respondents have evaluated correlating factor BPMC23 (Business process improvement efforts are important for the organization) high value and importance, it may explain that organization is working on process improvement, but slowly. Management should look into ways to make this process faster.

Epsilon could improve on how measuring the customer value, how important it is for the Epsilon to retain existing clients and Epsilon's employees also need to know how much it affects annual revenues. The employees could benefit from receiving information regarding the cost of customer acquisition, the annual value of a customer and the cost of a customer complaint.

BPMC32 (The organization extensively uses information systems.) Respondents slightly agree on this statement and they think it is important to use information systems. Organization should evaluate where in processes there are places to use information systems more efficiently.

BPMC34 (Existing information systems are reengineered if necessary.) Respondents slightly disagree with this statement. Organization should evaluate which legacy information systems may be in a need of reengineering.

BPMC35 (The information systems are aligned with the organization's strategy.) Organization could make it more clear that how IT systems support business processes. This matter might also be linked to lack of standardized process management system, which would make the links more visible. Organization should look into possibilities how to evaluate whether IT systems are aligned with BPM.

7.8.3 Background information

Background information shows what kind of respondents this survey had. All 51 respondents gave an answer to these background questions, so there were no missing values to handle.

7.8.3.1 General description

BPMC survey in Organization Epsilon was able to receive 51 responses. Target audience was 120 people, so it gives 43% response rate. The group of respondents did not contain a lot of managers (24%), so this survey mainly represents the opinions of Epsilon's employees. The survey was done during February 2013 - March 2013. The survey link was emailed to employees three times by one of the managers. Customer Centricity Team promoted answering to survey.

Anonymity of respondents was assured through general invitation that was sent in email to all employees in Organization Epsilon. So, no respondents can be traced back and this was mentioned in invitation letter. The survey system did not save any identification information about the respondents.

The graphs below show the basic information about the respondents:

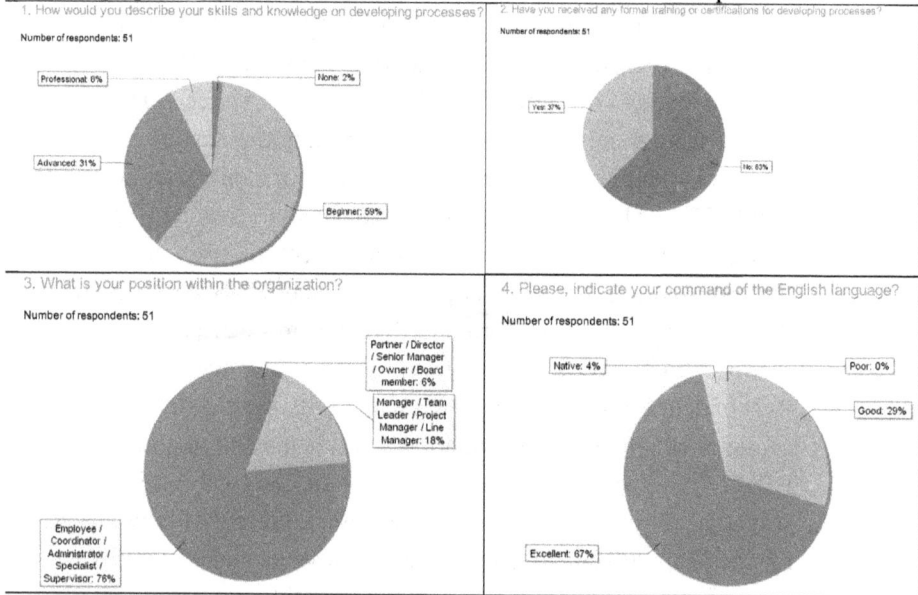

7.8.3.2 Relationship between process skills and formal training

How would you describe your skills and knowledge on developing processes? * Have you received any formal training or certifications for developing processes? Crosstabulation

			Have you received any formal training or certifications for developing processes?		Total
			No	Yes	
How would you describe your skills and knowledge on developing processes?	None	Count	1	0	1
		% within How would you describe your skills and knowledge on developing processes?	100.0%	0.0%	100.0%
	Beginner	Count	22	8	30
		% within How would you describe your skills and knowledge on developing processes?	73.3%	26.7%	100.0%
	Advanced	Count	8	8	16
		% within How would you describe your skills and knowledge on developing processes?	50.0%	50.0%	100.0%
	Professional	Count	1	3	4
		% within How would you describe your skills and knowledge on developing processes?	25.0%	75.0%	100.0%
Total		Count	32	19	51
		% within How would you describe your skills and knowledge on developing processes?	62.7%	37.3%	100.0%

Background information shows 39% of respondents feel that they are either advanced or professionals in process development. Only 37% of respondents have received some kind of formal training or certifications in developing processes. The table above shows that those who have received training on BPM, are stating their skills to he higher. Offering training in developing processes may raise people's own perception on their skills and knowledge on developing processes.

7.8.3.3 *Summary of background information*

Based on background information of 51 respondents, we can state that the survey has been able to receive responses from different organizational levels, though focusing more on the employee positions. Respondents have wide background in their experience in process development. All respondents had adequate command of English to be able to understand the questions in this survey.

Background information numbers also indicate, that offering training in developing processes may raise people's own perception on their skills and knowledge in developing processes. Since level of trained people in Organization Epsilon is quite low (37%), it is suggested to train more people for process development.

7.8.4 *BPMC – People factors*

BPMC Survey people factors contain BPMC factors from BPMC1 until BPMC15:

BPMC1 Managers share vision and information with you.

BPMC2 Senior management has confidence and trust in you and your managers.

BPMC3 Managers constructively use your ideas.

BPMC4 Managers have realistic expectations of process changes.

BPMC5 Managers have sufficient knowledge about process changes.

BPMC6 Managers frequently communicate with you.

BPMC7 Managers support changes in processes.

BPMC8 The organization has appointed responsible people for processes.

BPMC9 You are empowered to make decisions.

BPMC10 There is open communication between you and your managers.

BPMC11 Co-workers have confidence and trust in each other.

BPMC12 Teamwork between co-workers is the standard way to solve problems within this organization.

BPMC13 There is performance recognition among co- workers.

BPMC14 Managers evaluate customer expectations when establishing the organization's vision.

BPMC15 The organization uses external consultants when needed.

These factors were measured from two perspectives: how do respondents feel these statements apply to Organization Epsilon (value) and how important they think each statement is (importance).

7.8.4.1 BPMC People Value

People value describes how respondents valued Organization Epsilon in BPMC factors 1-15. This was measured by asking them how much do they agree or disagree with statements regarding this organization. Value questions were measured with Likert scale: 1 = Strongly disagree, 2 = Disagree, 3 = Undecided, 4 = Agree, 5 = Strongly agree

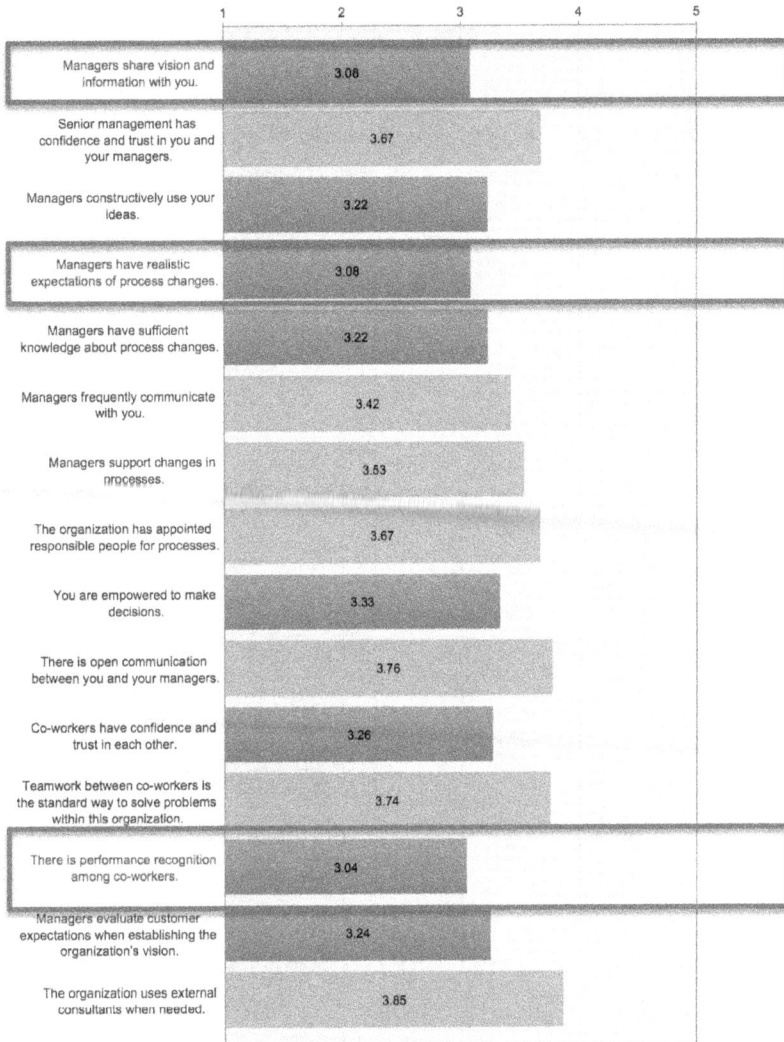

	1	2	3	4	5
Managers share vision and information with you.		3.08			
Senior management has confidence and trust in you and your managers.		3.67			
Managers constructively use your ideas.		3.22			
Managers have realistic expectations of process changes.		3.08			
Managers have sufficient knowledge about process changes.		3.22			
Managers frequently communicate with you.		3.42			
Managers support changes in processes.		3.53			
The organization has appointed responsible people for processes.		3.67			
You are empowered to make decisions.		3.33			
There is open communication between you and your managers.		3.76			
Co-workers have confidence and trust in each other.		3.26			
Teamwork between co-workers is the standard way to solve problems within this organization.		3.74			
There is performance recognition among co-workers.		3.04			
Managers evaluate customer expectations when establishing the organization's vision.		3.24			
The organization uses external consultants when needed.		3.85			

These mean values show that we can divide the responses into three categories: Negative (<2.8), Undecided (2.8 <= x =< 3.2) and Positive (>3.2). The researcher decided these thresholds for different categories. The thought pattern behind is that values close to 3 mean that respondents are undecided whether to have positive or negative standing. So, this undecided mean value is given +/- 0.2 units to sway on both negative and positive side. Any mean value differentiating more than 0.1 units from 3 are regarded either as negative (respondents disagree with statement) or positive (respondents agree with statement). This same logic is used also later on Process and Technology categories. Using the means values from above factors go into these categories in the following way: Undecided 20% and Positive 80%. In organization Epsilon there were no clearly Negative BPM capabilities.

7.8.4.2 BPMC People Factors' Importance

People factors' importance describes, how important respondents think BPMC factors 1-15 are. This was measured by asking them how important they think each statement is. Importance of these people factors was measured with scale: 1 = Low, 2 = Medium, 3 = High

Mean values for BPMC People Factors' Importance

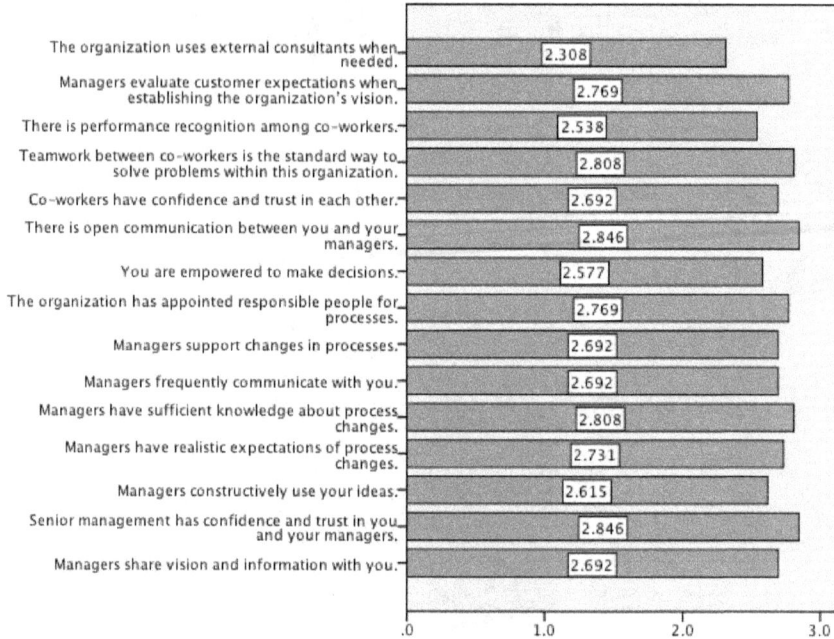

These mean values show that we can divide the responses into three categories: Low (<1.8), Medium (1.8 <= x =< 2.2) and High (>2.2). The researcher decided these thresholds for different categories. The thought pattern behind is that values close to 2 mean that respondents think the statement is of medium importance. So, this medium mean value is given +/- 0.2 units to sway on both low and high side. Any mean value differentiating more than 0.2 units from 2 are regarded either as low or high. This same categorization is used later also on Process and Technology importance. Based on mean values of importance in above table and graph we can conclude that respondents indicate that these people BPMC factors are important for organization. None of the factors were regarded as low (mean value below 1.8) or medium importance. All People BPMC factors were regarded as high importance.

7.8.4.3 Open ended comments on People Factors

What do you think Organization Epsilon should do to improve those People BPMC Factors that you answered either strongly disagree or disagree?

- Managers to share vision and more information with us - new developments in certain areas.

- By having regular team meetings whereby workers can express their concerns and grievances.

- Have a look at the Managers that doesn't know the process and how things work, and all of them is result driven, and will work someone to the bone, even if the system doesn't work at all. Expecting the unexpected.

- The Revision of Process management in the company should greatly incorporate and contain input from the employees, as they will be putting this blueprint in place.

- Epsilon should focus more on the employees, find out how managers got there positions, are they doing what is expected and treating the employees with respect.

Use the ideas the team gives and make each person feel like they are meant to be here. Epsilon is a very good company, but... management makes its tough to be here.

- Managers should share the company/departments vision and information with us as it helps interims of growth in the future

- They need to listen to their staff. Decisions are made at top level and opinions of staff actually doing these processes is not considered.

- Appoint managers who understand what employees do daily or understand the scope within which employees work and will then know what is needed to empower employees.

- They just need to be open with us and understand what we have to deal with on daily basis. They need to put themselves in the shoes of the consultant

- I think Epsilon should include the staff in their decision-making and empower the staff to make decisions, not to run to the manager for every minor issue. Co-workers do not trust in each other and have no confidence in each other. Epsilon should implement team buildings and workshops for staff to get to know each other better. Currently co-workers only think about covering their backs only.

- 1. Treat staff like adults and not children 2. Be open and honest

3. Listen to the staff

4. Up skill and empower staff 5. Have succession planning

- There is too much "personal competition" between co-workers - some are intimidated if you do well

- Senior management is still not transparent enough, people are expected to deliver excellence with sub-standard tools, the Epsilon way is being promoted and even practiced in some areas, but management changes the rules whenever it suites them. Consistency in managements' behavior and decision-making, more consideration for the customer and staff.

- Management should consult with the employees at ground level before deciding to change processes

- Management should support and not impose change on employees. They should inform employees and not just enforce it. Some people in managerial position seem to have gotten them according to who they know and

so they are not suitable and responsible enough for the position

- Decision-making should be placed in the hands of the person dealing with the query - they need to be trained properly and take responsibility for the decision

- Senior managers should share their vision for their respective departments and lead by example.

- Better communication- as I feel this is our downfall currently

- Interaction: Manager-employee

- Better understanding of roles.

- Listen to what staff has to say before decisions are made

- To work with each other and be there for each other. Manager needs to work with the employee

- Re-enforce the Epsilon cultures and values

- They could include us in changes or processes before implementing these processing and then only feel the need to get our input, and when consulting with us use our ideas because most times our ideas work better as we are the ones on a daily bases dealing with all the processes.

- I Disagree on the present processes.....

- Improve teamwork by using all the collaboration channels available to them.

- I FIND THAT A SIGNIFICANT FEW MANAGERS TEND TO HOLD ONTO INFORMATION. THEREFORE MISTAKES ARE MADE DUE TO LACK OF KNOWLEDGE OR INFO.

- Do checks to ensure that the same message is communicated to all. Use the feedback received from customers & implement the requests.

7.8.4.4 Summary of BPMC People Factors

Identified issues:

Organization Epsilon's managers should share vision and information with employees better.

Also Epsilon's managers should have more realistic expectations of process changes.

The employees should give performance recognition among co-workers more.

The employees are saying in open-ended comments that some of the managers are incapable and do not listen to employees enough. Giving leadership training to the managers would give them more skills to deal with employees.

Rest of the People BPMC factors in Organization Epsilon are on a higher level. Measuring them again later could give information on trend where they are moving.

Suggestions for improvement:

BPMC1 (Managers share vision and information with their subordinates) may be improved by having discussions between managers and subordinates about the ways in which they would like to receive information, how often and in what format. After that appropriate ideas from those discussions may be taken in use.

BPMC4 (Top management generally supports changes in processes) could be improved by clearer support from top management towards process changes. Top management should evaluate their views on process management and tell subordinates what are the ways they are willing to show support for changes in processes.

BPMC13 (There is performance recognition among co- workers) can be enhanced by promoting positive ways for employees to give each other appraisals. This should be on-going behavior and the appraisal should come from one employee to another as soon as there has happened something positive performance wise. The feedback should be genuine and timely.

Epsilon should consider regular team meetings whereby workers can express their concerns and grievances. Gathering and using the ideas presented by the team in those meetings make each person feel like they are meant to be here.

Epsilon should give leadership training to its managers, to enable them to communicate and deal with employees better.

7.8.5   BPMC – Process Factors

BPMC Survey process factors contain BPMC factors from BPMC16 until BPMC30:

BPMC16 The performance measurements adequately correspond to the process changes.

BPMC17 I know the cost of customer acquisition, the annual value of a customer and the cost of a customer complaint.

BPMC18 The bonus scheme adjusts to process changes.

BPMC19 There are training programs available to update my skills.

BPMC20 I know and understand Business Process Management (BPM) concepts and methodologies.

BPMC21 The plans for process improvement projects are adequate.

BPMC22 I am eager to improve the existing state of our processes.

BPMC23 Process improvement efforts are important for the organization.

BPMC24 Organizational structure can be easily changed when needed.

BPMC25 No one has to worry about losing his or her job because of process changes.

BPMC26 I feel comfortable with the new working environment after process changes.

BPMC27 The organization has a standard methodology for improving processes.

BPMC28 The organization is able to respond to changes in markets quickly.

BPMC29 Initiatives in the organization are heading in the same direction.

BPMC30 I know what I do within my organization and how it affects the result

The capability factors BPMC18 and BPMC25 were removed from the survey for Epsilon for political reasons. There are big process changes happening in Epsilon and the managers did not want to give employees ideas that could affect those efforts. Therefore those two questions were removed. Rest of the BPMC factors were measured from two perspectives: how do respondents feel these statements apply to Organization Epsilon (value) and how important they think each statement is (importance).

7.8.5.1 BPMC Process Value

Process value describes how respondents valued Organization Epsilon in BPMC factors 16-30. This was measured by asking them how much do they agree or disagree with statements regarding this organization. Value questions were measured with Likert scale: 1 = Strongly disagree, 2 = Disagree, 3 = Undecided, 4 = Agree, 5 = Strongly agree

285

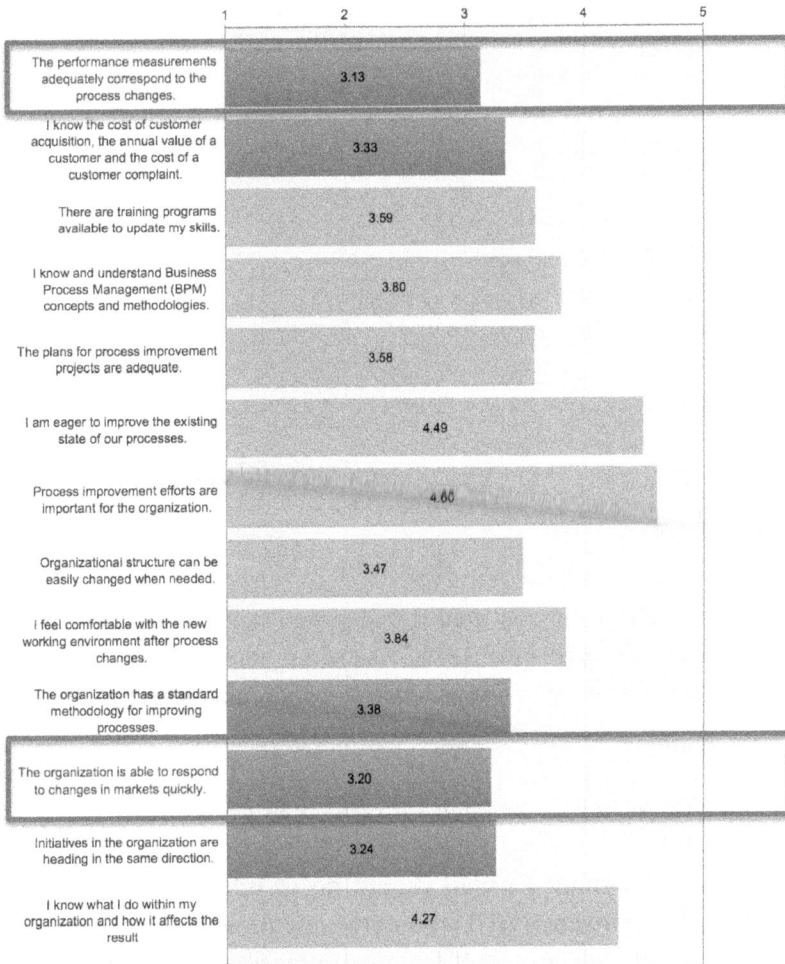

These mean values show that we can divide the responses into three categories: Negative (<2.8), Undecided (2.8 <= x =< 3.2) and Positive (>3.2).

7.8.5.2 BPMC Process Factors' Importance

Process factors' importance describes how important respondents think BPMC factors 16-30 are. This was measured by asking them how important they think each statement is. Importance of these process factors was measured with scale: 1 = Low, 2 = Medium, 3 = High.

Means for Process BPMC Factors

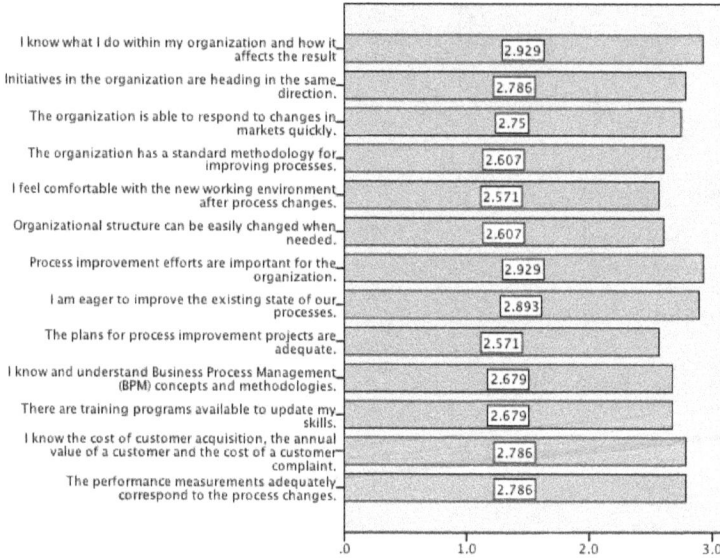

Factor	Mean
I know what I do within my organization and how it affects the result	2.929
Initiatives in the organization are heading in the same direction.	2.786
The organization is able to respond to changes in markets quickly.	2.75
The organization has a standard methodology for improving processes.	2.607
I feel comfortable with the new working environment after process changes.	2.571
Organizational structure can be easily changed when needed.	2.607
Process improvement efforts are important for the organization.	2.929
I am eager to improve the existing state of our processes.	2.893
The plans for process improvement projects are adequate.	2.571
I know and understand Business Process Management (BPM) concepts and methodologies.	2.679
There are training programs available to update my skills.	2.679
I know the cost of customer acquisition, the annual value of a customer and the cost of a customer complaint.	2.786
The performance measurements adequately correspond to the process changes.	2.786

Based on value in above table and graph we can conclude that respondents indicate that these process BPMC factors are important for organization. None of the factors were regarded as low or medium importance.

7.8.5.3 Open ended comments on Process Factors

What do you think Epsilon should do to improve those Process BPMC Factors that you answered either strongly disagree or disagree?

- As a Epsilon employee I feel that we need to get more training to update our personal skills and to learn more about business skills and management. Also motivational speakers can make a huge difference to our employees.

As a Epsilon employee we would like to know how important it is for us to retain clients and we also need to know how much it affects our annual values.

- Work closer to staff members and do take the ideas staff members have into mind and see if a newer quicker and cheaper process can be developed

- With regards to the process Epsilon follows, its either not working in a good order or the communication is not open.

- Changes are moving in snail pace and we are unlikely to get to the core sooner. System integration is also critical to excellent customer service focus.

- Open communication

- I've never received any communication about this "I know the cost of customer acquisition, the annual value of a customer and the cost of a customer complaint."

- Good communication between management and employees is of importance.

- Closing the gaps between senior management and agents on processes and the organizations vision.

- Better measurement tools/better communication at times.

- They can include us and involve us more in these processes and the impact it has on the company.

- TO START IMPLEMENTING THE NEW PROCESSES...

- More information and open communications should take place.

- Because the company has very rigid procedures and processes, there are so many channels that one needs to go through in order for any kind of change to take place

7.8.5.4 Summary of BPMC Process Factors

Identified issues:

None of the Process factors were negative in Epsilon. Two of the Process factors were undecided: BPMC16 (The performance measurements adequately correspond to the process changes) and BPMC28 (The organization is able to respond to changes in markets quickly).

These BPMC Process factors are barely on the positive side: BPMC17 (I know the cost of customer acquisition, the annual value of a customer and the cost of a customer complaint), BPMC27 (The organization has a standard methodology for improving processes) and BPMC29 (Initiatives in the organization are heading in the same direction).

Rest of the Process BPMC factors in Organization Epsilon are on a higher level. Measuring them again later could give information on trend where they are moving.

Suggestions for improvement:

Process factor BPMC16 (The performance measurements adequately correspond to the processes and changes into them) is disagreed by respondents slightly and they think it is medium importance. Organization Alpha should look into their performance measurements to see which parts of them are not adequately corresponding to processes.

BPMC28 (Organization is able to respond to changes in markets quickly) has been seen little bit on the positive side by respondents, but still it is very close to undecided. However, this factor is perceived to be of high importance, so management should work on being able to respond market changes quicker. Since respondents have evaluated correlating factor BPMC23 (Business process improvement efforts are important for the organization) high value

288

and importance, it may explain that organization is working on process improvement, but slowly. Management should look into ways to make this process faster.

Epsilon could improve on how measuring the customer value, how important it is for the Epsilon to retain existing clients and Epsilon's employees also need to know how much it affects annual revenues. The employees could benefit from receiving information regarding the cost of customer acquisition, the annual value of a customer and the cost of a customer complaint.

7.8.6   *BPMC – Technology Factors*

BPMC Survey technology factors contain BPMC factors from BPMC31 until BPMC35:

BPMC31 The business plan of the organization also takes the information systems into consideration.

BPMC32 The organization extensively uses information systems.

BPMC33 There are efficient communication channels for transferring information.

BPMC34 Existing information systems are reengineered if necessary.

BPMC35 The information systems are aligned with the organization's strategy.

These factors were measured from two perspectives: how do respondents feel these statements apply to Organization Epsilon (value) and how important they think each statement is (importance).

7.8.6.1 *BPMC Technology Value*

Technology value describes how respondents valued Organization Epsilon in BPMC factors 31-35. This was measured by asking them how much do they agree or disagree with statements regarding this organization. Value questions were measured with Likert scale: 1 = Strongly disagree, 2 = Disagree, 3 = Undecided, 4 = Agree, 5 = Strongly agree.

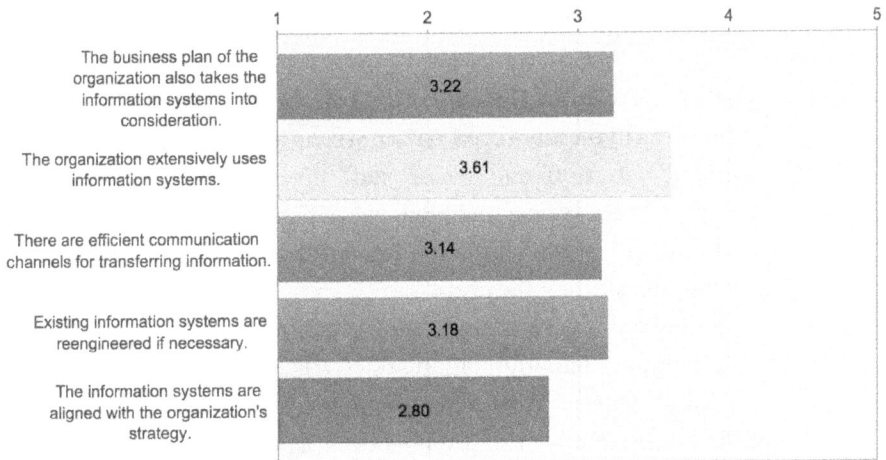

These mean values show that we can divide the responses into three categories: Negative (<2.8), Undecided (2.8 <= x =< 3.2) and Positive (>3.2). Using the means values from above factors go into these categories in the following way:

7.8.6.2 BPMC Technology Factors' Importance

Technology factors' importance describes, how important respondents think BPMC factors 31-35 are. This was measured by asking them how important they think each statement is. Importance of these people factors was measured with scale: 1 = Low, 2 = Medium, 3 = High.

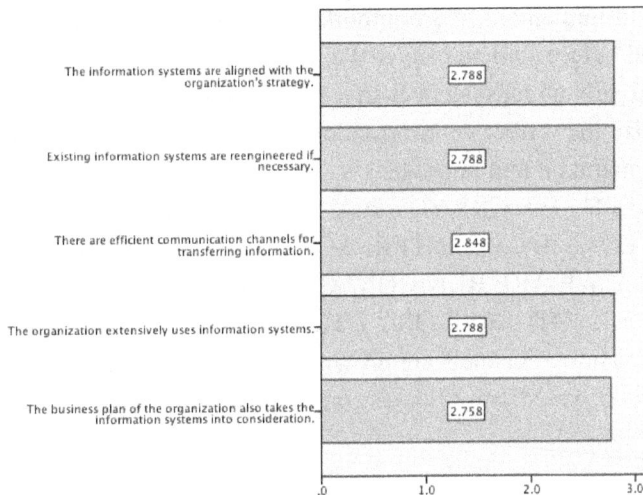

Means for Technological importance

Based on value in above table and graph we can conclude that respondents indicate that these technology BPMC factors are highly important for the organization. None of the factors were regarded as low or medium importance.

7.8.6.3 *Open ended comments on Technology Factors*

What do you think Epsilon should do to improve those Technical BPMC Factors that you answered either strongly disagree or disagree?

- Listen to staff and where staff gives ideas, take the ideas and work towards a better system and plan, cut out unnecessary long processes

- Communication with in the organization, improve the workers (giving me training), up skilling the agents.

Finding out if each person is doing as they were told.

- Changes to the information systems is long overdue

- A day doesn't go by without anyone [me included] complaining about IT or the system that we use [Being slow to respond]

- The systems really have to improve to meet the standards of growth. There are too many system issues

- A lot of system improvement is necessary - this would make the "new" processes either fail or succeed

- When the strategy is planned and implemented, systems should be in place to support the objectives.

- New CRM to enable measurement and strategy.

- we could make our systems accessible to everyone within the organization. Have one system

- Have CRM and SYSTEM on a single platform. Have more customer friendly applications for cellphones and Tablets. Encourage debit order payment instead of Bank deposits from customers.

- they should align there business decisions with the changes and process they decide to implement, more importantly products being rolled out should first be tested before sold and advised to clients.

- I feel strongly about system changes as it can improve productivity

- Recognize that effective information systems need proper funding and or resources to maintain and improve.

- WE NEED TO CREATE A SYSTEM WHERE MOST INFO IS INTEGRATED AND INTERFACES WITH ONE ANOTHER. CURRENTLY WE ARE RUNNIGN AROUND FOR INFO, SOME PEOPLE HAVE ACCESS, OTHERS DON'T ETC

- Communication channels are growing but sometimes as a mere agent you cannot use certain mediums without consultation with superiors

7.8.6.4 *Summary of BPMC Technology Factors*

Identified issues:

Only 40% of technology value factors are positive in Organization Epsilon. The BPMC31 (The business plan of the organization also takes the information systems into consideration) is barely on the positive side. There are two technology factors that are undecided, though little bit on the positive side. It is also notable that none of the technology factors are highly agreed either. This may show uncertainty amongst employees whether they agree or disagree to these statements in Organization Epsilon.

Technological capabilities to promote BPM success are on average level in Organization Epsilon. The statistics show that respondents do not feel that there are big hurdles in technological support, but they do not seem to strongly agree either. Respondents are quite undecided in this matter.

Suggestions for improvement:

BPMC32 (The organization extensively uses information systems.) Respondents slightly agree on this statement and they think it is important to use information systems. Organization should evaluate where in processes there are places to use information systems more efficiently.

BPMC34 (Existing information systems are reengineered if necessary.) Respondents slightly disagree with this statement. Organization should evaluate which legacy information systems may be in a need of reengineering.

BPMC35 (The information systems are aligned with the organization's strategy.) Organization could make it more clear that how IT systems support business processes. This matter might also be linked to lack of standardized process management system, which would make the links more visible. Organization should look into possibilities how to evaluate whether IT systems are aligned with BPM.

7.8.7 Open ended comments on overall process development in Organization Epsilon

What do you think Epsilon should do to improve its business processes?

- Involve all parties (Departments) in decision making when processes change. Do proper testing before implementing

- To implement one system, containing all details of customers, which allows Epsilon employees to assist clients immediately and not to transfer the customers from pillar to post?

I've also noticed that customers gets transferred from pillar to post due to the fact all the departments does not know who is dealing with what.

As from a legal point of view it will be nice of a client can add R20 or R30 per month to their sub as a agility product to make provision for clients who are unemployed (retrenchment).

- We need to always put the client 1st and ensure that our processes are in line with the promises we have made to the client.

- Send more staff members to this training in order for most staff members to understand the need to improve processes within the organization without any resistance from staff members.

- To better understand the different departments inter-dependencies on each other and collaborate more with each another to achieve each other's goals.

- Work closer with staff, relook all the processes and get away from long processes, there is unnecessary processes that is not cost effective nor efficient

- In order for the business processes to be changed the customer should be given first priority and the employee who directly speaks to the client should also be involved in change processes as they directly speak to the client and would have more views based on the clients expectations and experience.

- Make sure all the departments can work with the changes. A process might work with one department, but not with the other. Communication is very important.

- We need to have a higher level of communication within the different departments so we all are on the same page regarding processes, pricing etc. especially when we speak directly to clients

- Remove redundancies

- Remove all the unnecessary aspects.

Re-searching how each process works and simplify it

(mot, bp, br). Communication amongst managers and those who build the process for each department.

Making sure each person in the company understands the process in order to prevent angry and irate clients.

- They can follow the processes we did during the Centricity training as we are the ones that know which processes need to be eliminated in order for excellent customer service

- Update our systems

- The company needs to fortify the drive to keep employees motivated and the leadership within the organization needs to also join the party. The success of any entity lies on the people on the floor who will drive the processes to succession.

- Staff needs to be involved in any changes made to business processes as they ultimately do the work and deal with the inefficiencies of the information system.

- We need one information system to deliver excellent customer experiences.

- Get experts or consultants with experience to map up business processes as those started my managers did not live up to expectations.

- Communication between Dept as one might be automating a process and the other still doing it manually. Setup a team within the Dept's to review every 2 / 3 months with centricity team.

- Management needs to be more flexible to change & new ideas from agents.

- Involve floor staff

- I think as an organization Epsilon needs to go back to the drawing board and re- evaluate what is important.

We see customers cancelling daily because of sub standard service and negligence. Our processes are too rigid and there is no flexibility. Employees are unsure of processes within the company as they are changed often but not communicated to the entire organization. the changes are also not documented to be able to refer to them if and when the need arises.

- Combine the systems and make it more interfacing with clients.

- Consultation with all employees in the company

- Listen to the clients wants and needs and the employee's abilities - this will help with eliminating unnecessary steps when dealing with customer excellence

- Plan, organize, implement and communicate the objective so that everyone is on the same page and understanding.

- Mind set change is needed and system improvements

- Align itself with customer needs and wants, both internally and externally

- I think foremost each and every employee should be introduced to the Epsilon way and they need to live it, breathe it. Been a fairly new employee during my training the Epsilon way was drilled into us and i use it daily in my work and find it a success at all times, however some employees need to live the Epsilon way in order to adapt to change and to make Epsilon a greater place to be for us the employee and our customers

- Ask the customer..

- Not allowing intellectually challenged people to make decisions

- Epsilon needs to improve the systems we are currently using. we need to put the client first instead of numbers and we will avoid having to fix mistakes.

- Encourage debit orders with customers. Electronic statements as much as possible.

- Process between the manager and the employee, the system and the employee

- Publish successes; make it visible to the rest of the company

- Include all staff members in these decisions, especially the staff working directly in the channel they plan on making any changes, have the staff in that channel test the changes the process if it includes system changes, make us aware.

- to re-map the current process and re-look and take away a few stuff that is not necessary ...

- Make everyone involved and listen to ideas and try it before making a one-person decision

- Improve teamwork and inter-teamwork. Set realistic goals and communicate more. Improve all Staff skills on communication and computer literacy.

- be more interactive with employees and listen to employees instead of bringing them down and provide equal opportunities to everyone

- FIRSTLY, STREAMLINE ALMOST EVERYTHING BASED ON THE CLIENT'S NEED. OUR SYSTEMS CURRENTLY DO NOT CREATE A GREAT EXPERIENCE FOR CLIENT. OUR PROCESSES ARE QUITE REDUNDANT AND REPETITIVE.

- Epsilon could remove the unnecessary steps and procedure that need to be done for anything to happen as some of them are really a waste of time and delay if not affect customer satisfaction

- Cross-share department processes as part of training (show call center staff a finance process, etc.)

- I would say the departments need to start sharing information with each other

7.8.8   Summary of BPMC survey results for Epsilon

Following table shows number of negative, undecided and positive value factors in whole BPMC survey:

Factors	Negative	Undecided	Positive
People	0	3	12
Process	0	2	11
Technology	1	2	2
	TOTAL NEGATIVE: 1 (3%)	TOTAL UNDECIDED: 7 (21%)	TOTAL POSITIVE: 25 (76%)

As table above shows, Organization Epsilon is on the positive side regarding BPM capabilities measured in this survey. There are some areas to be developed especially on process capabilities, but people capabilities seem to be on a good level. Technological capabilities in Organization Epsilon are not very clear, since respondents indicated that they are something between undecided and positive. Organization should take measures to strengthen negative capabilities and to increase undecided capabilities to positive side.

Following table shows number of low, medium and high importance factors in whole BPMC survey:

Factors	Low importance	Medium	High importance
People	0	0	15
Process	0	0	13
Technology	0	0	5
	TOTAL LOW: 0 (0%)	TOTAL MEDIUM: 0 (0%)	TOTAL HIGH: 33 (100%)

Table above shows, that all capabilities measured in this survey are high importance.

7.8.9 Open ended comments on this BPMC survey

Please, share your thoughts and feedback on this BPMC survey?

- Very good, necessity

- I am positive by thinking about the future of Epsilon. I am proud to be a Epsilon employee. Epsilon always goes out of their way to make things better not only for their customers but also for their employees and managers. Epsilon's is really a great place to be.

- It was short and easy.

- That Epsilon Management needs to relook all the processes and honestly we can do with a good cost effective and efficient system change that works for everyone

- It is very informative.

- The survey is good enough for the course.

- The survey seems to focus more on how we perceive management, how involved we are in changes being made within the organization, whether we understand why changes take place and how we are effected by it but most importantly how our customer are effected by it .

- It was informative

- The idea that each person should go on training, up-skilling people is great .The survey is easy and touches each point.

- It has been great and very productive and hopefully it will have a major impact in improving customer service in Epsilon

- I am impressed and empowered.

- Surveys are good, however, are they ever put to good use?

- Will assist in spotting where processes are moving at snail pace and improve on those critical for excellent customer service enhancement.

- I hope it will help to bring about change at Epsilon.

- Very interesting - we just need to use it, otherwise it would be worthless and we will forget everything we learned

- The questions are relevant however I'm not sure weather the opinions will be taken into account or even considered going forward.

- If communication is good then things will fall into place.

- Direct, refreshing and gets an individual thinking.

- A few unnecessary questions.

- Is change happening?

- Fair

- I have done many of theses without seeing any results I hope with this one our opinions will be taken into consideration and some changes implements

- Thank you

- It was very nice and interesting

- I detest surveys

- its very enlightening to know that we have been given the opportunity to rate the course, it gives us the change to evaluate the course and let management know what working for us and what not working.

- It's good to know and it will definitely improve customer centricity

- Positive - and hope it will be implemented to make the Epsilon way a better environment to work.

- Do not know if the correct people will listen.

- I REALLY ENJOYED THE TRAINING, IT GAVE ME SCOPE AND WE OF THINKING THAT I INITIALLY DID

NOT POSSESS

- It allows view to be heard from different levels of the company thus allowing problems to be pointed from all sectors and levels of the company

- I would say the Survey needs to be a bit shorter

How easy did you find the questions in this survey to understand?

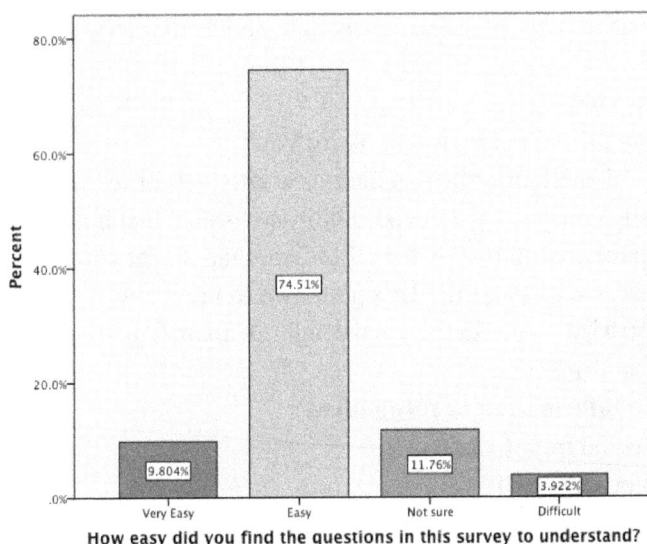

How easy did you find the questions in this survey to understand?

7.9   Appendix V – Interview format and questions

Welcome

Thank you very much for your interest in my research. This interview is part of Janne Ohtonen's PhD thesis for the Turku School of Economics, Finland.

This interview evaluates the BPMC factors that might contribute to success or failure in BPM initiatives. The purpose of the interview is to retrieve information about your opinions on the BPMC tool built in this research. In total, you will be asked to answer four sets of interview questions. It will take us about one hour to discuss this topic if you have gone through the BPMC tool beforehand. Altogether this interview process might take you about two hours.

For your protection, the researcher has obtained ethical approval for this study from the Turku School of Economics. If you have questions about or comments on this project or interview, please ask the interviewer for more details. Your participation in this interview is entirely voluntary and you can withdraw from the interview at any time without penalty or loss of privilege.

The information provided by you will be held totally anonymously and you will not be identified in any presentation or publication of this research. It will be almost impossible to trace your data back to you individually. You shall be identified with name "respondent" plus alphabetic letter such as A, B, C and so on.

Here are some preplanned questions for the interview. However, you are not restricted to discuss only about these questions and interview might ask you some other questions, too. Keep your mind open for discussion.

Do you have any practical questions about the arrangements of this interview?

Start of interview

Let's begin the interview, is that ok for you?

Can I record and transcribe this interview into text for research purposes?

Thank you. You will have the possibility to inspect that transcription later.

Did you have time to review the BPMC tool that I sent you earlier?

If yes: That is great! So, let's get down to interview.

If no: That's ok. Let's go through it after I have asked you some background information.

Background information of respondent

Where are you from (country)?

How do you define BPM?

How long you have used BPM approaches, tools or methods?

Which BPM conferences or seminars have you attended?

Have you published articles or books about BPM?

What kinds of BPM projects have you been involved with?

How would you describe your skills and knowledge on BPM?

Are you a member of professional BPM groups or associations?

Open questions on success capability factors

(If respondent had not gone through the BPMC artifact, go through success capability factors now.)

What is your view on the BPM success capability factors presented on that given list?

Which success factors can you relate to the most and why?

Which success factors you have not noticed in your work and why?

What do you think about the categorisation of these success capability factors?

How do you see these success factors could contribute to success in BPM initiatives?

Open questions on failure capability factors

(If respondent had not gone through the BPMC artifact, go through failure capability factors now.)

What is your view on the BPM failure capability factors presented on that given list?

Which failure factors can you relate to the most and why?

Which failure factors you have not noticed in your work and why?

What do you think about the categorisation of these failure capability factors?

How do you see these failure factors could contribute to success in BPM initiatives?

General questions on BPMC factors

What scale should be used to measure these BPMC factors?

How should the results received with that scale be analysed?

How do you see the potential of this BPMC tool for academic and practical fields?

What limitations might this tool have?

End of interview

That was all I have to ask. Do you have something more to add to this discussion?

Thank you very much on participating in this interview. Would you like to check this interview material after it has been transcribed into a textual format?

7.10   Appendix VI – BPMC Survey

Welcome to the BPMC survey!

Welcome to this survey on Business Process Management Capabilities (BPMCs) in [organisations' name]. The purpose is to find out your opinions on the capabilities of this organisation to develop its business processes. In total, you will be asked to answer four sets of questions. It will take you about 15 minutes to answer this questionnaire and all your answers will be saved anonymously.

Participating in this survey is completely voluntary and top management has authorised your participation. Your answers to this questionnaire cannot be traced back to you and all the information will be handled confidentially. For your protection, the researcher has also obtained ethical approval for this study from the Turku School of Economics and [organisations' name]. If you have any questions or comments on this survey or its technical operation, please e-mail Janne Ohtonen (jkohto@utu.fi) directly.

The results of this survey will be used to report the overall status of the BPMCs in [organisations' name]. The researcher will also use the information to evaluate the BPMC tool that is used in this survey as part of his PhD thesis. All information both at an individual and at an organisational level is handled anonymously. Please answer this survey according to your personal, genuine opinions. Your contribution will be highly valued by both your employer and the researcher.

Background information

How would you describe your skills and knowledge of developing processes?

[None, Beginner, Advanced, Professional]

Have you received any formal training or certifications for developing processes?

[No, Yes]

What is your position?

[Top management/Director, Middle management/Manager, Team leader/Project Manager, Specialist/Professional/Senior Consultant/Expert, Consultant/Employee/External/Trainee/Junior]

Please indicate your command of English?

[Poor, Good, Excellent, Native]

People BPMC Factors

Based on your personal opinions, how do the following statements describe your organisation?

[1= Strongly disagree, 2 = Disagree, 3 = Undecided, 4 = Agree, 5 = Strongly agree, 0 = I don't know]

And how important do you think these statements are for your organisation to succeed?

[1 = Low, 2 = Medium, 3 = High]

Managers share vision and information with their subordinates.

Managers place confidence in supervisors and their subordinates.

Managers constructively use their subordinates' ideas.

Top management generally has realistic expectations of process improvement projects.

Top management usually has sufficient knowledge about process improvement projects.

Top management frequently communicates with the project team and users.

Top management generally supports changes in processes.

The organisation has empowered process owners who are responsible.

Employees are empowered to make decisions.

There is open communication between supervisors and their subordinates.

Co-workers have confidence and trust in each other.

Teamwork between co-workers is the typical way to solve problems.

There is performance recognition among co-workers.

Management evaluates customer expectations when establishing the organisation's vision.

The organisation uses external consultants when needed.

What do you think [organisations' name] should do to improve those People BPMC Factors that you answered either strongly disagree or disagree?

What other comments do you have related to these People BPMC Factors in [organisations' name]?

Process BPMC Factors

Based on your personal opinion, how do following statements describe your organisation?

[1= strongly disagree, 2 = disagree, 3 = undecided, 4 = agree, 5 = strongly agree, 0 = I don't know]

And how important do you think these statements are for your organisation to succeed?

[1 = Low, 2 = Medium, 3 = High]

Performance measurements adequately correspond to the processes and changes to them.

Everyone knows the cost of customer acquisition, the annual value of a customer and the cost of a customer complaint.

The reward system adjusts to serve the employees after the changes.

There are training programs to update employees' skills.

BPM concepts and methodologies are known and understood.

The project plan for process improvement is adequate.

People are eager to improve the existing state of processes.

Business process improvement efforts are important for the organisation.

The organisational structure can be easily changed when needed.

No one has to be concerned about losing his or her job because of process changes.

Employees feel comfortable with the new working environment.

The organisation has a standard methodology for improving processes.

The organisation is able to respond to changes in markets quickly.

Initiatives in the organisation respect each other and are heading in the same direction.

People know the whole system they are part of.

What do you think [organisations' name] should do to improve those Process BPMC Factors that you answered either strongly disagree or disagree?

What other comments do you have related to these Process BPMC Factors in [organisations' name]?

Technical BPMC Factors

Based on your personal opinion, how do following statements describe your organisation?

[1= strongly disagree, 2 = disagree, 3 = undecided, 4 = agree, 5 = strongly agree, 0 = I don't know]

And how important do you think these statements are for your organisation to succeed?

[1 = Low, 2 = Medium, 3 = High]

IT is integrated into the business plan of the organisation.

The organisation extensively uses information systems.

There are efficient communication channels in transferring information.

Legacy information systems are reengineered if necessary.

IT is aligned with the BPM strategy.

What do you think [organisations' name] should do to improve those Technical BPMC Factors that you answered either strongly disagree or disagree?

What other comments do you have related to these Technical BPMC Factors in [organisations' name]?

Open Questions

What do you think [organisations' name] should do to improve its business processes?

Please share your thoughts and feedback on this BPMC survey?

Thank you for participating!

Thank you very much for participating in this BPMC survey. Your answers will be stored anonymously. In case you have any comments or questions on this survey, please send them to Janne Ohtonen on jkohto@utu.fi.

7.11   Appendix VII – Case Study Research Agreement

RESEARCH AGREEMENT FOR CASE STUDY ON BUSINESS PROCESS MANAGEMENT CAPABILITIES (BPMC)

This is a research agreement to **participate scientific case study on business process management capabilities** (BPMC). The study will focus on evaluating the BPMC tool developed by researcher Janne Ohtonen and analyzing the business process management capabilities of your organization.

AGREEMENT BETWEEN

RESEARCHER	AND	PARTICIPATING
ORGANIZATION		
Turku School of Economics		[organization name]
Janne Ohtonen		[responsible person name]
PhD Student		[responsible person title]
jkohto@utu.fi		[responsible person email]
+35844…		[responsible person phone]

RESEARCH DETAILS

Name:	Business Process Management Capabilities, BPMC
Researcher:	Janne Ohtonen, Turku School of Economics, Finland.
University:	Turku School of Economics
Supervisors:	Professor Hannu Salmela, dr. Timo Lainema, dr. Klara Palmberg-Broryd
Alias for organization:	Organization Alpha / Beta / Gamma
Duration of research:	From signed date until the end of year 2013.

CONTENT OF THIS RESEARCH AGREEMENT

1§   Researcher will sign the non-disclosure agreement with participating organization, if they wish so.

2§   Researcher will have access to necessary resources in organization to conduct the research, including but not limited to documentation, people, systems, etc.

3§   Researcher is allowed to conduct data collection in organization, including but not limited to following formats: interviews, documents and surveys.

4§   Researcher stores all the collected data in safe place and does his best to keep that information from spreading.

5§   Researcher will have access to organization's premises as needed for the research.

6§   Researcher is allowed to publish information and findings from organization in his PhD thesis and other related articles in anonymous format.

7§ Organization has right to read the public thesis and articles before they are published and to give comments. Organization has to send the comments to researcher within four weeks time when asked.

8§ Organization will receive both private and public report on findings.

9§ Organization will receive printed copy of researcher's thesis once it is ready.

10§ Researcher is allowed to share and discuss about all the information with his supervisors that are named in this agreement.

11§ The person signing this research agreement on the behalf of organization functions as a project manager and main contact for researcher. Organization has right to change this person or name a new person, if they wish. Also researcher can ask for a new contact person.

SIGNATURES

_____   _____   _____

Janne Ohtonen   [responsible person name]   [CEO name]
[date/place]   [date/place]   [date/place]

7.12   Appendix VIII – Post Survey Interview Questions

1.   What is your role and main duties within your organization?
2.   Who should receive our BPM Capabilities research report?
3.   What is the role of the person you think should be responsible for leading required actions to improve BPM Capabilities in your organization?
4.   What do you think your organization should do with BPM Capabilities that staff disagrees?
5.   What do you think your organization should do with BPM Capabilities were staff were undecided?
6.   What do you think your organization should do with BPM Capabilities that staff agrees?
7.   Was the research report useful for your organization? If yes, how? If not, how do you think it could ne improved?
8.   Was the research report useful for you personally? If yes, how? If not, how do you think it could ne improved?
9.   Would you recommend using the BPMC tool to other organizations? If yes, what kind of organizations do you think would benefit from using the BPMC tool? If not, what do you think needs to changed in order to recommend it to other organizations?
10.   Is your organization able use this BPMC tool independently? If not, what additions do you think are required to use it independently?
11.   Were the questions in the BPMC survey were hard to understand?
12.   Who do you think is the best target audience for the survey in BPMC tool?
13.   Were you able to follow the research process and draw your own conclusions from the report? If not, what changes do you think could be made to make it possible?
14.   How accurate do you believe the results provided by the BPMC tool are to your organization?
15.   Would it be useful if you were able to compare your organization's BPMC results to other organizations in your industry? Why would that information be useful?
16.   Do you think using the BPMC tool repeatedly would give useful information about the development of your organization's BPM Capabilities? If yes, how often do you think the BPMC tool should be used?
17.   Do you think the BPMC tool could be improved? If so, how?
18.   Do you have any other comments regarding this research or the BPMC tool? Please, elaborate.

A-1:2014   Kirsi-Mari Kallio
"Ketä kiinnostaa tuottaa tutkintoja ja julkaisuja
liukuhihnaperiaatteella…?"
– Suoritusmittauksen vaikutukset tulosohjattujen yliopistojen
tutkimus- ja opetushenkilökunnan työhön

A-2:2014   Marika Parvinen
Taiteen ja liiketoiminnan välinen jännite ja sen vaikutus
organisaation ohjaukseen – Case-tutkimus taiteellisen
organisaation kokonaisohjauksesta

A-3:2014   Terhi Tevameri
Matriisirakenteen omaksuminen sairaalaorganisaatioissa
– Rakenteeseen päätyminen, organisaatiosuunnittelu ja
toimintalogiikan hyväksyminen

A-4:2014   Tomi Solakivi
The connection between supply chain practices and firm
performance – Evidence from multiple surveys and financial
reporting data

A-5:2014   Salla-Tuulia Siivonen
"Holding all the cards"
The associations between management accounting,
strategy and strategic change

A-6:2014   Sirpa Hänti
Markkinointi arvon muodostamisen prosessina ja sen yhteys
yrittäjyyden mahdollisuusprosessiin
– Tapaustutkimus kuuden yrityksen alkutaipaleelta

A-7:2014   Kimmo Laakso
Management of major accidents
– Communication challenges and solutions in the preparedness
and response phases for both authorities and companies

A-8:2014   Piia Haavisto
Discussion forums
– From idea creation to incremental innovations. Focus on heart-
rate monitors

A-9:2014   Sini Jokiniemi
"Once again I gained so much"
– Understanding the value of business-to-business sales
interactions from an individual viewpoint

A-10:2014   Xiaoyu Xu
Understanding online game players' post-adoption behavior: an
investigation of social network games in

A-11:2014   Helena Rusanen
            Resource access and creation in networks for service innovation
A-12:2014   Joni Salminen
            Startup dilemmas
            – Strategic problems of early-stage platforms on the Internet
A-13:2014   Juulia Räikkönen
            Enabling experiences – The role of tour operators and tour
            leaders in creating and managing package tourism experiences
A-14:2014   Natalie S. Mikhaylov
            New school ties: Social capital and cultural knowledge creation
            in multicultural learning environments

A-1:2015   Hanne-Mari Hälinen
            Understanding the concept of logistics cost in manufacturing
A-2:2015   Arto Ryömä
            Mielelliset ja keholliset johtajuusprosessit yksilöllisyyttä ja
            yhteisöllisyyttä kietomassa
            – Empiirinen tarkastelu jääkiekkojoukkueen kontekstissa
A-3:2015   Kati Suomi
            Managing brand identity and reputation
            – A case study from Finnish higher education
A-4:2015   Jenni Jaakkola
            Essays on the decision-making in representative democracy
A-5:2015   Frederick Ameyaw Ahen
            Strategic corporate responsibility orientation for sustainable
            global health governance: Pharmaceutical value co-protection in
            transitioning economies
A-6:2015   Janne Ohtonen
            Business process management capabilities

All the publications can be ordered from

KY-Dealing Oy
Rehtorinpellonkatu 3
20500 Turku, Finland
Phone +358-2-333 9422
E-mail: info@ky-dealing.fi